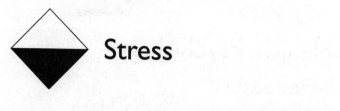 **Stress**

Health Psychology

Series editors:
Sheila Payne and Sandra Horn

Stress
Perspectives and processes

Dean Bartlett

Open University Press
Buckingham · Philadelphia

WITHDRAWN

Open University Press
Celtic Court
22 Ballmoor
Buckingham
MK18 1XW

email: enquiries@openup.co.uk
world wide web: http://www.openup.co.uk

and

325 Chestnut Street
Philadelphia, PA 19106, USA

First Published 1998

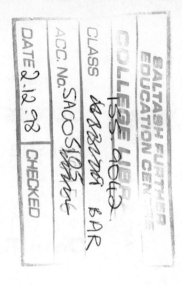

A catalogue record of this book is available from the British Library

ISBN   0 335 19928 3 (hb)   0 335 19927 5 (pb)

Library of Congress Cataloging-in-Publication Data
Bartlett, Dean, 1969–
    Stress : perspectives and processes/Dean Bartlett.
        p.   cm. – (Health psychology)
    Includes bibliographical references and index.
    ISBN 0–335–19928–3. – ISBN 0–335–19927–5 (pbk.)
    1. Stress (Psychology).   2. Stress (Physiology).   3. Medicine,
Psychosomatic.   I. Title.   II. Series.
RC455.4.S87B37   1998
616'.001'9–dc21   98–14536
                                                            CIP

Typeset by Graphicraft Limited, Hong Kong
Printed in Great Britain by Biddles Ltd, Guildford and King's Lynn

Contents

 # Series editors' foreword

This new series of books in health psychology is designed to support post-graduate and postqualification studies in psychology, nursing, medicine and paramedical science, as well as the establishment of health psychology within the undergraduate psychology curriculum. Health psychology is growing rapidly as a field of study. Concerned as it is with the application of psychological theories and models in the promotion and maintenance of health, and the individual and interpersonal aspects of adaptive behaviour in illness and disability, health psychology has a wide remit and a potentially important role to play in the future.

The study of stress, in particular its effects on health, now has a long but not untroubled history. The complex nature of the concepts of stress and health invites the use of a sophisticated metatheoretical framework, such as the biopsychosocial paradigm adopted and developed by health psychology. In this fourth book of the series, Bartlett has set about exploring and elucidating the various theoretical perspectives in which stress and its relationship to health have been cast. His stance is that it is the individual's experience of stress that determines the impact of stressful events, and that the experience is influenced by a host of factors, biological, psychological and social. By taking a phenomenological approach, Bartlett moves the debate away from unidirectional cause-and-effect models and provides a rich and distinctive account of the interactive elements of the stress process.

Sheila Payne and Sandra Horn

 # Acknowledgements

I would like to thank all of the people who have helped in the production of this book. These include Sheila Payne, Lawrence Warwick-Evans, Sandra Horn, Bogey Lou, Carol Hustler, Julien Binet, and others who know who they are.

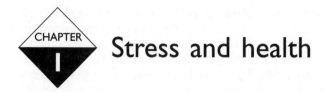

Stress and health

Learning objectives for this chapter

This chapter introduces the concepts of stress and health and presents a theoretical framework for studying the relationship between them. This framework is helpful in understanding how psychological, social and biological processes can interact with each other and mediate the effects of stress upon health. The chapter concludes by describing a number of different perspectives from which stress may be viewed, each of which provide a different insight into the stress process. After reading this chapter, you should be able to:

- explain what is meant by the concept of stress;
- explain the significance of the stress concept and why it has been so heavily studied;
- show a critical understanding of the difficulties surrounding the definition of both stress and health;
- describe the biomedical model of disease and understand its limitations;
- describe the biopsychosocial approach; and
- understand that stress may be viewed in a number of different ways, each of which adds to our understanding of how it can influence health but none of which constitutes a wholly adequate or sufficient explanation of this relationship.

Introduction

It has become an accepted wisdom that stress can influence our physical and psychological health, or more simply, too much stress can make you ill. This book explores how this is so and it therefore seeks to describe and explain the relationship between stress and health. If we are to understand this relationship, it is first necessary to consider exactly what is meant by each of the terms 'stress' and 'health'. This chapter therefore presents an overview of each of these concepts, explaining why the study of stress has attracted so much attention from social scientists over recent years, outlining the difficulty in developing precise definitions and explaining how the material presented in this volume is intended to add to current accounts of the stress process.

Why study stress?

It has been noted by many commentators in the field (e.g. Ursin and Murison 1984; Pollock 1988) that the notion of stress has become ubiquitous in our society and this is reflected in the popular discourse surrounding the term. Such discourse encompasses both our work lives in, for example, the stereotype of the 'stressed out' worker and our social arrangements, in terms of the social stress of modern urban living. The discourse of stress as reflected in the media, for example, influences common understandings and lay conceptions of exactly what constitutes stress. Consequently, the number and variety of phenomena that people have come to associate with increased levels of stress is staggering, ranging from 'road rage' incidents to so-called 'yuppie flu'. Furthermore, stress is thought to be 'on the increase'. It has been suggested that stress arises at least partly from the increasingly fast pace of modern life, as manifested in both the escalating degree of time pressure we each face in our daily lives and our becoming increasingly less able to keep apace with rapidly changing social attitudes, work practices and technological advances. This level of popular interest in stress is matched by a burgeoning academic and technical literature which has examined stress from a myriad of social and scientific perspectives, ranging in their level of analysis from the biochemical and cellular to the social–psychological and cultural.

Thus the notion that stress is bad for you and can make you ill has become a modern cultural truism. However, there is also a significant body of research evidence which lends support to this idea. The evaluation of this evidence is a difficult task for several reasons. Firstly, the sheer volume of research in terms of the number of published research findings is astonishing. During 1981, for example, 451 new articles appeared in the *Social Sciences Citation Index* with the word 'stress' appearing as a keyword in the title or abstract; by 1991, this had risen to over 1600 articles per year and during 1997 over 3000 such articles were published. As the research literature on stress continues to expand, it becomes increasingly impractical to conduct thorough and comprehensive surveys of the current status of the field. A second factor that causes difficulty in the evaluation of stress research and which explains why researchers have been unable to provide clear answers as to how stress could lead to ill health is that there is much confusion over the precise definition of what constitutes stress – is it a state of mind, a bodily reaction, a certain type of stimulus or something entirely different from each of these? A further source of controversy stems from the conflicting findings that have been reported in the research literature. Furthermore, and possibly as a result of some of these conceptual difficulties, research in the area is plagued by a host of methodological problems concerning how one can accurately and reliably measure stress. The fact that so much research has been published and that there are still so many questions to be answered provides good reason as to why it should be necessary to further study the phenomenon of stress.

The likelihood that stress can lead to ill health provides two more reasons as to why it is important to study stress. The first of these is that, if we are to intervene in this process, thereby preventing or ameliorating stress-induced ill health and the suffering that is associated with it, then we need to understand *how* stress causes illness. The second reason is based upon the economics of healthcare and, in particular, the escalating cost of providing healthcare to a population which is living longer, expecting greater standards of care and becoming increasingly 'stressed'. If we are able to develop ways either to reduce the levels of stress to which we are exposed, or else to reduce the impact of such exposure on health, then we can reduce the cost to society of stress-induced ill health. This will have benefits both in terms of reducing the lost productivity due to absence from work through stress-related illness and in terms of the cost of providing medical care to treat such illness. This is resonant with the more general argument put forward by Marks (1994: 113) who wrote that, due to changing economic and political agendas, 'the need to enhance our understanding of the multiple psychosocial dimensions of health and illness has never been greater'. Thus, by furthering our understanding of the stress process, we increase the likelihood of developing interventions which could be of benefit both to the individual, in that they reduce the human suffering associated with ill health, and to society as a whole, in that they reduce the burden placed upon an already overstretched healthcare system. The study of stress must, therefore, be central to the project of health psychology which concerns, at its most basic level, the role of psychosocial processes in health and disease.

One final reason as to why the study of stress represents such a fundamentally important element of health psychology and field of study generally concerns the way in which the stress concept draws together and integrates a much wider body of knowledge concerning human functioning in general. Elliot and Eisdorfer (1982) make this point in their book *Stress and Human Health: Analysis and Implications of Research*, arguing that many of the questions which the study of stress seeks to answer concern issues which lie close to the heart of the human condition. The extract which appears in Box 1.1 reinforces this point and also gives some clue as to the issues which will be addressed in this book.

Box 1.1   Stress: a challenging field of scientific inquiry

Elliot and Eisdorfer drew together most of the key pieces of research that have been conducted in the stress field and examined the findings and implications of this research. They identified some of the reasons why our efforts to understand exactly what constitutes stress and how it impacts upon our health represents such a challenging area of inquiry. The following extract gives an indication of how they view stress and highlights some of the key issues that are addressed in this book. It explains why it is necessary to focus upon the phenomenological experience of stress if we are to explain how reactions to stress differ between individuals and it suggests that, in doing so, we are likely to shed light upon a number of issues of importance in the study of human functioning.

. . . the same experience – painted in broad brush strokes – can have very different meanings for different people, even people as close as husband and wife. And the different meanings can elicit different emotional responses and hence very different physiological responses. To make matters still more complicated, different people may in many ways have different susceptibility to virtually the same experiences. For a given kind of stress, some are more vulnerable than others, and the sources of such variation are manifold. All well and good, but are there any general tendencies in the relation of stress and illness? Do certain kinds of experiences tend to increase the likelihood of illness, at least for certain kinds of people? . . . Are some more vulnerable than others? How can we find out? For that matter, how could stressful experience make someone ill? What processes or mechanisms could link human emotional experience and tissue damage? . . . Can science identify individual coping strategies that tend to be protective? What is the role of social support networks? . . . These are all fascinating subjects for scientific inquiry, not only for the satisfaction of long-standing human curiosity, but also for the future relief of much human suffering . . . Surely, a deeper understanding of human adaptability is a worthy quest. It is close to the heart of the human condition.

Elliot and Eisdorfer (1982: xxi) in the Foreword to their book, *Stress and Human Health: Analysis and Implications of Research*

Definitions of stress

Attempts to define stress have been many and varied and examples include: 'stress is the non-specific response of the body to any demand made upon it' (Selye 1974); 'stress is a particular relationship between the person and the environment that is appraised by the person as taxing or exceeding his or her resources and endangering his or her well-being' (Lazarus and Folkman 1984a); and 'stress is defined as any transactional process in which the organism experiences an alteration of psychological homeostasis' (Burchfield 1985). Conventional treatment of the definitional issues surrounding the stress concept usually divides the various definitions which have been proposed into three categories: stimulus-based definitions, response-based definitions and interactional definitions.

Stimulus-based definitions of stress

Stimulus-based definitions identify stress as an aspect of the environment (a stimulus) which causes a strain reaction in the individual exposed to the stressful stimulus. This type of definition is identified with the 'engineering approach' in reference to its counterpart in physics and engineering which relates to the elasticity of substances. In physics, when a load is applied to a substance, it produces a force inside the substance which tends to distort it. This force is known as strain and the substance is said to be under stress. In a similar fashion, stressful stimuli are said to set up a reaction called strain, and it is the strain reaction which leads to ill health in humans. The engineering approach provides a useful analogy as it refers also to the 'elastic limit' which, in the case of a physical substance, denotes the point at which no further stress can be applied without resulting in permanent damage. Thus the idea that people have a certain tolerance to stress, but will become ill if they are placed under too much stress, is encapsulated in the engineering approach.

Stimulus-based definitions of stress were popular in the 1940s and 1950s because of the military research being conducted at the time, which viewed the tasks soldiers had to perform in battle as stressful stimuli causing the observed breakdown in health when it became too intense. For example, Symonds (1947) wrote that 'it should be understood once and for all that stress is that which happens to the man, not that which happens in him; it is a set of causes, not a set of symptoms'. This research was later developed in the workplace where performance was measured as a function of the stress subjects were placed under by, for example, working in a noisy environment. The simple stress–strain relationship was elaborated upon by the proposal that there may be an optimal level of stress, above or below which performance deteriorates. Stress was viewed in terms of the demands placed upon the person by the intensity of stimuli from the environment and this relationship is often represented by the inverted-U shaped function, as in Figure 1.1.

The engineering approach is appealing because of its simplicity, but this simplicity has meant that the vast majority of researchers and practitioners find the model too limited in scope to explain and account for the complexities

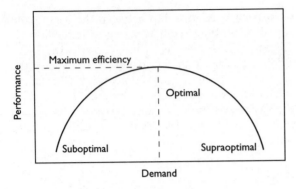

Figure 1.1 Stress and performance
Source: Reproduced from T. Cox (1978) *Stress*. The Macmillan Press Ltd.
With permission

of the stress process. Definitions based solely on the stimulus characteristics of the environment are not, therefore, in popular use. However, some approaches, particularly those that concentrate upon specific life events as the source of stress, do tend to focus more upon the stimulus than upon other aspects.

Response-based definitions of stress

The work of Hans Selye did most to popularize response-based definitions of stress because of his view that stress was a non-specific response of the body to any demand made upon it. In fact, Selye first used the term 'stress' to refer specifically to outside forces acting on the organism in his 1946 paper 'The General Adaptation Syndrome and Diseases of Adaptation', but by 1950 he had revised this definition and the term 'stress' now referred to the reaction of the organism to a given stimulus. This stimulus he then called a 'stressor'.

Although response-based definitions refer to the stimuli which lead to the stress response as stressors, they focus upon the occurrence of the response as the actual stress itself. The response is often viewed in terms of a physiological response pattern which leads to a disruption of normal homeostatic regulatory physiological functioning. As with stimulus-based definitions, defining stress merely in terms of a physiological (or other) response has proved inadequate in accounting for the complexities of the stress process. For example, the fact that we exhibit physiological stress responses during periods of excitement and pleasure is not consistent with the idea of stress as a cause of ill health. In this regard, Selye distinguishes between distress, being negative and resulting in damage to health, and eustress, being positive and enhancing health. As with stimulus-based definitions, very few people rely exclusively on a response-based definition.

Interactional definitions of stress

In response to the shortcomings of viewing stress solely as a characteristic either of the external environment (a stimulus) or of the physiological response, there has been a tendency to develop models in which aspects of both the environment and the person interact to produce stress. The interactional definition of stress is merely a fusion of the stimulus and response models and labels as stress the whole process from encountering stressful stimuli in the environment, through to the response of the body with its accompanying physiological changes and the phenomenological experience of stress. Popular interactional definitions of stress consist of the degree of mismatch between the person and the environment, sometimes called the person–environment fit, or P–E fit.

One of the most popular conceptualizations of stress is that proposed by Richard Lazarus and Susan Folkman (Lazarus and Folkman 1984a) and while many people view their theory of stress as interactional, in the most recent comprehensive explication of the theory, they quite clearly state that their model is not interactional but transactional. The concept of mismatch is viewed as structural and static, whereas the transactional framework which they propose is more process-oriented and takes account of the dynamic nature of the stress relationship between the person and the environment. The notion of stress as a dynamic process was, of course, not entirely new, as evidenced by the rarely cited work of Wolff (1977: 31) who defined stress as 'that state within a living creature which results from the interaction of the organism with noxious stimuli or circumstances, i.e. it is a dynamic state within the organism; it is not a stimulus, assault, load, symbol, burden, or any aspect of environment, internal, external, social or otherwise'. The differences between interactional and transactional frameworks will be discussed in Chapter 3 where the transactional model of stress is considered in greater depth.

Health and illness

Paradoxically, modern conceptions of health are intimately interwoven with ideas about the treatment of illness. Indeed the archetypal health profession, that of medicine, is dominated by a model of disease causation. This model is known as the biomedical model, but before going on to describe in greater detail exactly what the biomedical model says, it is worth giving some thought to the issue of exactly what is meant by the word 'health'. The very definition of health seems inextricably linked with the notion of disease, as the definitions given in Box 1.2 illustrate.

In simplistic terms, then, health may be considered as the state someone is in when he or she is not ill. Such a limited definition of health becomes problematic, however, when one starts to consider what it means to be 'not ill'. It is possible that while not suffering from a particular illness or

---

Box 1.2 Definitions of health

There are many different definitons of the word 'health' and three of these are presented below. The first two appear to define health only in reference to the state of being 'not ill' or 'without symptoms'. In fact the absence of disease is perhaps the primary indicator that is used to define health. The third definition does little to specify exactly what health is, merely offering the synonym 'well'. It is interesting to consider how the first two definitions bring the notion of optimal or vigorous functioning into the definition of health. How many of us usually have a feeling of 'vigour' or feel that we are functioning 'optimally' most of the time? Perhaps very few. Does this mean that most of us are not healthy, or are even ill?

The state of being bodily and mentally vigorous and free from disease.

(McCleod 1985)

The state of the organism when it functions optimally without evidence of disease or abnormality.

(*Stedman's Medical Dictionary* 1982)

The state of being well in body or mind.

(Allen 1985)

---

disease, a person is none the less not in a state of perfect or optimum health due to simply feeling a bit 'under the weather', for example. A more sophisticated way of conceptualizing the relationship between health and illness is to consider each of these states as opposite poles on a continuum ranging from 'healthy' at one end to 'ill' at the other. Yet even this way of thinking about health is not without problems because if these two states are at opposite ends on a continuum, one is naturally led to question what state actually constitutes each end-point of the scale. It is easier to define this for the 'illness' end of the spectrum, as the worst possible conceivable state of illness could be considered as death itself. But what is the best conceivable state of health? One could argue that this is represented not only by an optimal state of being well, but also by being positively resistant to disease. However, even this approach is problematic because what is optimal for one person may be suboptimal for another. The issue is further complic-ated when social and psychological aspects of health are taken into account as well as physical aspects. Thus, even if someone is physically fit and without physical symptoms, can they truly be said to be in a healthy state if they are also thoroughly depressed and miserable? These are issues which are, as yet, unresolved and which certainly fall beyond the scope of this book.

However, before leaving the subject of health and its relation to illness, it is worth considering the World Health Organization (WHO) definition of health which, although somewhat idealistic, perhaps goes furthest in specifying what it means to be healthy; health is 'a state of complete physical, mental and social well-being and not merely the absence of disease or infirmity'. Having highlighted the complexity of the health concept, the following sections provide a brief outline of two conceptual frameworks within which health can be studied; the biomedical model and the biopsychosocial perspective.

The biomedical model

The biomedical model is the predominant theoretical framework within which modern medicine is located. It is essentially a theory of disease causation and concentrates upon the physical bases of disease, asserting that disease is the result of physical changes caused either by exposure to an external pathogen, which invades the body or by inherited weaknesses or vulnerabilities in specific organ systems. The model is the result of various historical influences which have shaped the course of its development over many centuries.

Prior to early Greek thought, it was generally believed that disease was the result of mystical or supernatural influences such as possession by evil spirits. Around 400BC, the Greek healer Hippocrates laid the earliest foundations for modern medicine and earned himself the title 'the father of medicine'; even today, every doctor must abide by the principles of the 'Hippocratic oath'. He attempted to apply rational methods to the treatment of illness by examining symptoms, noting details of the patient's history and recording vital signs such as listening to the heart beat by placing his ear against the patient's chest. He charted the course of various diseases and was one of the first people to offer prognoses for diseases, based upon his knowledge of what had happened to patients exhibiting similar symptoms. Hippocrates also believed that in order to successfully treat illness, it was necessary to adopt a holistic approach, taking into account the thoughts and feelings of the patient as well as the physical symptoms.

It was Galen who, around AD200, first attributed the cause of disease to specific agents which he labelled pathogens. At the time, it was thought that pathogens consisted of bad air or bodily fluids like bile and it was not until the Renaissance and the discovery of the microscope in the sixteenth century that microorganisms were discovered and found to play a role in the causation of disease. At around this time, important advances in the physical sciences were being made and these coincided with the philosophical influence of René Descartes who proposed that the mind and the body are completely separate entities which work on very different principles – the mind, or soul, is of an incorporeal or spiritual nature and the body, which is of a corporeal nature, functions in a mechanistic way. According to Descartes, then, human beings consist of both spiritual and mechanistic, or incorporeal and corporeal parts, both of which function independently and in tandem to make up the living person.

This splitting of the person into two distinct parts (a dualism) by Descartes is known as 'Cartesian dualism' and it resulted in an almost complete separation of the mind and the body in scientific thinking. In the field of medicine, this logically implied that the causes and treatment of physical diseases would be found by concentrating purely upon the physical body of the patient, rather than on their thoughts and feelings which exist only in the mind. Thus medicine was conceived as a mechanistic science in which physical diseases could be treated solely by physical procedures aimed at changing the biological state of the body, for example by surgery or vaccination. Since this early period of medical science, the discovery of an increasing number of specific external pathogens such as bacteria, viruses and chemicals and the development of numerous drugs to combat these has increased confidence in the sufficiency of the biomedical model in explaining the disease process.

The twentieth century has seen greater advances in medicine than any other period. Increasing knowledge about cellular and subcellular mechanisms has shifted the analytical emphasis away from the level of organs and tissues and towards the microscopic. At the beginning of the century, Pasteur's work established the role of bacteria and microbes in the causation of specific diseases, an idea which has become known as germ theory. This notion of specificity in disease causation, along with the view that disease is largely the result of a singular external cause or pathogen, has been reinforced by the dramatic success of vaccines and antibiotics in the prevention and treatment of disease. These successes have been further enhanced in more recent times through the use of increasingly sophisticated medical technology which has served to underline the biomedical model and has led to an increased acceptance of it as the predominant explanatory framework within which illness may be understood.

Problems with the biomedical model

The widespread and unquestioning acceptance of the biomedical model is perhaps understandable; its scientific basis has made it attractive in our scientific age and it has proven extremely successful thus far in controlling, treating and even eradicating disease. The biomedical model has become accepted as an integral part of our 'common knowledge' and this acceptance has been reinforced by the medical profession itself which, perhaps for reasons of professional interest, has socialized and indoctrinated medical practitioners into this way of thinking throughout their period of professional training. In this respect, the biomedical model has become dogma.

However, there have been a number of serious challenges to the conceptualization of illness and the corresponding notions of health which it implies. Many of these challenges have come from within the field of medicine itself in the form of a reaction to the overemphasis upon the physical causation of disease and the exclusion of the role of psychological and social factors. For example, psychosomatic medicine sought to explicitly reject the dualistic thinking which pervades the biomedical model and to reintegrate psychological and physical functioning by examining the interaction between the mind, or the psyche (as in psycho-), and the body, or the soma (as in -somatic).

The psychosomatic movement resurrected the concept of multicausality in medicine and it is possible to trace two relatively distinct strands in its development. The first of these was the pioneering work of Freud who founded a distinctive new approach in psychology which became known as the psychodynamic or psychoanalytic approach. Freud described a condition called hysterical paralysis in which patients presented with apparently complete paralysis of one or more limbs, but where no organic pathology could be identified. Freud believed that this was the result of repressed emotions and sexual desires which were too psychologically threatening for the patient to face. He argued that these psychological problems manifested themselves in physical symptoms, thereby suggesting a direct link between psychological and physical functioning. The second strand which contributed to the development of psychosomatic medicine stemmed from psychophysiological experiments which demonstrated an association between the experience of emotions and certain accompanying physiological changes in the body, such as an increased heart rate when a person experiences anger and, once again, this suggested a direct link between the mind and the body.

Following the emergence of psychosomatic medicine came the development of a much broader discipline which examined the influence of psychological and social influences on health and which has become known as behavioural medicine. Behavioural medicine placed a far greater emphasis upon holistic thinking, consisting of elements from the whole range of the behavioural sciences, most notably psychology and sociology. Furthermore, it adopted a largely preventive perspective resulting partly from the foundations upon which it was based. These included the observation that many chronic diseases, such as heart disease and hypertension, were related to certain behaviours such as cigarette smoking and overeating. Thus by educating people as to the dangers of these behaviours, it was hoped that the illnesses associated with them could be prevented.

Psychological interventions, or therapies, which aimed to help individuals change their behaviour have become a legitimate part of behavioural medicine and, following on from the psychophysiological traditions of psychosomatic medicine, behavioural medicine has also adopted techniques aimed more directly at physiological functioning including, for example, the method known as biofeedback. Biofeedback consists in giving patients information (feedback) about certain physiological parameters, for example heart rate or electrical activity in the brain (brainwaves) and asking them to attempt to control that activity, for example slow down or speed up the heart rate. Experiments have shown that, over time and given some training, people can learn how to bring such bodily responses, which had previously been considered involuntary responses, under voluntary control.

The most recent challenge to the biomedical model has come from the subdiscipline of health psychology which has built upon both psychosomatic and behavioural medicine and adopted and developed a distinct alternative to the biomedical model: the biopsychosocial approach.

The biopsychosocial model

The biopsychosocial model was developed by George Engel (1977) and it asserts that the biomedical model must be supplemented by paying greater attention to the psychosocial aspects of health and illness. The model constitutes more than a merely abstract conceptualization; it is implicitly based on actual organismic functioning. It is, in one sense, a reaction to the exclusive emphasis on biological functioning inherent in the biomedical model and has, therefore, been associated with a radical fringe (Temoshok 1990). It is important in this respect, however, to note the powerful influence of the medical profession who have a vested interest in maintaining the status quo of the biomedical model and therefore dismissing or attempting to minimize the influence of any challenge to it. Despite such opposition, the biopsychosocial model is becoming increasingly mainstream and while these influences may perhaps explain its moderate scientific impact, others have argued that its current status is more a change in perspective or attitude than a well-articulated scientific paradigm.

Although the model emphasizes the importance of interactions between factors at the three levels which it encompasses, these three levels may be examined in isolation from one another in order to gain a deeper understanding of the scope of the model. The 'bio' (biological) component of the model represents the types of influence that are encapsulated in the biomedical model such as bacterial or viral infection, genetically transmitted diseases and structural weaknesses. The 'psycho' (psychological) component of the model accounts for the psychological aspects of health and illness in terms of the cognitions (thoughts), emotions (feelings, sometimes called affects) and behaviours of the individual. The 'social' components include sociological and cultural factors such as social class, the social influences of friends, family and the workplace and the way in which the wider cultural values of society relate to health. Thus the model is extremely broad in its conceptualization of the types of things which influence health and it seeks to explain how each of these factors contribute to the overall well-being of the individual through interactions between each of the three components (biological, psychological and social). From a biopsychosocial perspective, illness must be examined in a holistic way, resulting from a combination of interacting factors, none of which is sufficient in itself to explain the manifestation of a particular pattern of symptoms. Correspondingly, the treatment of illness involves treating the whole person in their social situation, rather than focusing exclusively upon the physical symptoms with which they present.

The biopsychosocial model incorporates a general systems perspective which means that, while it is possible to describe the independent functioning of each of the three systems, it is necessary to examine the interactions between them in order to explain fully the causes of illness and how it may be treated. This is because any change in one of the systems will cause changes in the other systems. To take a very simple example, spending a long time thinking about a troublesome worry (a psychological phenomenon) may lead to the experience of headache (a physical symptom) which may lead to the avoidance of social contact (a social effect).

General systems theory is a way of describing natural phenomena which states that nature may be viewed as a number of circumscribed, and therefore individually specifiable, systems which are organized in a hierarchy and which interact with each other. One of the main consequences of thinking about natural phenomena in this way is that each of the systems may be described as being a part of a larger system in the hierarchy or, conversely, each system is made up of smaller systems. This provides a method of analysing the system, that of reductionism – reducing each element to its constituent elements. However, the theory also asserts that each of the systems interact with each other and it places great emphasis upon looking at those interactions as the primary focus of analysis. It therefore adds to the strictly reductionistic approach of the natural sciences upon which the biomedical model was founded in that, as we progress up through the levels in the hierarchy of systems, each system may be understood only by considering it in relation to the other systems. While at any particular point in time (i.e. in a static analysis) each component system may be understood in terms of the subsystems which constitute it and the suprasystems which provide the context in which it exists, we may only fully understand that system if we are also familiar with the ways in which it interacts with the systems above and below it in the hierarchy. This has two very important consequences. Firstly, it means that we need to understand how changes in each of the subordinate and supraordinate systems affect the system in question. This means that we need to look at how the system changes over time if we are to understand fully its functioning and must therefore adopt a dynamic analysis of any phenomena which we choose to examine from a systems perspective. The second important consequence of focusing upon the interactions that occur in any given system is that we need to specify the mechanisms of interaction within the system. Some of these mechanisms are specific (that is, they explain interactions only between certain subsystems) while others are more general and are therefore able to explain interactions between several of the component systems. One very important general way in which systems interact is through a mechanism known as negative feedback, which operates at the three main levels of analysis specified in the biopsychosocial model and which will be referred to at appropriate points in subsequent chapters. These features of general systems theory which apply also to the biopsychosocial model make it particularly useful in examining the phenomenon of stress.

Despite early resistance to the biopsychosocial model, which arose in particular from the medical profession, it is this perspective which has become the accepted model within health psychology. This is largely because of the scope it offers psychologists in explaining the role of psychological factors in health and illness. However, there are other benefits in adopting this model which are particularly useful in the field of stress. Firstly, it has the advantages which derive from the systems perspective upon which it is based and which have already been discussed. Secondly, it incorporates a rejection of mind–body dualism and forces us to address the issue of exactly how these systems interact by considering the mechanisms and pathways by which psychological processes impact upon biological ones. It is very important that we understand these pathways, both to gain a fuller understanding of the stress phenomenon and in order to develop strategies for intervening in that process. The third main benefit which derives from adopting a biopsychosocial perspective is that it ensures that we avoid myopic thinking about the stress process. The biopsychosocial model is perhaps the only one which is sophisticated enough to account for the complexity and multifactorial nature of the stress process. As Chapter 2 makes clear, one of the main failings of stress researchers has been to focus too narrowly upon highly specialized subdisciplines and areas of study. While it is not possible for one individual to have sufficient expertise in every area of relevance to the stress process and at every level of analysis, by individual stress researchers locating their analyses within a common integrative framework such as that offered by the biopsychosocial model, we are more likely to arrive at a seamless and more comprehensive explanation of stress. For all of these reasons, the biopsychosocial model constitutes the overarching framework, or paradigm, within which specific theories of stress can be described and evaluated.

Perspectives on stress

There is a large body of theoretical material in the stress field which may be loosely referred to as 'stress theory' and which consists of a diverse range of specific theories of stress, some more widely accepted than others, some focusing on particular mechanisms which are thought to mediate the stress–health link and some which employ particular sets of theoretical ideas and reject or exclude others. Thus we are offered a number of perspectives on stress which have stemmed from different academic disciplines and traditions, each with their own pedigree and appeal. Some of these theories are fairly general in their scope and consequently attempt to explain a wide range of stress phenomena, while others have a much more restricted range of convenience. It is possible, however, to discern a more limited number of perspectives on stress which are implied by the approach that they have each adopted in trying to understand how stress can influence health. In order that the various theories of stress which will be introduced in subsequent chapters may be more easily integrated into an overall understanding of the stress process, a number of these perspectives on stress are described here.

The fact that the body of theoretical knowledge relating to the stress phenomenon is extremely diverse has led to disparity within the field. However, the fact that we have so many discourses upon which we may draw in our attempts to locate and explain the stress phenomenon makes it a particularly rich and challenging field of enquiry. Indeed the very notion of 'discourses of stress' offers one perspective from which to view the stress phenomenon – the discursive perspective. This approach draws upon people's experiences of stress which are influenced by – indeed constructed through – their everyday understandings of the notion of stress and which, as outlined earlier in the chapter, draw upon the prevalent lay theories in the social and cultural milieu. One powerful proponent of the discursive approach to understanding health and illness is Alan Radley who has written about biographical and cultural perspectives on health and illness (Radley 1993) and suggests that the study of health and illness, must include an analysis of the way in which people take up or refuse the dominant discourse in Western culture that defines these things as 'medical matters' (ibid: 6). The discursive approach emphasizes the need to take account of the individual's own experience, understanding, interpretation and perception of stressful events in order to explain how such events come to influence health. This approach to understanding stress is very new. Indeed, it may be argued that it lies at the 'cutting edge' of the field, and consequently there is a dearth of research which has adopted this perspective. Furthermore, such research requires a fundamental reconsideration of what constitute appropriate methodological and analytical techniques, necessitating a move away from hypothetico-deductive, quantitative methods and towards rigorous qualitative methodology and grounded forms of analysis. It has been limited, to some extent, by the lack of researchers trained in this relatively new methodological movement in psychology. However, Pollock (1993, 1988) has conducted some empirical work in the area in relation to the ideology of stress and coping and how this can determine the course of both stress episodes and illness more generally.

Another popular way in which stress is often viewed is known as the evolutionary perspective. From this perspective, the pathogenic origins of stress result from the disparate time scales of biological and cultural evolution; our bodies evolved slowly, those responses which enhanced our chances of survival in an uncivilized world being preserved by natural selection, while the sudden (in evolutionary terms) advent of society made these responses redundant. The types of bodily responses which enhance the chances of survival of a species are those which increase the capacity of individual members of that species to deal with and overcome the threat posed by predators, namely fighting the predator or running away from it. The types of responses which perform such functions are the catabolic physiological processes which are under autonomic control and which are activated by adrenaline. These responses result in a condition of extreme physiological arousal in preparation for running very quickly or fighting and they are discussed further in Chapter 2 where the work of Walter Cannon on the 'fight or flight' syndrome is considered in more depth. Unlike our ancestors, the types of stresses which we face in the modern world, such as time pressure, for example, have a far higher psychological element to them than the more physical types of challenges or stresses that our species may have faced in prehistoric times, which consisted largely in physical threats to survival. The catabolic processes invoked, therefore, are not appropriate reactions to more modern types of stressors as they are superfluous. Not only do they serve no useful function, but by repeatedly leaving our bodies in a state of extreme physical arousal with no ensuing outlet, they can cause damage to the 'aroused' organ systems, such as sclerosis in the arteries and thromboses in the heart. According to the evolutionary perspective on stress, it is this inappropriate physiological response which constitutes the link between stress and disease and thereby causes ill health.

The notion of a state of 'general physiological arousal' constitutes a recurrent theme in the stress literature and, in this sense, acts as a further perspective upon the stress process. Appley and Trumbull (1967) have referred to this as 'the hourglass model' which describes a wide range of psychological, biological and social stimuli, each feeding in to a common element (the bottleneck of the hourglass) and resulting in a wide range of responses. This perspective integrates a variety of stimuli and responses by asserting that the process which intervenes between them is common and consists in the physiological bodily arousal that has been described. The hourglass model does not, however, elaborate on the psychological or social processes which constitute the stressor and it thus provides a scant description, rather than a detailed explanation, of how these higher-level processes influence the hypothesized 'common element' and how this in turn initiates further physiological changes and affects subsequent thoughts and behaviour. With respect to the precise biological pathway or mechanism which constitutes this common element, or general state of arousal, the various candidates are considered in subsequent chapters. However, it would seem overly simplistic and highly unlikely that one individual biological pathway could fulfil such a function.

A further perspective on stress is related to the notion of adaptation – the challenge represented by a threatening or changing environment and the resources drawn upon during the process of adaptating to those changing environmental conditions. This perspective has several variants including the life change–health change paradigm (e.g. Garrity and Marx 1985), the conservation of resources model (Hobfall 1988, 1989) and the 'diseases of adaptation' approach (Selye 1983b).

The life change–health change paradigm states that life changes, both positive and negative, are stressors in that they tax our adaptational resources causing psychological and physiological strain, thereby leading to a greater probability of a negative change in health. This approach is comparable with more simple models such as the hourglass model, although it invokes the concept of psychophysiological strain which refers to the repeated bodily arousal previously described. Also, it elaborates the antecedents and sequelae of this strain, specifying that the most important element of a stressor is that of a change in circumstances, rather than the absolute level of stress in a person's environment.

The conservation of resources model also states that stress is the result of the draining of our resources. However, it incorporates a much more sophisticated conceptualization of the notion of 'resources' than simply bodily or physical resources and includes concrete objects which we own, states or conditions which we value, personal skills and characteristics and valuable commodities such as time, money and knowledge. Hobfall (1988: 25) suggests that 'people have an innate as well as learned desire to conserve the quality and quantity of their resources and to limit any state that may jeopardize the security of these resources'. The model adopts a response-based definition of stress, stating that stress is the response to one of three conditions: the threat of a net loss of resources, the actual net loss of resources or the lack of resource gain following investment of resources.

The diseases of adaptation approach was formulated by Hans Selye. It proposes that during our efforts to adapt, physiological strain is placed upon various organs in our body (such as the heart or stomach) and that this repeated strain has a pathogenic effect upon one or more of these organ systems, resulting in the manifestation of diseases such as coronary heart disease. The approach is in some ways similar to another perspective on the stress phenomenon which takes as its starting point the end disease state, rather than the stress process itself, as the phenomenon requiring explanation. This may be called the disease-specificity perspective and whole literatures have sprung up around certain diseases which have become linked with the idea that stress can play a major causal role in their genesis. These diseases include coronary heart disease, myocardial infarction, hypertension (high blood pressure), bronchial asthma and cancer and stress has been labelled as a risk factor in all of these illnesses. A risk factor is something which makes someone more likely to develop a particular disease than an individual who does not have it and such factors tend to involve things like family history, lifestyle and cultural and socio-economic conditions. This perspective has several components and it brings together a number of important and recurring concepts in the study of stress: specificity, vulnerability and stress diathesis.

The stress-diathesis model suggests that individuals may have particular weaknesses or vulnerabilities in one or more organ systems which are known as diatheses. Specific illnesses then result from stress experienced by people with a constitutional predisposition towards that illness, due to a particular weakness. This weakness may either be inherited or could be due to defects arising from previous damage or pathology. Alternatively, there may not be a specific weakness or fault in any particular organ system, but as it is unlikely that all systems are equally resilient, one particular organ or system is likely to be the 'weakest' and therefore break down or succumb to disease before the others. When placed under stress, it is the weaker, or most vulnerable, organ system which is likely to develop pathology and a wide array of general stressors can thereby result in damage to the same bodily system, resulting in the manifestation of a specific disease.

An opposite view on specificity states that it is not the end result which is specific, but the initial stress. That is, different types of stress can result in particular types of response which result in certain diseases. A third possibility with respect to specificity is that a wide variety of general stressors can result in specific types of responses which mediate the effect on their associated organ systems, an idea known as 'response patterning'.

The notion of specificity can apply to the stressor, the mediating response, the end disease state or two or more of these in combination. When one adds to this already complex set of ideas, the possibility that specificity, response patterning or diathesis may apply to the psychological as well as the physical responses to stress and that the physical responses themselves may involve specificity at a neural and/or hormonal level, one begins to see exactly why no single perspective is sufficiently detailed to account for the processes involved in the mediation of the stress–health link.

The notion of mediation, and the various mechanisms which are implied in the link between stress and health introduces another perspective towards stress which involves the idea of 'intervening variables'. An intervening variable is one which is used to explain the relationship between two other variables and is said to intervene between, for example, the cause and effect, the dependent and independent measure or the precursor and outcome. There are many types of intervening variables in the study of stress which can be psychological, social or biological and which mediate the impact of stress upon health. Such mediating mechanisms may involve specific vulnerabilities to stress, such as a weak organ system, an overactive adrenal gland or an inability to cope with demanding or pressured situations. Just as stress has been identified as a risk factor in particular diseases, there may exist certain risk factors, or vulnerabilities, which make someone more susceptible to suffer from stress, either simply in terms of ill health or in a more experiential way as well. Some common types of intervening psychological mechanisms include cognitive styles, personality traits and coping repertoires (which are considered in greater depth in Chapter 3 where the stress and coping paradigm is presented). Some of the vulnerabilities which have been mentioned constitute mediating mechanisms in that they are involved in the actual transmission of stress through particular biopsychosocial pathways. Other variables serve to moderate the effects of stress upon health, as opposed to directly mediating those effects. Some moderating variables constitute vulnerabilities in the same way as the types of mediating mechanisms which have been described. However, others do not constitute vulnerabilities, but conversely serve to reduce or 'buffer' the effects of stress upon health. Such variables are known as 'buffering variables' and consist of things which are useful in helping to cope with stress and which therefore constitute resistance resources which ward off stress-induced ill health, such as good social support networks, a sense of personal control or high socio-economic status.

Another perspective on stress is the behaviourist perspective. Burchfield (1979) suggested that stress may arise from the learning of predictive and consequential cues in the environment. She proposed that organisms learn which cues precede stressor onset and, after repeated exposure, learn the threat potential of that particular stressor, thereby allowing them to initiate a physiological stress response in anticipation of the subsequently required level of defence. Rather than viewing stress as an inappropriate physiological response which has not yet become extinct, the model claims instead that individual organisms learn to moderate their stress response to an appropriate level. This particular model emphasizes physiological conditioning and is concerned more with physiological stimuli and responses than psychological ones. However, it does highlight the possible involvement of basic learning processes and further enriches our multiperspectival understanding of the stress phenomenon.

The final perspective on stress to consider is the cognitive perspective. Cognitive perspectives on stress focus upon the cognitive decision-making and information processing strategies that describe and explain the perception, experience, interpretation and resulting effects of stress. Lazarus and Folkman's theory of stress is an example of a cognitive approach which is known as the stress and coping paradigm and which is described more fully in Chapter 3. Another cognitive model is Brown's (1980) stressor-processing model which describes some of the psychological processes which mediate the link between stress and health. According to the model, stress arises as a result of disparity between preconceived expectations and perceptions. Such disparity results in a rumination process which consists in generating social threats, constructing mental images of the threats or stressors and also invokes unconscious defence mechanisms. Such processes lead to physiological arousal and, once under stress, perceptions are distorted and problem-solving ability is impaired. The model is useful in that it brings into consideration a wider set of cognitive components than many other approaches. For example, it highlights the role of expectations which are multidimensional, depend upon individual history and are determined, modified by and linked to aspirations, motives and situational cues. The model is, however, not well cited in the literature and it fails to elaborate to any great depth upon the precise role of these various cognitive elements in determining exactly how stress can influence health.

Concluding comments

The preceding review of a number of perspectives on stress, while inevitably selective, serves to highlight the fact that there is no single approach which is sophisticated enough to capture the multidimensional nature of the stress concept or account for the complexity of the stress process. Rather, each of the approaches that has been described offers a different insight into the overall process. With respect to the multifarious nature of the stress concept, Lazarus suggests that 'stress be treated as an organizing concept for understanding a wide range of phenomena of great importance in human and animal adaptation. Stress, then, is not a variable, but rather a rubric consisting of many variables and processes' (Lazarus and Folkman 1984a: 11–12). The perspectives that have been described give substance to that rubric and provide a number of theoretical ideas upon which we may draw in attempting to develop a more integrated description of the stress process and an explanation of how it can influence health. These perspectives may be considered as a basic theoretical 'tool-kit' from which appropriate components can be taken to describe particular elements of the stress process. Such a conceptualization makes redundant some of the simplistic theoretical accounts of stress and prepares the ground for a more determined effort to find ways of describing and explaining the role of individual subjective and experiential aspects of the stress phenomenon. It is aspects such as these which, although they are likely to exert an important influence upon how stress impacts upon health, are the least well understood and researched components of a potential explanatory framework. Such meaning-centred inquiry necessitates a critical approach which both recognizes the limitations of previous efforts in elucidating our understanding and which accounts for the way in which stress is experienced by individuals. In order to achieve the former of these two aims, Chapter 2 provides a critical historical overview of the development of the stress concept. This permits a fuller appreciation of current debates in the field than some of the briefer overviews available elsewhere. The latter of these aims, accounting for individual subjectivity in the stress process, is addressed in subsequent chapters where a cognitive–phenomenological framework is described and elaborated. Such a framework places central importance upon the subjective meanings that individuals attach to events and it treats the phenomenological experience of stress and the cognitions associated with it as the fundamental psychological datum from which contributions to a biopsychosocial account of the stress process must be developed.

Further reading

Hinkle, L.E. (1977) The concept of stress in the biological and social sciences. In Z.J. Lipowski, D.R. Lipsitt and P.C. Whybrow (eds) *Psychosomatic Medicine: Current Trends and Clinical Applications*. New York: Oxford University Press.
Mason, J.W. (1975a) A historical view of the stress field. Part 1. *Journal of Human Stress*, 1(1): 6–12.
Selye, H. (1983b) The stress concept: past, present and future. In C. Cooper *Stress Research: Issues for the Eighties*. Chichester: John Wiley.

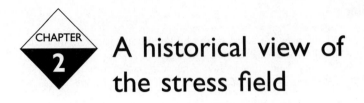 # A historical view of the stress field

Learning objectives for this chapter

In this chapter, which adopts a critical historical perspective, the development of stress theory over the past century or so is outlined, tracing the emergence of the stress concept from its roots in psychosomatics, through the interest in how life events impact upon health, to current times and its integration into the field of health psychology. The chapter describes how social and political forces have influenced theorizing in the area and introduces a body of highly critical literature, labelled the 'anti-stress movement'. After reading this chapter, you should be able to:

- outline the history of the stress concept;
- identify the various strands of work which have shaped the field as it stands today;
- identify some of the psychological and biological mechanisms implicated in the mediation of the stress–health link;
- appreciate how the social and political context in which stress research is conducted influences the formulation of research questions and the types of influence in the stress process which are deemed to be important;
- critically assess the current status of the stress concept;
- outline the key arguments which have been presented against further investigation in the area of stress; and
- explain why further investigation of stress is warranted and why it continues to be an important area of enquiry within health psychology.

Introduction

Taking a historical perspective aids a deeper understanding in several ways because it provides a portrayal of how and why current issues have emerged and it permits an understanding of the way in which the socio-political context in which previous research and theorizing in the area has influenced these emerging issues. This is an important, but often neglected endeavour because the wider cultural context in which research takes place both influences, and is influenced by, the research itself. Examining the nature and consequences of this bidirectional relationship in previous stress research provides an insight into the way in which such dynamics influence current research. These dynamics are particularly powerful in the field of stress due to its absorption into popular culture and current popularity in the scientific research community, as outlined in Chapter 1.

A second reason for examining the history of the stress concept revolves around the prevailing sense of confusion which dominates the field, as pointed out by Elliot and Eisdorfer (1982: 5) who wrote, quite simply, that 'stress research is filled with confusion, controversy and inconsistency'. It is only by understanding the sources of this confusion that strategies for resolving some of the persistent problems in the area may be developed and clarity may emerge. Of course, this requires that the field be examined historically. A third reason for taking a critical historical perspective is to dispel the 'presentism' which is apparent in many of the available overviews of the area. Such constructions can be misleading as they portray the research process as strictly cumulative, one finding building upon another as more information about the phenomenon is accumulated. These accounts are often a little overoptimistic and tend to engender a way of thinking about stress which does not accurately reflect the reality. They draw upon the discourse of 'scientific progress' and present investigation into the stress phenomenon as a strictly objective enterprise, uncovering the 'true' nature of stress and building upon the already substantial collection of 'facts' that have been 'discovered'. Of course, such representations do not provide an accurate description of the practice of science as the work of Kuhn, Popper and modern deconstructionists has taught us. Indeed, such accounts may actually serve to mask the underlying state of confusion, plastering over the cracks in our knowledge, rather than attempting to highlight and directly address them. The application of the types of constructionist approaches referred to in Chapter 1, such as discourse analysis and discursive psychology, have gone some way towards remedying the situation. However, it is still necessary to exercise caution and maintain a warranted scepticism when reading many of the accounts of stress research which are available.

The evolution of the term 'stress'

In a pointed and oft-cited critique of the stress concept, Hinkle (1977: 29) describes how the term 'stress' evolved over a period of several hundred years, from around the seventeenth century when it was commonly used to mean 'hardship, straits, adversity or affliction' until the eighteenth and nineteenth centuries when this usage had largely been replaced by that denoting the 'force, pressure, strain or strong effort exerted upon a material object or a person, or upon a person's organs or mental powers'. During this period, the physical sciences had undergone huge developments and were integrated into a relatively coherent body of knowledge used to describe the physical world. The words 'stress' and 'strain', having already been thoroughly absorbed into common culture, were employed in physics to describe the behaviour of elastic materials under load. Often, the use of terms in a scientific sense affects their meaning in the wider culture and vice versa and, by the nineteenth and early twentieth century, the word had come to be used as an analogue in the social and biological sciences to describe a possible cause of ill health and mental disease. This is evidenced by the following quote, as cited in Lazarus and Folkman (1984a) and Hinkle (1977), among others, from Sir William Osler in his Lumleian Lectures of 1910:

> Living an intense life, absorbed in his work, devoted to his pleasures, . . . the nervous energy of the Jew is taxed to the uttermost, and his system is subjected to that stress and strain which seems to be a basic factor in so many cases of angina pectoris.

Thus by the beginning of the nineteenth century, the word 'stress' was in use in the social and medical sciences. The concept can, no doubt, be traced even further back in time as implied by Buell and Eliot (1979: 22) who, with reference to the relationship between stress and cardiovascular disease, wrote that 'almost 2000 years ago, Celsus recognized that emotional states could influence the heart . . . [and] . . . In 1628, William Harvey reaffirmed the observation by stating that every affection of the mind that is attended with either pain or pleasure, hope or fear, is the cause of an agitation whose influence extends to the heart'. Thus the concept of stress and, in particular, the notion that it can influence health has a long history.

It comes as something of a surprise, then, when surveying the vast stress literature to come across many seemingly authoritative sources which state that 'the concept of stress was first introduced into the life sciences by endocrinologist Hans Selye in 1936' (Appley and Trumbull 1967: 1). As Mason (1975a: 6–7) points out, this statement is factually incorrect:

> In fact, Selye himself has remarked that he did not use the term 'biologic stress' in his initial papers in 1936 on the subject because of 'violently adverse public opinion', with the further explanation that 'There was too much criticism of my use of the word stress in reference to bodily reactions, because in everyday English it generally implied nervous strain.' He also remarked that such expressions as nervous stress and strain had long been commonly used by psychiatrists to describe mental tension.

Selye did not, in actuality, use the term 'stress' until 1946, ten years later than the time Appley and Trumbull suggest, but not only are they incorrect about *when* the stress concept was popularized in the life sciences, they are also mistaken about *who* popularized it, for the work of Selye was predated by that of Walter Cannon who developed the stress concept from his work on the fight-or-flight response in 1914.

The fight or flight syndrome

The fight of flight syndrome is a response which prepares the body for action (either fighting or fleeing) in an emergency situation. This response involves the activation of the adrenomedullary system (see Chapter 5) which mobilizes the body's resources by releasing glucose stored in the form of glycogen in the liver and increasing cardiovascular activity by raising cardiac output. This results in an increase in heart rate, stroke volume and force of contraction and an alteration of haemodynamics by vasoconstriction of the blood vessels which supply the skin and viscera, vasodilation of the blood vessels which supply the muscles and brain and biochemical alteration of the blood-clotting mechanism. Cannon conceived of stress as disturbing homeostasis, causing a movement away from physiological equilibrium which results from exposure to both physical and psychological stimuli. Other bodily changes normally associated with autonomic arousal include an increase in rate and depth of breathing, bronchodilation, pilo-erection and pupo-dilation. Such bodily responses would obviously have survival advantages and form the basis of the evolutionary perspective on stress. Cannon's research on the fight or flight syndrome converged with the work of Freud and Pavlov to pave the way for the rise of the psychosomatic movement in medicine which started in Germany but, by the 1930s had spread to England and North America (Wittkower 1977). It was over twenty years after the appearance of Cannon's work, in the 1936 paper entitled 'A Syndrome Produced by Diverse Nocuous Agents', that Hans Selye introduced a concept which has had a profound impact on modern stress research and which he called the general adaptation syndrome (GAS).

The general adaptation syndrome

A revealing account of the research process leading up to the publication of this seminal paper was provided by Selye in his book *The Stress of Life* (1956). Selye was researching the discovery of new sex hormones and during this research frequently injected rats with hormones, usually consisting of crude ovarian extracts. He found that such injections produced a triad of morphological changes consisting of adrenocortical enlargement and hyperactivity, atrophy of the thymus gland and lymph nodes and the appearance of gastrointestinal ulcers. Because no existing ovarian hormone

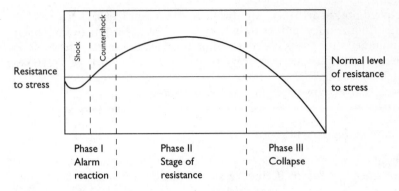

Figure 2.1 The general adaptation syndrome
Source: Reproduced from T. Cox (1978) *Stress*. The Macmillan Press Ltd.
With permission

was known to produce such changes, Selye believed he had discovered a
new hormone and, in order to test out this hypothesis, prepared extracts
from other organs such as the pituitary, kidney and spleen. To his initial
disappointment, he discovered that these extracts also produced the changes
outlined above and this led him to suspect that, rather than the biochemical
action of the injections, it was in fact their toxicity (due to their impurity)
that caused the syndromal response. In order to test the toxicity hypothesis,
Selye tried injecting other toxic fluids and these also produced the same
effects. In a series of later experiments designed to examine the degree of
specificity of the response he replicated the results with a much wider array
of stimuli including insulin injection, excessive cold and heat, mechanical
restraint and vibration, sleep deprivation, water deprivation, foot shock
and X-irradiation. It was only later, in a paper published in 1946, that Selye
associated this syndrome with stress and expanded upon the concept of the
GAS. In this paper he also introduced the idea of the 'diseases of adaptation' as
the result of abnormal or maladaptive reactions to stress, a position which
was refined and consolidated in later works such as *The Stress of Life* (1956).

The GAS consists of three identifiable stages (see Figure 2.1). The first of
these, the alarm reaction, has two phases: an initial shock phase, during
which resistance to the stressor is lowered; and a countershock phase where
defensive mechanisms become activated. These mechanisms increase their
activity in the second stage, the stage of resistance, until maximum adaptation occurs, after which and under conditions of continued stress, the stage of
exhaustion is reached during which adaptive resources are stretched beyond
their limit and collapse leading to disease and, ultimately, death.

Like Cannon's theory, Selye's is based largely upon physiological functioning, although it focuses upon the role of the pituitary–adrenocortical
system (see Chapter 5). The GAS is concerned with the homeostatic maintenance of psychoendocrine functioning and says little about psychological

aspects of stress, other than to include psychological stimuli as one category of possible stressors. However, Selye used mainly physical stressors, such as foot shock, water deprivation and physical restraint and vibration and the issue of whether such stressors produce reactions similar to stressors of a more psychological nature remains debatable.

Thus, one may question the relevance of both Cannon's and Selye's contribution to our understanding of the psychological aspects of stress, as Lazarus and Folkman (1984a: 3) state: 'although the enormous volume of work on hormonal stress secretions that stemmed from Selye's work had obvious implications at the sociological and psychological levels of analysis, it did little to clarify the latter processes'. Despite this caveat, and in common with many other commentaries on the subject, when referring to the recent expansion of interest in the stress phenomenon in the social sciences, they go on to say that his work had played a dominant role. Frankenhauser (1980) correctly points out that the work of Selye and Cannon forms the basis of today's *psychoendocrine* research into stress but many psychological researchers appeal to this body of work to validate their psychological models, with which they are fundamentally incomparable (Pollock 1988). Martin (1984: 461) has argued that, in the context of the 'psychologisation' of stress, Selye's ideas have become 'outmoded and are no longer appropriate guidelines for stress research' while others (e.g. Miller 1996) have suggested that the work of Selye merely requires modification.

The transition from the physiological work of Cannon and Selye to the types of psychological models presented in this book is often portrayed in terms of the former providing an impetus for the latter in a continuous flow of ideas, but there is actually discontinuity in moving from one to the other as was pointed out by Radloff and Helmreich in 1968 who argued that calling psychological stress an analogue of Selye's physiological construct is inappropriate because of the psychologist's inability to specify a psychological equivalent of physiological homeostasis and to deal with complications introduced by higher mental processes. It certainly seems that the physiological work of Cannon and Selye both preceded and was contiguous with that of psychological approaches, but the first truly psychological attempts to describe and explain stress were spawned largely independently of this (Fleming *et al.* 1984).

Scientific and historical developments

At around the period of Selye's work, several other developments influenced the course of stress research. Firstly, in the medical profession, physicians such as Harold Wolff (1953) were expounding the idea that life stress played a role in the aetiology of disease and this idea was becoming more widely accepted in medicine. Secondly, within psychology the emphasis on psychoanalytic concepts in their application to psychosomatic problems was decreasing, while the rising behaviourist paradigm saw an increasing amount of research conducted on animals. Consequently, the results of Selye's animal experiments were seen as being highly relevant to the study of stress in human beings. Thirdly, the advent of the Second World War gave renewed impetus to research and theorizing in the area of stress as evidenced by the 1945 publication *Men Under Stress* by Grinker and Spiegel which contains an extensive discussion of stress in a military context. In particular, the military were interested in the effect of combat stress on performance and efforts to identify the role of individual differences in vulnerability to stress were generated from the observation that large individual differences existed in the performance of troops under combat stress (Harris *et al.* 1956).

The contribution of combat psychiatry had a prolonged influence on stress research extending over the next twenty years or so, especially in North America where, with the advent of the Korean War, many studies were directed at the effects of stress on the performance of the increasingly skilled tasks that soldiers had to perform. Advances in biochemistry permitted the extraction and analysis of stress hormones such as adrenaline and cortisol, which were considered to be reliable, objective indicators of stress while parallel developments in psychophysiological technology allowed the precise measurement of variables such as heart rate, galvanic skin response and other indices of autonomic arousal. The effects of the Vietnam War increased the interest in combat stress and again provided the impetus for a host of studies which used this new technology in the study of individual differences and performance under stress. These studies identified the individual's perception of potentially stressful events as the major variable determining their physiological response to stress (Rose 1984). Towards the end of the 1960s and into the 1970s, the interest in how humans perform under stress provided the conceptual basis of research into how people coped with the rapid pace of technological development. Stemming from military work in the area, this research began to address issues such as the stress associated with travel in space, which was being pioneered at the time. Studies were also conducted which examined the effects of noise on performance and this research was developed and applied to the workplace, leading to the development of research into what is today referred to as 'occupational stress'.

By 1960, the stress concept had become firmly established within psychology (Haward 1960) and developments throughout the 1960s meant that any attempt to produce a coherent theoretical account of stress had to explain how individual differences arose. In 1966, Richard Lazarus proposed that individual differences in performance under stress were due to the fact that not everyone perceives potentially stressful situations in the same way. He argued that stress is psychologically mediated by a process which he labelled 'cognitive appraisal' and thus an event is only stressful if it is appraised as such by the individual. The idea that stress was mediated by some psychological process was not new and formed the basis of much of the work at this time, but it was Lazarus who elaborated the idea by invoking the concept of cognitive appraisal and extended it to focus on the process of coping. The stress and coping paradigm is presented in detail in Chapter 4.

It was also the 1960s that saw the advent of an approach known as 'life events research' which is based upon the life change–health change paradigm. Holmes and his associates began looking at the effects of life changes, both positive and negative, upon health, arguing that such changes constitute stressors in that they tax our adaptational resources causing psychological and physiological strain, thereby leading to a greater probability of a negative change in health status. The instrument they used to investigate this theory is the well-known Social Readjustment Rating Scale or SRRS (Holmes and Rahe 1967), a device which measures the relative stressfulness of life events (see Box 2.1).

The life events approach has been criticized by various researchers (e.g. Schroeder and Costa 1984) on several grounds, but perhaps the most damning criticism is that such an approach fails to take account of the individual variation in response to life events shown by different people. The scale provided the impetus for a whole era of stress research into life events and several good reviews are available which all suggest that stressful life events are associated with negative changes in health status (e.g. Dohrenwend and Dohrenwend 1979; Brown and Harris 1989; Theorell 1992).

Also during the 1960s, the concept of stress at the social level became popular in sociology and social psychology. As Lazarus and Folkman (1984a) have noted, riots, panics and other social disturbances such as increased

---

Box 2.1 Life events research and the Social Readjustment Rating Scale

Life events research is based upon a stimulus-based conception of stress in that it assumes that certain life events act as stressful stimuli which lead to ill health. It uses the Social Readjustment Rating Scale to measure stress. The scale is presented below and consists of a checklist of 43 commonly reported events which were rated on a scale of stressfulness from 1 to 100, with marriage being assigned the arbitrary value of 50. These weightings were then averaged over a large number of people to give the 'average stressfulness' of each of the events. Hence the level of stress to which a particular individual had been subjected over a given period can be measured by ascertaining how many of these events he or she had experienced. This type of standardized measure is useful as it allows direct comparisons to be made between different studies. However, it fails to account for how individuals see the events listed in the scale and the meanings they attach to them. Consequently, the approach does not account for differences in the subsequent amount of 'strain' they cause.

Rank	Life event	Mean value
1	Death of spouse	100
2	Divorce	73
3	Marital separation	65
4	Jail term	63
5	Death of close family member	63
6	Personal injury or illness	53
7	Marriage	50
8	Fired at work	47
9	Marital reconciliation	45
10	Retirement	45
11	Change in health of family member	44
12	Pregnancy	40
13	Sex difficulties	39
14	Gain of new family member	39
15	Business readjustment	39
16	Change in financial state	38
17	Death of close friend	37
18	Change to different line of work	36
19	Change in number of arguments with spouse	35
20	Mortgage over $10,000	31
21	Foreclosure of mortgage or loan	30
22	Change in responsibilities at work	29
23	Son or daughter leaving home	29
24	Trouble with in-laws	29
25	Outstanding personal achievement	28
26	Wife begins or stops work	26
27	Begin or end school	26
28	Change in living conditions	25
29	Revision of personal habits	24
30	Trouble with boss	23
31	Change in work hours or conditions	20
32	Change in residence	20
33	Change in schools	20
34	Change in recreation	19
35	Change in church activities	19
36	Change in social activities	18
37	Mortgage or loan less than $10,000	17
38	Change in sleeping habits	16
39	Change in number of family get-togethers	15
40	Change in eating habits	15
41	Vacation	13
42	Christmas	12
43	Minor violations of the law	11

Source: Holmes, T.H. and Rahe, R.H. (1967), The Social Readjustment Rating Scale, Journal of Psychosomatic Research, 2, 213–18.

rates of suicide, crime and mental illness were analysed in terms of the effects of social stress or strain. The idea of social stress has also influenced stress research in psychology, for example the focus on demographic variables has highlighted differences in vulnerability to stress due to factors such as age, sex, employment status, social class and urbanization (Jenkins 1991). The concentration on social aspects of stress led to a growing interest in the concept of social support which is a measure of the number and quality of social relationships that a person enjoys. Social support may take various forms such as emotional support or instrumental help in a material or practical way and it may therefore act at more than one level, reducing the impact of stress on health by spreading responsibilities and providing resources which help deal with the after-effects of stress, including helping someone to cope with the illness itself. There is some research evidence that social support reduces the effects of stress on health. However, in a meta-analysis of studies of the effects of social support, Schwarzer and Leppin (1989) pointed out that findings have been inconsistent and suggest that further theoretical refinement is necessary.

At the same time as the life events research was taking place there was an extensive literature developing from the ongoing eight-and-a-half-year prospective Western Collaborative Group Study (Rosenman *et al.* 1975). This study demonstrated the association of the Type A Behaviour Pattern (TABP) with coronary heart disease (CHD). The TABP consists of a constellation of character traits constituting hostility, an aggressive and competitive drive for achievement and a chronic sense of time urgency. This research stemmed from the observation firstly that traditional physiological risk factors for coronary heart disease accounted for less than half its incidence and, secondly, that not all of those who lead a similarly stressful life are equally likely to develop CHD. It was therefore hypothesized that stress could have a causal role (Buell and Eliot 1979). Type A behaviour was reported to be characteristically displayed by those who were particularly prone to stress-induced CHD and the notion of the 'stress-prone' personality became firmly entrenched in psychology. Other approaches to individual differences at around this time also focused on the role of personality variables as mediating, moderating or buffering variables and this type of research has remained popular since the 1960s. Thus an enormous literature has developed around individual differences in the stress process and a large number of variables have been isolated. These variables are reviewed in Chapter 3 and they include Kobasa's (1979) work on the concept of hardiness, Bandura's (1977) self-efficacy theory and Rotter's (1975) work on locus of control. A typical finding is, for example, that of Crandall and Lehman (1977) who reported that external locus of control correlated with scores on Holmes and Rahe's SRRS, suggesting that externals experience more stress.

The rise of cognitivism in the 1970s influenced stress research by encouraging the development of cognitive theories of stress and through the contribution of cognitive-behavioural therapy. The 'cognitive revolution', coupled with the persistence of social approaches and the emergence of socio-cognitive theory in psychology led to the formulation of intricate models of the role of cognitive processes in moderating the effects of stress on psychological and physical health (e.g. Hamilton and Warburton 1979). Accordingly, the literature on cognitive–behavioural therapy identified certain cognitions as pathological, for example Lohr and Hamberger, in their 1990 review of the cognitive–behavioural modification of the coronary-prone behaviour pattern identified the following types of cognition as contributing to the pathogeny of type A behaviour: appraisals of harm or loss, paralogical reasoning such as selective abstraction, overgeneralization, arbitrary inference, minimization of success and maximization of failure and irrational beliefs caused by inappropriate syllogistic reasoning processes such as attitude statements, meta-rules and belief systems and negative, internal, stable, global attributional styles. Cognitive–behaviour therapy focuses on how people construe situations as a central factor in the stress process (Hamberger and Lohr 1984) and attempts to change thoughts, as well as feelings and action. This approach has led to the development of cognitive interventions (e.g. Meichenbaum 1977) and stress inoculation training (e.g. Novaco 1977). Research in the field of cognitive–behaviour therapy has continued to develop throughout the 1970s and up to the present but has, as is often the case with applied research, been relatively neglected by the mainstream academic community. Cognitive–behavioural research continues to make an important contribution to our understanding of the stress process in developing the application of cognitive theories to the stress phenomenon. Chwalisz *et al.* (1992), for example, examined the role of attribution theory in the mediation of the stress–illness link, while Croyle (1992) has developed an interesting application of social comparison theory in explaining the mediation of psychological stress.

As cognitive-behavioural approaches were being developed throughout the 1970s and into the 1980s, life events research was simultaneously being questioned, since although reliable correlations between life events and illness had been obtained in both prospective and retrospective studies, these correlations were generally quite weak ranging from 0.2 to 0.3; at best, stressful life events seemed to account for less than 10 per cent of the variance in health outcome (Martin 1989). The relative lack of predictive power of life events in isolation from other factors contributed to the increase in popularity of notions of cognitive mediation and the influence of moderating variables, such as those of social support and individual differences. Martin (1989) argues that something of a 'paradigm shift' occurred at around this time which led to an increased focus upon the role of individual psychological factors in mediating the stress–health link. During this period, developments in neurobiology provided a pertinent and powerful stimulus to stress research.

Psychoneuroimmunology

The brain and endocrine systems were generally viewed as separate entities until the development of psychoendocrinology which, inspired by neurobiological findings, uncovered the way in which these systems interact. Psychoendocrinology allowed more detailed study of the hormonal response to stress, bringing to the fore once again the research of Cannon and Selye. Selye's claim that the stress response was non-specific was, however, being questioned by researchers who had found specific patterns in the hormonal response to stressors, known as response patterning (e.g. Mason 1971). Throughout this period, due partly to these developments in psychobiology, stress research became increasingly popular. In his review of the psychoendocrinology of stress, Rose (1984) points out that during the period from 1968 (when Mason produced his classic review of the 200 articles available at the time) to 1984, there was an increase of greater than an order of magnitude in the number of publications relating to changes in endocrine functioning in response to a wide variety of stressful stimuli.

The psychoendocrine research into stress produced two essential findings. Firstly, that wide individual differences existed in endocrine responses, depending largely upon the individual's perception of the potentially stressful event (Rose 1984). Secondly, the range of hormones and neurotransmitters involved in the endocrine response was extended to cover a wide array of substances, including catecholamines, growth hormone, prolactin, testosterone, thyroid hormone, insulin, aldosterone, gonadotropins, enkephalins, 5-HT, gamma-aminobutyric acid and beta-endorphin, which were implicated in an equally wide range of diseases.

The psychoendocrine research of the 1960s and 1970s did much to stimulate research at the interface between psychology and biomedicine. Indeed Frankenhauser (1984) suggests that psychobiological stress research has become a meeting place for questions concerning health–behaviour relations. In this respect, a major development of the period was an influential article by Engel (1977) entitled 'The Need for a New Medical Model: A Challenge for Biomedicine' in which he proposed the biopsychosocial model. This reinforced the notion that stress and disease always affect the organism as a whole and do not restrict their influence to any particular level of analysis or specific modality.

The other main development in the biomedical field which has influenced modern stress research also stemmed from advances in neurobiology and concerns the relationship between psychology and immune functioning. The psychoendocrine research uncovered hormones and neurotransmitters that were important in immune functioning and new immunoassay techniques permitted the detailed study of psychological, neural and immunological interactions. The term 'psychoneuroimmunology' (PNI) was coined by Ader (1981) to describe such research. The central tenet of PNI is one of cognitive modulation of immunocompetence. Environmental and psychosocial stimuli are perceived and interpreted according to an individual's history before they exert a top–down influence on the hypothalamus which controls both the autonomic nervous system (ANS) and the pituitary gland, thus effecting neural and hormonal regulation of the immune system. There exist several good reviews of PNI research (e.g. Solomon *et al.* 1985; Kiecolt-Glaser and Glaser 1988, 1995; Schulz and Schulz 1992) which have evaluated the effects of stress upon immune functioning and which all suggest that there is evidence that both major stressors, such as bereavement, and the types of minor stresses known as 'daily hassles', can have a suppressive effect on the immune system, thereby increasing susceptibility to illness. The role of more minor forms of stress, sometimes referred to as 'microstress', is examined in greater depth in Chapter 4.

The anti-stress movement

As is evident from the historical outline of the stress field presented in the previous section, there have been many approaches to studying stress. Perhaps unsurprisingly, therefore, the attempt to integrate this huge diversity within a single concept has generated considerable debate, controversy and confusion. The nature of debates waged within the study of individual differences in the stress process, some of which have already been mentioned, is symptomatic of the deep malaise in the field of stress where conceptual confusion and theoretical controversy seem to be an accepted feature. These conceptual and theoretical issues are considered in more detail in this section where a body of highly critical literature, referred to collectively as the 'anti-stress' movement, is reviewed.

The anti-stress movement argues that the concept of stress is so confused that it has become worthless. Ader (1980: 312), for example, wrote that:

> . . . there is little heuristic value in the concept of 'stress'. 'Stress' has come to be used (implicitly, at least) as an explanation of altered psychophysiological states. Since different experiential events have different behavioural and physiologic effects that depend upon the stimulation to which the individual is subsequently exposed and the responses the experimenter chooses to measure, the inclusive label, 'stress', contributes little to an analysis of the mechanisms that may underline or determine the organism's response. In fact, such labelling, which is descriptive rather than explanatory, may actually impede conceptual and empirical advances by its implicit assumption of an equivalence of stimuli, fostering the reductionistic search for simple one-cause explanations.

Given such damning criticism, one is led to question the very notion of a unified concept of stress. Indeed, some researchers have suggested that the stress concept should be abandoned altogether. Buell and Eliot (1979), for example, suggested that the term 'stress' affords little understanding because it means stimulus to some people, response to others, interaction to some, and complex combinations of these to still other workers. In their analysis, Buell and Eliot identify one of the major causes of confusion within the stress field and that concerns its definition; different researchers use the term to mean different things. The problem is not merely one of definition, though, and in their exhaustive review and evaluation of stress research, Elliot and Eisdorfer (1982: 5) identified a related, but separate problem:

> Starting from a set of reasonably well-defined concerns about the effects of certain types of stimuli on the body, the stress concept has broadened markedly as different investigators have invoked it to explain their data. It now encompasses a wide array of empirical studies and a descriptive literature of uneven quality that is scattered throughout almost the entire range of the behavioural, biological, and medical sciences.

The attempt to integrate a huge and diverse literature under the single concept of stress represents the second reason for current confusion and controversy in the stress field. Perhaps there is a good theoretical reason to attempt to integrate the diverse phenomena studied under the rubric of stress, in line with Appley and Trumbull's (1967) hourglass conception of stress as feeding from a wide source of stimuli through a narrow common element to a spectrum of responses. If stress is, indeed, such a ubiquitous phenomenon which pervades many of our interactions with the world, then this would explain the intense interest it has received from the academic community. There is also, however, a different and rather more cynical interpretation of the relatively recent sharp increase in the number and range of papers throughout the social scientific and biomedical literature which invoke the stress concept. This interpretation concerns the more pragmatic social and political forces to which researchers find themselves subject. The more benign of these interpretations relates to the fact that 'stress' has become something of a 'buzzword' in recent times, thus initiating a 'bandwagon effect'. Indeed in a scathing attack of the stress concept entitled 'Stress: The Creation of a Modern Myth', Briner (1994) noted that one can hardly pick up a popular newspaper or magazine without coming across the word stress. In this paper, Briner suggested that the attachment of such widespread cultural significance to a word like stress influences the development of such concepts, drawing an analogy with the word 'nerves' in the 1940s and 1950s when people were said to be 'suffering from nerves' and went to the doctor to get treatment for their 'nerves'. A similar point was made by Ursin and Murison (1984) who refer to the 'attributional power' the word stress has acquired in popular language. There remains, however, another interpretation of such widespread usage of the term 'stress' and this relates to the very real financial pressure applied to academics both to obtain funding for research projects and to produce an ever-increasing number of publications per year. By including the concept of stress in grant proposals and publication titles, the likelihood of acceptance by refereeing bodies is, perhaps, augmented because of the current popularity of the concept and the sheer number of publications dealing with the subject.

The two main sources of confusion in the stress field relate firstly to disagreement over its definition and, secondly, to an extension of its application to a huge and diverse array of phenomena. The two problems are, of course, interrelated; a concept which is not clearly defined, or has more than one popular definition, is likely to be applied to a wider variety of phenomena than one which is confined to a more restricted range of affairs. Appley and Trumbull (1967: 2), for example, suggested that while the use of common language might lead to the establishment of useful relationships and is therefore an advantage, the use of common terms in different ways may lead to confusion. This, they wrote, 'is quite apparent to anyone studying or confronted by the burgeoning stress literature'. In the face of confusion over such fundamental conceptual issues as the definition of stress, further empirical research is unlikely to provide clarification; the more fundamental problems must firstly be addressed and rectified.

Current controversies

One of the most persistent controversies in the stress field is the issue of whether the various processes studied under the rubric of stress do, in fact, share a common element. When Appley and Trumbull (1967) compared stress to an hourglass feeding from a wide source of stimuli through a narrow common element to a spectrum of responses, they implied that the relationship between the diverse phenomena studied under the umbrella of stress consisted of the fact that they shared a mediational pathway. They proposed that a possible mechanism could be the physiological stress response identified by Selye. However, they go on to caution that, as research findings accumulate, such a conception could turn out to be an oversimplification of the facts. In concluding their seminal book on issues in stress research, they predicted that the study of idiosyncratic psychobiological patterns would emerge as a major area of stress research and much of what they foresaw has certainly transpired.

Appley and Trumbull's idea of a common element was not, however, without its critics and even they themselves warned stress researchers to avoid treating stress as if it were a unitary, all-or-none phenomenon. Similarly, Mason (1975a: 12) wrote that '. . . the question of the extent to which there may be logical continuity or compatibility of concepts developing in the psychological stress field with Selye's concept of stress as a non-specific physiological response pattern is an issue which very much needs to be confronted directly and resolved, if we are to move towards clarification of thinking in this field'.

Many researchers propose that these two levels at which stress may be viewed are discontinuous. For example, Appley and Trumbull (1967: vii) make a clear distinction between the psychology and the physiology of stress, writing that there are '. . . clear shifts in emphasis and in concern for detail as one moves from considerations of physiological to social factors and from microcosmic to macrocosmic units of discourse'. Other writers have also differentiated between physiological and psychological aspects of stress according to the vast differences in the size levels of their respective units of analysis (e.g. Elliot and Eisdorfer 1982) and Hamberger and Lohr (1984) distinguish between physical and psychological stress, suggesting that psychological stress results from loss, frustration, conflict and failure, while physical stress consists of burns, infections, injuries and the like.

Mason (1975a: 10–11) states that 'relatively few workers at present use the term [stress] exactly according to Selye's particular definitions and formulations . . . [and it] . . . remains curiously "in limbo" – in the state of not being generally recognised as either proven or refuted beyond reasonable doubt'. The reasons for such a state of affairs are complex, however, and Mason goes on to discuss some of them suggesting that the actual practice of stress research has long been conducted in two largely separate and distantly removed arenas, physiology and psychology. Interest in the physiology of stress has dwindled in comparison to the flourishing interest in its psychology. This fact, coupled with the proclivity by psychologists to look upon stress as a broad and multidimensional concept, has meant that psychologists have found it easy to subsume Selye's physiology in their formulations of stress. Thus the relatively independent development of psychological stress concepts has proceeded based on an assumption by psychologists that the particular psychological process or construct which they are studying is related to and indeed triggers the physiological processes studied by Selye, an assumption which may or may not be true. This assumption constitutes one of the primary reasons that confusion reigns in the field of stress.

A major reason why attempts by psychologists to elaborate the stress process have been fraught with conceptual and methodological difficulties is the lack of theoretical and empirical collaboration between psychological and physiological stress researchers. On the one hand, many contemporary stress theorists insist that stress is, by its very nature, interdisciplinary, while on the other they proceed quite independently of the disciplines which are so essential to a full understanding of the problem. Furthermore, the nature of theorizing within health psychology tends to be somewhat piecemeal and unconcerted due to its relative immaturity as an academic discipline. The on-going cycle of thesis and antithesis allows many competing theories to coexist quite happily side by side as it has not yet achieved the synthesis of the physical sciences. The problems faced are a function of both the historical context in which the stress concept has developed and the attempts to integrate an extremely varied series of phenomena within a single unitary concept. Indeed, as Elliot and Eisdorfer (1982: 11) wrote, 'some definitions are so broad that they include essentially anything that might happen to someone'. The concept of a general level of arousal which is heavily drawn upon in the stress literature shares a similar problem in that it is simply too wide ranging and poorly defined to be of any significant practical use or explanatory power and as a consequence it has now been largely rejected as a serious explanatory variable in many areas of psychological theorizing.

It certainly appears that for most people working within the field, the account of stress offered by Selye is too simplistic to account for the available data (Cox 1978; Cox and Ferguson 1991). It does not elaborate on the role of individual subjectivity in the perception of stress or account for individual differences, it fails to distinguish between the pathogenic effects of positive and negative events and empirical research into the specificity of response patterning (e.g. Mason 1971) discredits the notion of a single 'stress response' which is elicited by all stressors. These criticisms of Selye's approach have, of course, been countered; for example, Selye claims that response patterning is merely the superposition of specific effects on top of the stereotypical response (Selye 1980). Despite such claims, the notion that the hormonal mechanisms which Selye studied constitute the single explanatory common pathway remains untenable in the face of the criticisms which have been outlined.

The types of hormonal responses upon which Selye's formulation of the stress concept is based are unlikely to represent the full picture with respect to isolating a common mediating pathway which unites and explains all of the areas studied under the stress rubric. However, this does not preclude the possibility that there exists some other common mediating pathway. Also, there remains the possibility that such a pathway could consist of some degree of commonality in its subcomponents which act in combination with other differentiated elements. Such differentiated elements could explain the observed response patterning and may themselves vary according either to the types of stressors to which individuals are exposed or else according to individual constitutional factors. In this connection, it would appear likely that commonalities in mediating pathways exist at the various levels of analysis encompassed in a biopsychosocial analysis. These would involve different mediating mechanisms at each of these levels, including not only common biological pathways such as the types of hormonal axes studied by Selye but also common cognitive and emotional mediating mechanisms in the psychological domain. Although the role of emotions in the stress process is considered in greater detail in Chapter 5, it is worth noting here that it is a widely held, but often implicit, assumption in much theorizing in the stress field that emotions or affective mechanisms play a crucial mediating role in the stress process. There have been relatively few attempts to elaborate exactly which emotions are crucial in this process and precisely how affective mechanisms may mediate the effects of psychosocial stress upon physical health. Once again, this is due to an overreliance upon biological mediating pathways as possible candidates for a common element in the stress process, to the relative neglect of common psychological processes. This is symptomatic of a more general tendency in the field of health psychology, as Marteau and Johnston (1987) pointed out when they warned against the danger of neglecting psychological models. Only in recent times is this situation being fully recognized and addressed by professionals working in the field.

In considering cognitive mediation as a common element in the stress process, as opposed to the physiological mediation outlined by Selye, care must be taken not to merely substitute one set of problems for another. Also, such a proposition moves from one level of analysis (the physiological) to another (the psychological) and therefore takes us no further along the path towards understanding exactly how events at one level influence processes at the other. The suggestion that the link may involve an element of cognitive mediation still leaves unaddressed the 'conceptual hiatus' described by Brown (1980: 22):

> The most obvious conceptual hiatus concerns the mechanisms operating between the external psychosocial factors and the activation of the internal psychophysiological mechanisms during reactions to psychosocial stress . . . cognitive mediation is known experientially and subjectively to occur, but . . . Despite the tacit understanding and pragmatic acceptance of cognitive mediation, the most popular notion of psychosocial stress is the vast oversimplification that psychological stressors excite the varieties of neural, endocrine and immune systems that implement stress reactions, as defined by Selye.

Brown goes on to identify the main theoretical omissions and, in particular, points to the fact that systematic analyses of the nature of psychosocial stressors fail to suggest how such stressors are processed neurally or cognitively to result in activation of physiological processes that manifest the observed changes in health status. Despite the problems which Brown identifies and those which have been outlined in earlier sections of the book, an observation made by Mason (1975a: 6) suggests that the one must not accept too unquestioningly the persuasive rhetoric of the anti-stress movement:

> Perhaps the single most remarkable historical fact concerning the term 'stress' is its persistent, widespread usage . . . despite almost chaotic disagreement over its definition. This fact alone would seem to suggest both that the term has a curiously strong popular or intuitive appeal and that it fills widely recognised needs for describing biological phenomena not adequately covered by other generic terms at present. It is sometimes said that durability provides a good index of the validity or usefulness of scientific concepts. If this is true, then the durability of stress concepts in the face of so much confusion over terminology suggests that a continuing search for what is solid and valid in these concepts may eventually prove rewarding.

Aside from the intuitive wisdom of what Mason says, there are a number of sound reasons as to why investigation of the stress phenomenon should remain an important scientific endeavour and area of study more generally and these were outlined in Chapter 1. Also, until the hypotheses of common cognitive or emotional mediating mechanisms are actually tested and disproved, they cannot be rejected. Even though such mechanisms may only provide a common psychological element, we must entertain the possibility that they may, at some stage be tied, either neurally or hormonally, to a physiological mechanism or mechanisms which in turn effect the changes in health status which empirical research has demonstrated.

The sometimes hostile nature of debates within the field of stress research is exemplified by the exchange between Lazarus and Dohrenwend on the pages of the July 1985 issue of *American Psychologist* (Lazarus *et al.* 1985; Dohrenwend and Shrout 1985) and was highlighted by the title of an article by Deutsch (1986) which read 'Calling a Freeze on Stress Wars: There is Hope for Adaptational Outcomes'. Such an atmosphere does little to encourage tentative attempts at theoretical integration, which are further hampered by the prevailing empirical *Zeitgeist* in psychology. This was summed up by Selye (1983a: 441) who wrote, in relation to the stress field, that:

> . . . now we see an entirely unwarranted over-emphasis upon fact-finding, accompanied by what often amounts to an actual disdain for theories and interpretations . . . Indeed the prejudice against 'mere theorising' has become so serious . . . that many an investigator who describes facts makes a special point of emphasizing that he does not attempt to interpret their meaning. What is the value of facts without meaning?

The latter chapters of the current volume develop one possible integrative framework within which many of the available facts which have been gathered in the enormous stress literature may be interpreted. Before describing this theoretical approach, however, Chapter 3 describes some of the frameworks which have been used in the study of how stress influences health.

Further reading

Haward, L.R.C. (1960) The subjective meaning of stress. *British Journal of Medical Psychology*, 33: 185–94.

Martin, R.A. (1984) A critical review of the concept of stress in psychosomatic medicine. *Perspectives in Biology and Medicine*, 27(3): 443–64.

Mason, J.W. (1975b) A historical view of the stress field. Part 2. *Journal of Human Stress*, 1(2): 22–37.

Pollock, K. (1988) On the nature of social stress: production of a modern mythology. *Social Science and Medicine*, 26(3): 381–92.

Frameworks for studying stress phenomena

CHAPTER 3

Learning objectives for this chapter

This chapter presents a number of frameworks for examining the stress process. It describes in detail the stress and coping paradigm and suggests that in order to understand fully the stress process and how it influences health, it is necessary to adopt a transactional approach. The transactional framework is described and its relationship to the stress and coping paradigm and the biopsychosocial model is discussed. The chapter also examines the methodological issues raised by research into the stress phenomenon and looks at how minor forms of stressors known as 'daily hassles' have been shown to influence health status. After reading this chapter, you should be able to:

- understand the difference between a theory and a metatheoretical framework;
- describe the stress and coping paradigm;
- describe the transactional metatheoretical framework;
- understand the processes of cognitive appraisal and coping;
- outline the main methodological problems in studying stress; and
- describe and explain the phenomenon of microstress.

Introduction

Many theories of stress have been proposed by various researchers and theorists in the area and several of the predominant ones have been presented in earlier chapters. Each of these theories reflects the particular areas of interest and expertise of those individuals who have formulated them and, as the previous chapters have made clear, it is necessary to draw upon

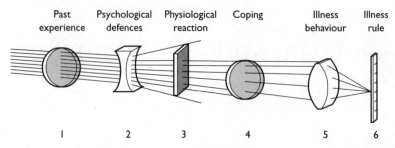

Past experience | Psychological defences | Physiological reaction | Coping | Illness behaviour | Illness rule

1   2   3   4   5   6

Figure 3.1 The path through which a stressor traverses before it impacts upon health
Source: Reproduced from R.H. Rahe, A model for life changes and illness research, *Archives of General Psychiatry*, 1974, 31, 172–7 Copyright 1974. American Medical Association. Reprinted with permission

a number of them in order to develop an overall understanding of the stress process. Aside from these specific theories, there exists a number of higher-level conceptualizations of the types of influences which are important in explaining the stress–health link and these may be considered as frameworks within which the lower-level theories may be located.

One useful framework developed out of the life events research described in Chapter 2. It proposes that stressors do not exert their effect upon health directly, but rather that they are transmitted through a number of psychological processes which either attenuate or accentuate their potential to cause changes in health status. These psychological processes are conceived of as a series of 'perceptual lenses and filters' (Rahe 1974) which can 'filter-in' or 'filter-out' various components of a particular stressor and thereby influence the impact of that stressor (Figure 3.1). The elements which cause such effects consist of the past experience of the individual, the psychological defences they have available to them, differences in the types of physiological responses these cause, the things people do to cope with the stressor and the illness behaviours in which individuals engage following the onset of illness.

A similar framework, again stemming from the life events approach was proposed by Dohrenwend and Dohrenwend (1979) who argued that life events and illness are subject to mediating factors such as personal characteristics and social situations. The personal characteristics which they proposed mediate the stress–health link consisted of abilities, needs, psychological defences and coping, genetic predispositions and attitudes towards illness and medical care. Their framework centred around life events as constituting objective stressors which lead to the experience of subjective stress, causing affective, physiological and behavioural strain leading to illness and illness behaviour. They presented the model in diagrammatic form and commented that '. . . the utility of this metatheoretical diagram is in its blank spaces. We can each fill in variables to suit our own hypotheses. The great advantage of the framework provided in the diagram is that it reminds us to be complex in our thinking as we seek to explain the mechanisms by which life events influence our health' (p. 155).

Elliot and Eisdorfer (1982) divided mediators into those which mediate between the objective stressor and the individual reaction to stress and those which mediate between this reaction and its consequences, or outcome. Their framework described the way in which events in the environment can affect the individual and it consists of three primary elements, activators (X), reactions (Y) and consequences (Z). Examples of X are perceptions of threat, burning your hand or exposure to a virus; those of Y are an increase in adrenaline secretion, the activation of cell-mediated immunity, or jumping up and down screaming expletives; those of Z are an increase in blood pressure, falling into a deep depression or terminating a life-long friendship. It can be seen, then, that each of these components consists of a wide array of events at many different levels and this is reflected in the nature of the mediators. For example an X–Y mediator may be the process of cognitive appraisal or the hypothalamic–pituitary–adrenocortical axis while an example of Y–Z mediation may be structural arterial damage (leading to hypertension) or feelings of inadequacy (leading to social withdrawal).

While frameworks such as these are alluring in their scope, they have serious shortcomings when one considers exactly how they can be of practical use. For example, the distinction between each of the X–Y–Z elements in the framework suggested by Elliott and Eisdorfer is often blurred, as in the example of a transient increase in blood pressure – is this a reaction, a consequence or a mediator? Such broadly integrative models, in their attempt to account for such a diverse number of theoretical perspectives and empirical results seem simply to remove problems at one level of abstraction by substituting different problems at another. While frameworks such as these are a useful device for interdisciplinary communication, they often tend to be of little explanatory value.

The stress and coping paradigm

The stress and coping paradigm was developed by Richard Lazarus and his colleagues over a period of some thirty years (e.g. Lazarus 1966; Lazarus and Folkman 1984b) and it is based upon the assertion that an event is only stressful if it is perceived as such by the individual. Lazarus considers stress as arising from the way in which the individual perceives and interprets events which occur in their external environment. He therefore asserts the primacy of cognition in what he labels as stressful 'transactions' or 'encounters' with the environment (Lazarus 1966, 1967, 1984a). The cognitive process which Lazarus proposed to intervene between an encounter and the reaction is that of cognitive appraisal. The process of cognitive appraisal describes how a person construes an event and it is divided into two types: primary appraisal and secondary appraisal. Primary appraisal determines the meaning an event has for the individual because it constitutes an assessment of the relevance, significance and implications of the event for that particular individual. Primary appraisal is therefore about determining whether or not the individual has anything at stake in the encounter. Events are appraised as being either (i) irrelevant for the individual, (ii) relevant and positive, or (iii) relevant and negative. This third type of appraisal is called a 'stressful appraisal' because it is events which are appraised in this negative way which, Lazarus proposes, constitute stress. Secondary appraisal involves an assessment of the individual's ability to cope with the event. Primary appraisals are therefore about the assessment of events which occur in the environment, while secondary appraisals are about an assessment made by the individual of his or her ability to cope with those events.

Appraisal processes have been characterized as a number of questions which the individual asks about an event. Primary appraisal is the process whereby an individual asks, 'Am I in trouble or being benefited, now or in the future and in what way?,' while secondary appraisal involves asking the question 'What, if anything, can be done about it?' (Lazarus and Folkman 1984a: 31). The individual only experiences a stress response if they judge that the event is stressful and feel that they are unable to cope with it fully. Thus Lazarus defines stress as a relationship between the person and the environment which the person appraises as taxing or exceeding his or her resources and endangering his or her well-being.

According to this formulation, the stress process cannot be fully understood without reference to the process of coping, which is defined as the process of managing the demands that an event which is appraised as stressful places upon the individual (Lazarus and Folkman 1984b). Secondary appraisal refers, then, to the process of judging what resources the individual has access to and what options are available in dealing with the event. Such judgements may, once again, be considered as a number of questions: 'What options are available?,' 'Do I have the ability to do each/any of these?' and 'What is the likelihood that they will work?'. Each type of appraisal is continually changing as the stressful transaction with the environment unfolds and the individual reappraises the stream of events (Cohen and Lazarus 1983).

There are several criticisms of the stress and coping model. For example, although the model is particularly wide ranging within the psychological and behavioural levels, it extends little across to other levels, such as that of physiology. Furthermore, Lazarus does not specify the mechanisms by which stress may influence health, writing for example merely that '. . . the nature of the link between cognitive processes, adaptational behaviour and physiological outcomes remains obscure' (Lazarus *et al.* 1980: 91). Lazarus has suggested that Selye's GAS (see page 25) could be significant, as could the role of emotions in mediating the link between the psychological processes which the model describes and health outcomes. Empirical research by Lazarus and his colleagues has, however, failed to yield significant relationships between these variables and somatic health status (e.g. Folkman *et al.* 1986) and has, generally, not even attempted to measure physiological functioning.

Lazarus implies that affective mechanisms are involved in the relationship between stress and somatic health and his theory of stress has, in fact, been extended to one broad enough to encompass emotion (Lazarus 1968, 1982, 1984a; Lazarus *et al*. 1970, 1982; Folkman and Lazarus 1985, 1988a,b) as well as psychopathology (Lazarus 1981, 1989; Folkman and Lazarus 1986). Indeed Lazarus has been criticized for confusing the concepts of stress and emotion (Eisdorfer 1981) and this confusion is manifest in statements such as the following: 'Stress emotions play a key role in illness because under conditions of harm or danger the body mobilises as part of the effort to cope' (Lazarus 1974: 321). Lazarus has even suggested that emotions should be the prime focus for studying the effect of psychological processes on health (Lazarus 1990b).

A further criticism of the stress and coping paradigm is that it invokes the concept of arousal which, as discussed in Chapters 1 and 2, is oversimplistic and unable to account for the influence of stress upon health. The notion of coping has also been criticized in that it is often difficult to see exactly what coping is and, while Lazarus clearly defines it, it remains an exceptionally wide-ranging concept and seems to include much of human activity, as well as sharing much in common with the concept of adaptation. Others have employed concepts similar to that of coping in order to elucidate their ideas on stress and some of these models even use it as an alternative to Selye's GAS in an attempt at theoretical integration. For example, Buell and Eliot (1979: 22) suggest that various stress-related illnesses are interrelated because they share some common denominator and that 'the pivotal point of this common denominator might well be the ability of the individual to cope with life changes and dissatisfactions from the perspective of personal success or failure within his or her environment'.

In evaluating the theoretical contribution of Lazarus, it is helpful to distinguish between his *cognitive theory of stress and coping* and the *metatheoretical transactional framework* in which the theory is located. While it is difficult to decide exactly where the demarcation line for such a distinction should be drawn, there are certain features of the approach as a whole which clearly fall within the category of either a characteristic of the theory, or a characteristic of the metatheoretical framework. For example, the cognitive process of appraisal is clearly a part of the theory of stress and coping, whereas the notion of a bidirectional person–environment interaction clearly falls within the category of a characteristic of the metatheoretical transactional framework.

The transactional perspective

Coyne and Lazarus (1980) give some reasons as to why a transactional perspective on stress is superior to other approaches. With the ever-expanding scope of stress theory and the movement towards a biopsychosocial approach in the health field, the limitations of simple concepts of drive, tension reduction or stimulus–response models have become apparent. The transactional perspective involves extensive psychological mediation and reciprocal feedback loops which cannot be reduced to stimulus–response terms. Current person–environment interactional models of stress, which emphasize environmental stressors, dispositional properties of persons and stress responses, are limited to an interactional level of analysis. The problem with such models is that they are static and structural, assuming that the person and the environment exist as substantially separate entities and that key person and environment variables can be described prior to connection to each other. Lazarus also makes the point that, even when the conceptual system allows for mediation as in stimulus–organism–response (S–O–R) psychology, such models still presume linear, sequential causation (Lazarus and Folkman 1984b) and treat the person–environment transaction as a static 'snapshot'.

The problem with thinking about stress in these more limited ways becomes apparent if one carries out the following thought experiment. Think of a stressful stimulus. Think about how that stimulus, or event would be interpreted and perceived and what type of response it would elicit. Now consider what happens when one allows the transaction to proceed. The response may, in turn, have an impact on the person through feedback and altered evaluations or 'reappraisals' of the situation. Thus variables can only be designated as antecedent or consequent for that particular, frozen moment in time. In contrast, a transactional approach views the person and environment in a dynamic, mutually reciprocal, bidirectional relationship and views the stressful transactions, or 'stressful commerce' with the environment, in a process-oriented way.

In a transactional formulation, stress becomes a relational concept and the separate variables of person and environment are combined into a new concept at a higher level of analysis (Lazarus and Launier 1978). Each component of the system is dependent for its specification upon the other parts of the system; no constituents of the ongoing flow can be specified independently from the others and the designation of variables as independent and dependent, antecedent and consequential is only ever provisional and can be revised as needed. Variables can therefore be redesignated, redetermined and renamed as the observer's interest in phases of on-going events shifts. Such a perspective is much more in harmony with a biopsychosocial approach. As described in Chapter 1, the biopsychosocial model adopts a systems approach which makes it compatible with the transactional framework described by Lazarus and his colleagues.

According to Coyne and Lazarus (1980), rather than concentrating on mechanisms or inherent structures, psychological *processes* and their contexts become the units of analysis in a transactional framework. The boundaries of the process and its relevant context are then determined by the purposes of analysis and therefore vary as the focus of the analysis changes. As pointed out by Lazarus and Launier (1978), when working from an interactional perspective, one adopts the logic of analysis of variance in the search for determinants: the separate person and environment antecedent variables are partitioned in accordance with the proportion of outcome variation they account for separately and by interaction. The analysis is therefore deterministic. From a transactional perspective, however, designating certain variables as coming first and others as being determined by them is dependent upon where, in the ongoing dynamic transactions, one chooses to break the continuity of the process. As Coyne and Lazarus (1980: 146) write, 'when one thinks in process-oriented, transactional terms and acknowledges the existence of feedback loops, one is forced to abandon firm notions of linear causality'.

Cognitive appraisal

This section considers in more depth the nature of the appraisal process and identifies a number of criticisms of the theory of cognitive appraisal. Primary appraisal may be thought of as an evaluative process of categorizing the encounter and its various facets with respect to its significance for well-being. The three types of primary appraisal previously mentioned (irrelevant, relevant and positive, and relevant and negative) reflect differing judgements about the significance of an event for the well-being of the individual concerned. Lazarus described these three types of appraisal in the following way. 'Irrelevant' appraisals are arrived at when an encounter with the environment carries no implication for a person's well-being. 'Benign-positive' appraisals occur if the encounter is construed as preserving or enhancing well-being. 'Stressful' appraisals are arrived at when a demand is placed upon a person's adaptational resources. Stressful appraisals are further subdivided into: (i) appraisals of 'harm or loss' when some damage has already been done to the person; (ii) appraisals of 'threat' when harms or losses are anticipated; or (iii) appraisals of 'challenge' which are similar to those of threat but focus on the potential for gain or growth in the encounter and are characterized by pleasurable emotions such as eagerness, excitement or exhilaration. In contrast to primary appraisals, secondary appraisals relate to evaluations about what the individual is able to do to cope with a stressful event, however the two processes of primary and secondary appraisal do not occur independently. Lazarus argues that the two processes are interdependent because, from a transactional perspective, the processes are ongoing, with new primary appraisals following on from earlier secondary appraisals and leading to further primary and secondary appraisals as the encounter unfolds. This is what Lazarus refers to as 'reappraisal'.

A major criticism of the theory of cognitive appraisal concerns the inferred status of the theoretical construct of appraisal. Lazarus suggests that cognitive appraisal is biologically functional in that it allows us to distinguish between benign and dangerous situations, arguing that such a mechanism is likely to have been naturally selected through the process of evolution. However, it is less clear how we are able to tell whether or not this inferred theoretical construct actually has any true analogue in reality, either as a cognitive process or, for instance, a neural substrate. Lazarus proposes that the appraisal process is sometimes unconscious and may be implicit, automatic and virtually instantaneous. This may explain why it is not always possible to obtain self-reports of appraisals. However, it also means that it is not possible to confirm empirically whether or not the appraisal process is a necessary theoretical construct in explaining the link between stress and health. It is arguable as to whether or not the appraisal process always operates during stressful transactions with the environment. According to the stress and coping paradigm, certain types of cognitive appraisal are a necessary condition for stress to occur. However, aside from the hypothetical argument that, in the course of evolution, human beings must have evolved some mechanism for distinguishing between benign and dangerous situations, there is no persuasive evidence for the primacy of the specific cognitive appraisals suggested by Lazarus and Folkman in the stress and coping paradigm. On the other hand, it is likely that some form of evaluative perceptual process does usually operate during the transmission of psychological stress and although it is possible that such perceptions may be slightly different in their specific form, they are also likely to be of a similar nature to the types of appraisal processes described by Lazarus. The hypothetical status of the appraisal process was hinted at by Lazarus when he wrote that 'in speaking of harm-loss or threat . . . [which are primary appraisals] . . . we are only attempting to describe the hypothetical psychological relationship that underlies the observed pattern of reaction, not explain or predict it' (Lazarus and Launier 1978: 288).

The proposal that the appraisal process is the cognitive mediator of stressful person–environment transactions is seductive because it provides a theoretical framework, based upon cognitive principles, which accounts for individual subjectivity and meaning in the stress process. The attractiveness of this approach is based upon a simple fundamental principle which Lazarus described thus: 'cognitive activities – evaluative perceptions, thoughts and inferences – are used by the person to interpret and guide every adaptational interchange with the environment' (Lazarus et al. 1980: 91). While this principle appears to represent a sound basis for the development of a cognitive account of the stress process, it does not necessitate invoking the concept of cognitive appraisal. Furthermore, even if the concept of appraisal does prove a useful means of describing one of the psychological processes involved in the transmission of stress, there are surely other types of psychological processes involved, some of which may turn out to be of far greater significance than that of appraisal.

Lazarus claims that some of the most important factors that influence appraisal are the individual's beliefs and commitments. He claims that these influence the hypothesized appraisal process by determining what is salient for the individual and shaping that person's understanding of the event. In consequence, the commitments and beliefs of the individual determine the nature of his or her emotional reaction and therefore the types of coping efforts which are appropriate for dealing with the stressor. Finally, they provide the basis for evaluating outcomes (Lazarus and Folkman 1984a). Commitments are described as expressing what is important to a person and what stressful transactions mean for them in terms of their significance to valued ideals and personal goals. Beliefs are described as notions about reality which serve as a perceptual lens and which enable people to create meaning out of life. They may, therefore, be partly existential in nature referring to a god or some natural order in the universe. Lazarus claims that the commitments and belief systems of the individual influence the subjective situation as perceived by that person. The extent to which an encounter between the person and the environment is stressful depends on the meaning or significance of that encounter which, in turn, is based upon the personal agendas and coping resources the person brings to it.

Coping

According to the stress and coping paradigm, stress can only be fully under-stood if we also take into account the ability of the person to cope with a potential stressor. Coping is defined as the process of managing external and/or internal demands that are appraised as taxing or exceeding the resources of the person (Lazarus and Folkman 1984a). This definition is quite a complex one and it encapsulates the dynamic nature of the stress process which a transactional approach engenders. Thus as soon as cop-ing efforts begin, the situation is changed, either in terms of its objective characteristics (if the person actually does something to help deal with the situation) or in terms of how the individual subjectively views the situ-ation. Furthermore, coping may begin prior to a stressful event actually happening and this is known as 'anticipatory coping'. Coping is divided into two fundamental types. The first is labelled 'problem-focused coping' because it consists of efforts to work towards solving the problem which the stressor represents, while the second is called 'emotion-focused coping' as it aims to deal with the emotions that arise as a result of the stressful transaction. These coping efforts result in the transformation of the situ-ation, either objectively or subjectively or, more usually both objectively and subjectively. This changed situation is then reappraised, which alters the subjective meaning of the ongoing flow of events and results in new coping efforts. Thus not only are the two processes of primary and second-ary appraisal interdependent, but also coping is interdependent with appraisal. The way in which an individual copes with an event is determined partly by appraisals of what is at stake in the encounter, whether or not anything can be done about the situation and which types of emotions earlier appraisals have generated.

During their empirical research on coping, Lazarus and his colleagues have identified eight main ways in which people cope with stress. Two such 'ways of coping' are primarily problem-focused and these are confrontive coping, which involves standing up for yourself and fighting for what you want and planful problem-solving which is about actively developing solutions to the problem. Five of the remaining six ways of coping are emotion-focused and these are: distancing (oneself from the situation psychologically); self-control (which involves exercising self-control over the expression of feelings); accepting responsibility (for the events which led to the stress); escape avoidance (which involves getting away from the problem) and positive reappraisal (which involves trying to see the situation in a more positive way). The final method of coping, that of seeking social support, may be both problem-focused and emotion-focused and involves engaging others to help either in a practical way (also known as instrumental social support), or simply by providing emotional support (sometimes referred to as emotional social support). These eight types of coping were identified by factor analysing a list of 67 different types of cognitive and behavioural strategies people use to deal with stress which constitute the 'Ways of Coping' measurement scale. Of course, they represent only one way in which coping may be categorized and other people have developed different classification systems. Wong and his colleagues, for example, have described five different clusters of coping behaviours which they view as different types of coping 'schema' (e.g. Peacock *et al.* 1993). These include both problem and emotion-focused schema as described by Lazarus and his colleagues, and also a 'preventive schema' which deals with anticipated problems and which shares much in common with what Lazarus calls 'anticipatory coping', an existential schema which attempts to make sense of loss, suffering, hardship and the conditions of life and finally a spiritual schema which refers to concepts such as God, fate and destiny. Carver *et al.* (1989) offer yet another classificatory system which again overlaps with the two that have already been mentioned but also includes other strategies such as suppressing competing activities and turning to religion.

Aside from the three categorizations of coping responses which have been described, there are many other types of specific coping strategies which have been studied by various researchers. These strategies include denial of the problem, seeking information about the problem (also known as 'monitoring') and the opposite of this which has become known as 'blunting', and finally prospective coping which is similar to anticipatory coping and which is known variously as preventive coping, anticipatory coping, prospective coping or prophylactic coping. Interestingly, the notion that prospective coping which pre-empts a problem can have a prophylactic effect is becoming increasingly popular in psychology and is sometimes referred to as an 'inoculation effect'. The term 'stress inoculation' can, however, also refer to two other phenomena: firstly, the idea that prior exposure to stress can mitigate the impact of subsequent exposures by making one better able to cope with those subsequent exposures; and, secondly, the idea that people can be taught specific coping techniques which prove useful in moderating against the effects of stress. This is a cognitive–behavioural therapeutic procedure which is known as 'stress inoculation training'.

Coping is, then, a constellation of many acts and in the coping literature, just as in the field of stress generally, different people use the same words to mean different things and different words to mean the same thing. For example, denial and avoidance are often mistakenly assumed to describe the same process. However, some theorists have differentiated between the two, using denial to mean direct negation of the problem and avoidance to mean that the problem is accepted by the coper, but that person makes a deliberate effort not to think about it.

The various ways of coping which have been discussed may usefully be considered as a repertoire of different strategies. To take the eight ways of coping identified by the Lazarus group as an example, the extent to which all people use all eight of the coping strategies which comprise the complete repertoire is an issue of some controversy. Some people have argued that individuals tend habitually to use a limited number of these strategies and therefore have a limited repertoire of coping responses. Others have argued that most people use all of the strategies, but apply particular types of strategies to particular types of problem. A third possibility is that most people apply most of the strategies to most problems, but in varying degrees.

There are many factors which influence both the choice of coping strategies that a person employs in dealing with a stressor and how successful those strategies are. For example, people are more likely to use problem-focused coping when they feel that they have some degree of control over a situation, whereas if it is one over which they have little or no control, they are more likely to use some form of emotion-focused coping. Some people may only have access to a limited repertoire of coping strategies because they have not developed the ability to use certain other forms of coping. Alternatively, individuals may have access to a complete repertoire of coping strategies, but due to stable characteristics of the person, tend to use only a limited number of them. This is referred to as a 'coping trait' or 'coping style' and may result either from a conscious preference or may be due to more unconscious heuristic processes. Some of the factors influencing the ability of the person to cope with a potentially stressful event include the physical condition of the person, their problem-solving skills, the amount of social support and material resources available to them and their social skills, which give them the ability to enlist more easily the help of others in dealing with the stressor, rather than taking everything upon their own shoulders. Coping, then, can involve anything that someone does in order to help them deal with stress and it is therefore a very wide-ranging concept.

As Lazarus points out, 'the definition of coping functions depends upon the theoretical framework (if there is one) in which coping is conceptualised' (Lazarus and Folkman 1984a: 149).

The stress and coping paradigm encapsulates a complex and dynamic view of the stress process which captures the cognitive and emotional richness and complexity that is an integral part of human functioning. It requires that any attempts to study how stress can influence health must also adopt methodological techniques which are capable of dealing with this complexity. Indeed, the lack of suitably complex and sophisticated research methods constitutes one of the major limitations in our quest for a deeper understanding of the stress process. Some of these methodological issues are considered briefly in the following section.

Methodological issues in studying stress

There are several good reviews of methodological issues in the area of stress research (e.g. Zimmerman 1983; Frese and Zapf 1988; Kaplan 1990a; Schafer and Fals-Stewart 1991). The issues which they address generally fall into the following categories: conceptualization and operationalization; measurement of stress and health outcome; study design; and statistical analysis. While there is much that could be written about the methodological problems associated with research into stress and coping, this section is divided into appropriate subsections which deal briefly with each of the main issues listed above.

The conceptualization and operationalization of stress

Compounding the definitional problems outlined in Chapters 1 and 2 is the lack of specific, detailed and well-articulated theories about stress. Such theories would permit operationalization of the stress concept; however, it appears that the more theoretically rich a model becomes, so the more fuzzy and difficult to operationalize become the constructs that it employs. The poor operationalization of some of the transactional concepts described in Lazarus' theory of stress and coping has limited the extent to which that theory has been adequately tested. In contrast, an approach such as the life change–health change paradigm has clearly defined stressors which are neatly operationalized in the form of the Social Readjustment Rating Scale (SRRS), but the approach appears to be theoretically impoverished and fails to capture the richness and complexity of the stress process. Schafer and Fals-Stewart (1991) suggested that, in operationalizing theoretical constructs, the following three tasks must be performed: (i) distinctions, to distinguish what the construct is and what it is not; (ii) dependencies, or basic components from which the term is formed; and (iii) relations to other terms. A clear example of confusion over terminology is provided by the two terms stress and strain. These terms are used to mean different things by different people and often heavily overlap, thereby violating the principles of discriminant and convergent validity.

The measurement of stress and health outcome

The biggest source of controversy surrounding the measurement of stress concerns the distinction between objective and subjective measures of stress. Objective measures are seen as being more reliable and resilient to confounding factors such as neuroticism, whereas proponents of the view that a stressor is only stressful if it is subjectively perceived as such maintain that objective indicators of stress tell us little. Another problem associated with objective measures such as those used in the life events research is that they are often contaminated with symptoms and may thus lead to spurious significant relationships emerging between the stress measure and the symptom measure (Zimmerman 1983).

The development of life event measures has tempted many researchers to simply administer the checklist and use this as a measure of stress. This becomes problematic when attention is not given to exactly what the instrument purports to measure, the referent population, the biases which are inherent in the measure and which statistical treatments are appropriate. Often, the search for reliability indices takes priority over these more basic, but fundamentally more important concerns. Life event checklists have also been criticized for containing only a limited subset (43 items in the case of the SRRS) of all potentially stressful life situations and for concentrating on change *per se*, rather than differentiating between desirable and undesirable change. Kanner *et al.* (1981) criticized the life events approach because of the modest degree of correlation between life event ratings and health outcome measures and the lack of insight gained into possible processes intervening between change in life and change in health. They suggested that the popularity of life event measures was due to a combination of the difficulty of studying stress in more sophisticated and complex ways, the simplicity of using the SRRS and the lack of alternative measures of stress. They contrasted the major life events approach with one that concentrated on 'the relatively minor stresses and pleasures that characterize everyday life'. Recent research has suggested that these minor forms of stress, known also as 'microstress' or 'daily hassles', can exert a negative effect on health and they are considered in more detail below.

Many of the problems which have been discussed in relation to the measurement of stress also apply to the measurement of health status. Indeed, researchers have tended to adopt an even wider array of outcome measures than they have measures of stress itself. Scores on the sorts of stress scale mentioned earlier have been correlated with a number of outcome measures which purport to measure health. Again a primary distinction in the type of outcome measure adopted is that between objective and subjective measures. Objective measures include the number of visits to a medical practitioner over a given period or the length of stay in hospital, while subjective measures include overall ratings of health or well-being. More detailed assessment of health outcome consists of an assessment of the nature and severity of symptoms. Such ratings tend to be made by the research participants themselves which introduces considerable variation in the score on health outcome due to individual differences in style of responding, as opposed to actual differences in health status or differences due to differential exposure to stress. Of course, differences due to response-style constitute the basis of the neuroticism effect which would suggest that those people who score highly on subjective measures of stress are likely also to score highly on subjective measures of health outcome, thereby leading to spurious correlations. A large number of studies have been conducted which examine the effects of stress on particular illnesses. In such studies, the measurement of outcome can be more precise because researchers are focusing upon particular parameters of known illnesses, such as the duration of tension headaches or the severity of specific illness episodes. Even so, the popular use of subjective, self-report ratings does not address the problem of neuroticism effects. The most popular type of outcome measure consists of self-report symptom checklists on which the participant indicates the particular symptoms they have experienced over a specified period. A typical paradigm would be to administer one of the currently popular stress scales to a particular sample, followed by the administration of a symptom checklist. The data is then examined for significant relationships between scores on the two measures.

Design considerations

Obviously, ethical considerations render most experimental designs inappropriate for research into stress. Researchers are therefore limited to naturalistic observation or quasi-experimental designs. Although most stress researchers recognize the superiority of longitudinal designs in such studies, these can be prohibitive in terms of time and money and thus much research is published which uses cross-sectional data. The main problem associated with cross-sectional designs is that they do not permit the inference of causality and it becomes impossible to determine how the outcome variable is related to the predictor variable; the predictor could cause the outcome, the outcome may cause the predictor, or both may covary owing to their relationship to some other factor, such as neuroticism or some other, non-trivial causal factor.

Longitudinal designs also have drawbacks; for example, they are based on 'snapshots' of time and although the point at which to take these snapshots may be important for theoretical reasons, such design decisions are often driven by more practical considerations. Furthermore, many purportedly longitudinal studies incorporate only two measurement occasions, treating the first as a baseline measure. Such limited observation periods make it difficult to gain any depth of insight into the processual nature of stress.

Statistical analyses

In analysing the data from studies into stress and health, there are several problems faced by researchers. Many studies use simple correlations and this type of statistical analysis is problematic for several reasons. Of primary importance in this regard is the fact that correlational data do not predict the direction of causality and therefore suffer from the same lack of explanatory power as cross-sectional studies in general. Also, correlations do not permit the inference of latent variables or allow for the possibility of intervening variables. Some of the more advanced statistical techniques such as factor analysis do allow for these possibilities, but they require certain types of experimental design which may be suited to some research questions more than others.

ANOVA techniques do not permit the researcher to account for the transactional complexity of the stress process and thereby distort the phenomenon to fit experimental designs which are not necessarily the most appropriate. Furthermore, such techniques rely on aggregated data which may serve to mask much of the underlying processual data and within-subject variation. This problem has been addressed by the use of structural equation modelling techniques, but these are time consuming and also have problems relating to their inability to distinguish between analytically distinct concepts which use the same measure (Kaplan 1990a). A final problem concerns the lack of statistical techniques which simultaneously account for the intra- and intersubject variation over a number of repeated measurement occasions.

Minor forms of stress

The notion that relatively minor life events can have a negative influence on health has cropped up periodically throughout the stress literature over the past sixty years or so, but until the mid-1980s such events had not been widely used to study the impact of psychological stress on general health outcomes (Lazarus and Folkman 1984a). Lazarus and his colleagues suggested that daily hassles may intervene between major life events and health, arguing that major life events often result in the manifestation of day-to-day problems. It is the cumulative impact of these day-to-day problems which, they suggested, may cause a decrement in health status (via some unspecified physiological mechanism) and thereby explain the association between major life events and illness. They also proposed that it may be of importance to consider positive daily events as well as negative ones, suggesting that just as negatively toned stress (such as daily hassles) can cause neurohumoral changes that result in the diseases of adaptation, positively toned experiences may serve as emotional buffers against stress disorders. They referred to these negative and positive experiences as 'daily hassles' and 'daily uplifts', respectively, defining them thus:

> Hassles are the irritating, frustrating, distressing demands that to some degree characterize everyday transactions with the environment. They include annoying practical problems, such as losing things or traffic jams and fortuitous occurrences such as inclement weather, as well as arguments, disappointments, and financial and family concerns.
>
> (Kanner *et al.* 1981: 3)

> Daily uplifts . . . [are] . . . positive experiences such as the joy derived from manifestations of love, relief at hearing good news, the pleasure of a good night's rest, and so on.
>
> (Kanner *et al.* 1981: 6)

They presented these ideas in a seminal paper (Kanner *et al.* 1981) which went on to present the meagre amount of previous research that had been conducted involving the types of events that could be classified as either daily hassles or uplifts, of which only two papers attempted to systematically assess hassles in daily life; before the publication of this paper the terms 'daily hassles' and 'daily uplifts' were unheard of in the stress literature, not appearing as keywords on many electronic databases until the mid-1980s. The paper described the results of a study in which scores on the hassles and uplifts scales were compared with scores on a major life events scale (based on the SRRS) with respect to how well each predicted psychological symptoms. The results showed that the hassles scale was a better predictor of concurrent and subsequent psychological symptoms than the life events score and shared most of the variance in symptoms accounted for by life events. Contrary to expectations, uplifts were positively related to psychological symptoms, but for women only; there was no effect of uplifts for men.

In describing the theoretical rationale underlying their suggestion that focusing on daily hassles may be more productive than examining the effects of major life events, Kanner *et al.* make several implicit assumptions. Firstly, with their reference to neurohumoral changes that can result in the 'diseases of adaptation', they imply not only that the mechanism linking major life events to changes in health status is something resembling Selye's GAS, but also that this same mechanism could be responsible for inducing illness as a result of daily hassles. Secondly, by suggesting that daily uplifts might serve as emotional buffers against stress, they imply that the stress health link is mediated or moderated by an affective mechanism. Both of these untested assumptions were identified by Mason (1975b) as two of the primary sources of confusion in the stress field.

In his formulation of the stress and coping paradigm, Lazarus states that the person–environment transaction is mediated by the process of cognitive appraisal, which in turn influences and is influenced by an individual's beliefs and commitments. In transactions involving major life events, the relevance of the transaction to those, sometimes deeply held, beliefs and commitments is far more apparent than in transactions involving minor life events. In the former case, the beliefs and commitments are likely to be more cognitively accessible than in the latter due to cognitive priming effects; one can see how the death of a loved one may influence one's belief in God or in a just world, but the connection between such beliefs and events such as temporarily misplacing the TV control, or a sudden shower of rain is less obvious. Given that one of the main tenets of Lazarus' stress and coping theory is that the pathological potential of stressful events derives from their perceived potential for harm, loss, threat, or challenge, it is difficult to see why the types of events listed in the hassles scale should exert a more powerful influence on these appraisal dimensions than their more devastating major life counterparts.

Lazarus (e.g. 1980b) states that an event is only stressful if it is appraised as such by the individual; if, that is, it is appraised as taxing or exceeding resources and endangering well-being. Do the types of hassles described by Kanner *et al.*, such as a broken shoelace, represent a danger to well-being? Such wording seems rather strong for such a minor occurrence and this raises once again the question of the ontological status of Lazarus' appraisal processes. Does the cognitive appraisal process actually occur, or is it merely a heuristic device used to describe the relationship between the inputs and outputs of the cognitive 'black box'? If Lazarus is claiming that it does occur, then the notion that the sorts of events which he labels as hassles represent a 'danger to well-being' must be revised because it is unlikely that the average person could interpret a broken shoelace, for example, as a danger to well-being; it represents more of a slight inconvenience. Similarly, such events are unlikely to be interpreted as representing a harm, loss, threat or challenge.

Looking at the rationale and assumptions underlying Lazarus' suggestion that one consider minor, rather than major life events in the stress–health link, the notion that minor life events may influence health by the same neurohumoral or emotional mechanisms as major life events seems intuitively unlikely. Kanner *et al.* claimed that it is these minor events that ultimately should have proximal significance for health outcomes and whose cumulative effect should therefore be studied, without appearing to present any sound theoretical reasons as to why this should be so. Lazarus suggested that the effects of major stressors on health may be mediated by minor events, but in the context of his assumption regarding the mechanisms by which those major events were thought to exert their effect, this seems unlikely. This is because the sort of physiological activation in Cannon and Selye's work is not subject to the type of cumulation to which

Lazarus refers. For example, ten incidents of misplacing things or bad weather does not equal one death of spouse; it would seem likely that the two types of events involve different psycho- and sociodynamics.

The notion that a hassle may be perceived as stressful, depending on the particular beliefs and commitments of the individual does, however, seem plausible, though such perceptions may not necessarily be mediated by the process of cognitive appraisal. For example, Brown's (1980) model of stress highlights the importance of subjective perception and interpretation of events, but does not deem it necessary to invoke the concept of appraisal as a necessary mediator of the stress process, though it is possible that appraisal may be a significant component in some cases. Given that the Lazarus–Folkman model was developed in the context of more major stresses, it should not seem surprising that, given its focus on harm/loss, threat and challenge, it may not be generalizable to more minor life events such as daily hassles and uplifts.

The publication of the paper by Kanner *et al.* stimulated a considerable amount of empirical work into the effects of daily hassles and uplifts on health and following their demonstration that the hassles scale predicts psychological symptomatology, the Lazarus group set out to determine if it also predicted somatic health. Their results, which were comparable to those relating to psychological health, indicated that it did (DeLongis *et al.* 1982). They found, however, that uplifts exerted no influence on somatic health and concluded that 'despite considerable theoretical speculation and the intuitive appeal of the theme, there is at present little support for the notion that positive events in any form protect, enhance, restore or damage health' (p. 132). Because of this finding, interest in the role of uplifts in physical well-being waned considerably.

Since these seminal publications, there has been little theoretical development of the hassles concept, or the scale used to measure hassles. The scale has been revised slightly and Lazarus and his colleagues have expanded somewhat upon their theoretical position with regard to daily hassles. Following the publication of the finding that hassles proved a better predictor of ill health than major life events scales, two influential researchers (Bruce and Barbera Dohrenwend) who had devoted the whole of their professional careers to studying the influence of major life events on health published an article claiming that this result may be due to a confounding of items on the hassles scale with outcome measurements of psychological symptoms. A tit-for-tat battle thus ensued with each side claiming superiority in measuring stress (Dohrenwend *et al.* 1984; Lazarus *et al.* 1985; Dohrenwend and Shrout 1985; Lazarus and Folkman 1986; Dohrenwend and Shrout 1986). The dispute centred around the issue of confounding, Dohrenwend and colleagues saying that 'nothing correlates with symptoms like other symptoms' (Dohrenwend and Shrout 1985: 780), while the Lazarus group argued that the Dohrenwend group had, in an attempt to eliminate possible redundancy, 'abandoned the hard-won insight that there are no environmental stressors without vulnerable people whose agendas and resources influence whether or not they will experience stress' (Lazarus *et al.* 1985: 776). The debate was followed closely by researchers in the field and others soon became embroiled in the conflict (e.g. Weinberger *et al.* 1987; Rowlison and Felner 1988; Reich *et al.* 1988; Pearlstone *et al.* 1994) which simply added to the polemic within the already adversarial stress field.

The salience of particular hassles is determined by 'person factors', a major one of which is the personal agenda the person brings with them to an encounter. Hassles which are central to important personal agendas would therefore have a bigger impact on health and the concept of 'centrality' was formalized and defined in a further article by the Lazarus group (Gruen *et al.* 1988). Central hassles were defined as those that reflected important on-going themes or issues of particular concern in the person's life and were distinguished from peripheral hassles which did not. Gruen *et al.* argued that central hassles should be more important in predicting health outcomes for the following reasons: firstly, being more closely related to important patterns of goals, commitments and beliefs, they should generate more distress; secondly, because of their psychological salience, they should have a longer-lasting effect in the form of preoccupation; and, thirdly, they should occur more frequently because individuals' stable belief systems, coping ineptitudes or other personal agendas, should propel them into similar kinds of situations. Central hassles were found to be significantly more dependent upon the following things than peripheral hassles: lack of personal control; personal skills; personal needs, goals, expectations, beliefs or values; the characteristics of the other person(s) involved; physical resources; material resources; society's rules, expectations and values and, finally, the personal habits of the individual, or their 'ways of doing things'.

Central hassles are more likely than peripheral hassles to contribute to psychological vulnerabilities to stress, as both psychological symptoms and central hassles may tap into common variables such as particular efficacy beliefs or coping ineptitudes. Vulnerability consists of both person and environmental factors that result in a greater risk of experiencing stress. Suggestions were made for possible environmental factors (including economic and social factors that endanger jobs or create harmful living conditions) and person factors (for example, stable values and patterns of commitment and generalized beliefs about oneself and one's relationship to the world) which contribute to these vulnerabilities.

When DeLongis *et al.* (1982) reported that the hassles scale predicted somatic health better than the life events scale, a flurry of studies appeared comparing the two ways of measuring stress (e.g. Monroe 1983; Ivancevich 1986; Wolf *et al.* 1989; Chamberlain and Zika 1990; Williams *et al.* 1992; Landreville 1992). The vast majority of these studies revealed hassles to be better predictors of both somatic and psychological health and validated these findings across a wide range of demographic and cultural contexts. These findings increased the popularity of the hassles scale as a way of measuring stress and an increasing number of studies adopted the hassles scale as the main predictor variable for a wide variety of health outcomes (e.g. Zarski 1984; Scheidt 1986; Stone *et al.* 1987; Johnson and Bornstein 1991; Lu 1991; Kohn and MacDonald 1992a; Wu and Lam 1993; Johnson and Bornstein 1993). Studies also began appearing in the psychoneuro-immunological literature (see Chapter 5) which linked exposure to daily hassles with suppressed immunity. Brosschot *et al.* (1994), for example, showed that a high number of daily hassles is associated with immunosuppression. Taken together, these studies provided further empirical support for the notion that daily hassles could influence health across different demographic and cultural groups, although the studies did report that different groups tend to report different types of hassles, as would be expected.

Other types of research have examined the effect of hassles as a pre-cipitating factor in the acute onset of symptoms in specific 'stress-related' illnesses. In this research, hassles have been conceptualized as a 'trigger' to illness episodes and have been empirically demonstrated to precede the onset of symptoms in a wide variety of illnesses. A brief search of the medical databases gives an indication of the variety of illness that have been associated with daily hassles, which range from tension headache (Holm *et al.* 1986; De Benedittis and Lorenzetti 1992), epilepsy (Temkin and Davis 1984), herpes labialis (Schmidt *et al.* 1985) and postpartum depression (Powell and Drotar 1992) through to a decreased sex drive (Morokoff and Gillilland 1993).

Implicit in the conceptualization of daily hassles is a stimulus-based defini-tion of stress. According to the stress and coping paradigm, however, the occurrence of events in the environment does not actually constitute stress; rather, it is the way in which they are perceived that results in the experi-ence of stress. This inconsistency arises as a result of focusing upon the hassles themselves while, at the same time, holding the view that it is their psychological significance which determines the stress they cause. The tension created by these conflicting views is reflected in the recent shift in emphasis by Lazarus, away from stress *per se* and towards the emotions which, presumably, constitute a significant component of the experience of stress. A further problem results from holding a transactional view of stress and the difficulty of operationalizing relational constructs. As Lazarus has pointed out, the difficulty lies in how one captures the ever-changing person–environment relationship in a way which takes account of the rich-ness, complexity and individual subjectivity which characterizes human life. The problem appears to be an intractable one which requires a radical reconceptualization of how to go about investigating the stress phenom-enon. Some possible solutions are presented in the latter chapters of this book. Firstly however, Chapter 4 considers the numerous variables which have been used to explain and elaborate the stress process.

Further reading

Coyne, J.C. and Lazarus, R.S. (1980) Cognitive style, stress perception and coping. In I.L. Kutash, L.B. Schlesinger and associates. *Handbook on Stress and Anxiety.* London: Jossey-Bass.

Kaplan, H.B. (1990b) Measurement problems in estimating theoretically informed models of stress: a sociological perspective. *Stress Medicine*, 6: 81–91.

Lazarus, R.S. (1990a) Theory-based stress measurement. *Psychological Inquiry*, 1(1): 3–13.

Lazarus, R.S. and Launier, R. (1978) Stress-related transactions between the person and environment. In L.A. Pervin and M. Lewis (eds) *Perspectives in Interactional Psychology.* New York: Plenum.

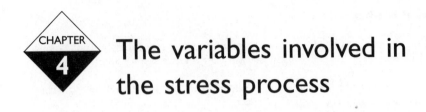

The variables involved in the stress process

Learning objectives for this chapter

This chapter will provide an overview of some of the main variables which have been implicated in the link between stress and health. These variables derive from different theoretical approaches and have spawned a number of distinct strands in the stress literature which have built up around classic personality constructs, such as the Type A Behaviour Pattern, or fields of study such as stress in the workplace. These approaches are contrasted with a more integrative approach such as that implied by a transactional perspective and the relationship between varying definitions of the stress concept, understandings of the stress process and outcomes in terms of health status is discussed. After reading this chapter, you should be able to:

♦ understand the difference between those variables which moderate the impact of stress upon health and those which mediate the relationship;
♦ explain the concept of person–environment fit (P–E fit);
♦ describe some of the main personality variables which have been implicated in the stress process;
♦ describe the types of environmental characteristics which are associated with higher levels of stress and recognize the limitations of focusing upon purely environmental influences in the stress process;
♦ outline the types of factors which have been identified in the workplace as contributing to stress at work; and
♦ explain how the interplay of definition, methodology, process and outcome necessitate more sophisticated approaches to the investigation of stress phenomena.

Introduction

Wide individual differences have been found in the literature on stress and health, both in the number and types of stress reported and in the association of such stressors with ill-health. A large number of variables have therefore been examined to determine if they moderate or mediate the stress–health link. There has been some debate over precisely what constitutes a mediating variable and how this differs from a moderating variable. Folkman and Lazarus (1988b) suggest that moderator variables consist of antecedent conditions such as gender, socio-economic status (S.E.S.) or personality traits that interact with exposure to stress and other environmental variables to affect the outcome. That is, antecedent variables such as these moderate, or modulate, the impact of stress upon health, either increasing or decreasing the magnitude of change in health status. In contrast, mediator variables do not interact with stress to affect outcome; rather they intervene in the link between stress exposure and health outcome. From a transactional perspective, mediating variables are not separate antecedent entities, but are actually generated during the stressful encounter and transmit the effects of stress exposure, being impacted upon by stress and in turn impacting upon the outcome in terms of enhancing or diminishing changes in health status. For example, Lazarus views the concept of appraisal as a transactional cognitive mediator, generated only when the person encounters a situation which taxes or exceeds his or her resources and endangers well-being. Both moderator and mediator variables affect the degree of impact a stressful event exerts upon health status and, if they reduce this impact, are said to be 'protective'. Protective moderating variables are also referred to as 'buffering variables', as they serve to soften or cushion the impact of stressful events.

Considerable conceptual confusion exists as to how those variables which have been implicated in the link between stress and health exert their influence (Zika and Chamberlain 1987). They have been treated variously as having a direct, mediating (or intervening) or moderating (buffering) effect. The term 'direct' refers simply to the relationship between predictor and outcome variables so that the predictor is said to have a 'direct effect' (as opposed to an interactive effect) on the outcome variable. Exactly how each type of variable should be treated depends on the theoretical model one adopts and the types of statistical analyses required to adequately test each type of influence are quite different. The main distinctions, however, remain those between direct and interactive effects and between those types of interactive effects which involve actual transmission of influence (mediation) and those which act to moderate an influence (moderators).

Individual differences in the stress process are best viewed from an interactional perspective which posits that factors in the environment interact with factors within the individual to result in stress. Although, as discussed in Chapter 3, the processual elements of the stress phenomenon are best accounted for by a transactional perspective, in identifying and understanding the various factors which are involved in such transactions the interactional perspective proves most useful. Interactional psychology adopts the theory of person–environment fit (P–E fit) which is concerned with how characteristics of the person and characteristics of the environment affect well-being

(Caplan 1983). At its most basic level, P–E fit theory examines the degree of fit between the demands of the environment and the ability of the person to meet those demands. Alternatively, the degree of fit between the needs and values of the person and the opportunities the environment offers to meet those needs can be measured. The opportunities that the environment offers to engage in certain actions or types of behaviour are sometimes referred to as the 'affordances' of the environment and one can say that the environment 'affords' this or that action or behaviour.

The characteristics of the person (P) and of the environment (E) can be considered either from an objective perspective, or else can take into account the individual subjectivity of the person involved in the interaction and how that person perceives the characteristics of both the environment and of themself. The perceptual distortions which result in these subjectivities constitute one primary mechanism by which individual differences in the stress process may be explained, along with the differences between people accounted for by the P variables in a P–E analysis. According to a transactional perspective such as the stress and coping paradigm, subjective fits would seem to be more important as they would determine the amount of stress one actually experiences. In this sense, subjective fits are said to be more 'proximal' with respect to health outcomes than objective fits.

From a P–E fit perspective, stress is the result of a lack of fit between P and E, while successful coping can be viewed as a change in either P or E such that the degree of fit is improved. This can come about either through changing the environment (environmental mastery) or else by changing P (adaptation). By taking account of time and the dynamics of the stress process, the interactional model becomes much closer to the more suitable transactional perspective. This may be achieved by extending the principle of fit to consider retrospective fit and anticipated fit. However, this approach does not overcome all of the problems addressed by a transactional approach. For example, a P–E fit model, even one extended to account for the time dimension, is still reliant upon being able to express the characteristics of P and E separately and cannot, therefore, account for the dynamic nature of transactional variables which are generated during the interaction. In contrast, models which adopt an ecological perspective maintain that this simply does not reflect reality as people are never removed from their environment. Instead, they focus upon what is referred to as 'situated action' and always examine the 'person in context', as opposed to just 'the person'. In this sense, ecological models are similar to the transactional approach outlined in Chapter 3; however, the transactional perspective emphasizes the temporal dynamics of situated actions and the influence of P variables somewhat more than ecological models, which tend to emphasize E variables. Lazarus claims that coping is a transactional variable in that it is not possible to specify the P components independently of the person situated in the environment, that is independently of E, but coping only arises as ongoing sequences of action unfold over time.

Personality variables in the stress process

It is important to consider personality variables in the stress process if we are to account for and explain the individual differences which have been observed in responses to stress. Of course, personality variables are not the only source of individual differences. Other types of P variables include genetic and biological differences, differences in skills or cognitive capacities and differences in the goals and motivations which propel people into different kinds of situations. All of these variables constitute differences which arise from internal sources within the person. In a transactional biopsychosocial analysis, however, it is the interactions that occur along the internal–external dimension and between the biological, psychological and social levels of analysis which are of interest.

The concept of personality in psychology has been conceived of as the result of unconscious psychodynamic processes, psychological constructs, character traits, socially conditioned responses, information-processing strategies and cognitive styles to name but a few approaches. What all of these approaches share in common is that they attempt to explain the differences between individuals and similarities within individuals during their interactions with the environment over time; that is, they attempt to explain patterns of behaviour. Personality variables are therefore very useful in explaining how individuals relate to and interact with other people and the world in general, and they have therefore been studied extensively in relation to individual differences in the stress process.

Furthermore, and partly as a result of where the personality construct is located in terms of what it attempts to explain (that is, at the internal–external interface), personality research offers us a particularly rich set of concepts which more adequately address the cognitive–phenomenological elements of the stress process than many other types of P variables, such as biological predispositions, for example. For these reasons, this chapter is concerned primarily with the personality variables that have been used to explain individual differences in the stress process. The biological and social components of the biopsychosocial analysis presented in this book are given fuller consideration in Chapter 5, while some of the E variables involved in the stress process are discussed towards the end of this chapter.

The Type A Behaviour Pattern

The Type A Behaviour Pattern (TABP) consists of an exaggerated sense of time urgency, an excessive competitiveness and drive for achievement and hostility or aggression. The TABP was reliably associated with an increased risk of developing coronary heart disease (CHD) by Rosenman *et al.* (1975) during the Western Collaborative Group Study. This study was a longitudinal, prospective field study during which 3524 men aged 39–59 years were followed over a period of eight-and-a-half years and which found that those individuals assessed as Type A were more than twice as likely to develop CHD than Type B individuals, who are defined by default as not exhibiting these behavioural characteristics.

There has been an enormous amount of research into the TABP, to the extent that researchers in the field rarely attempt to produce comprehensive reviews of the multitude of individual studies in the area; instead, there is a trend towards reviewing the reviews, or meta-analyses, of the subject (e.g. Contrada 1989; Edwards 1991). Rather than a personality trait *per se*, the TABP is a stereotypical set of behavioural responses which a predisposed individual (known as a Type A or coronary-prone person) exhibits when faced with a situation which she or he interprets as challenging (Haney and Blumenthal 1985). In their review of the literature, Cohen and Edwards (1989) concluded that the evidence for the stress-moderating effects of the TABP are at best suggestive. The association between TABP and coronary heart disease (CHD) seems to depend on the way in which it is measured (see Box 4.1), the structured interview (S.I.) yielding the most consistent associations and the Jenkins Activity Survey (a questionnaire) the least.

A further issue in assessment of the role of the TABP in CHD revolves around the question of exactly which aspects of it are pathogenic; re-analyses of data from the Western Collaborative Group Study have revealed that only some aspects of the TABP (e.g. hostility) are important for understanding the origins of coronary risk (McCann and Matthews 1988). Other researchers (e.g. Schaubroeck and Ganster 1991a) claim a role for the triad of anger, hostility and aggression, which have become known as the AHA! (Taylor and Cooper 1989). Much research effort has been aimed at identifying the mechanisms that link TABP to CHD and this effort is based on the hypothesis that coronary risk is increased by the cardiovascular responses to psychological stress, which are more pronounced in Type A individuals. The research findings indicate that reported associations account for only a small proportion of the variance and that the strength of association is dependent upon how TABP is assessed. Also, the association between TABP and physiological reactivity to stress is greater when the relationship is examined separately for hostility and anger, particularly anger which is suppressed rather than expressed, with those individuals who suppress their anger showing nearly twice the mortality risk of those who express it (Julius *et al.* 1986; Contrada 1989).

Lohr and Hamberger (1990) offer a cognitive–behavioural conceptualization of the TABP which they locate within a cognitive appraisal framework. However, the appraisals upon which they focused were very different from the primary and secondary appraisal processes described in the stress and coping paradigm. The concept of cognitive appraisal has recently become far more generalized than when it was originally used by Lazarus and his colleagues to describe the specific forms of primary and secondary appraisal outlined in Chapter 3. It is now customarily used to signify a wide variety of general evaluative perceptions and Lohr and Hamberger refer to a number

Box 4.1   Assessment of the Type A Behaviour Pattern

The Type A Behaviour Pattern was identified in the Western Collaborative Group Study using a special type of structured interview consisting of 26 questions designed to elicit Type A behaviour. An assessment is made not only by examining the answers the interviewee gives, but also by looking at how the interviewee responds; rapidly, impatiently, tapping fingers on the table and similar types of non-verbal behaviour are indicative of the Type A personality. Furthermore, the style of the interviewer is important and the interview is conducted at a fast pace, with many rapid questions, prompts and follow-ups so as to create a situation in which the interviewee feels suitably challenged and pressured to exhibit Type A behaviour. Once this atmosphere is created, the interviewer uses a clever device about half way through the interview where they suddenly appear to have lost their concentration. They ask the question 'Most people have to get up fairly early in the morning to go to work. What time do you . . . um, usually, um . . . get up, in the uh . . . morning?' It is obvious what the question is going to be and the interviewer notes down whether or not the subject starts to answer before the end of the question and also if they answer in an impatient or even hostile way (which Type A individuals are likely to do).

An alternative form of assessment of the TABP consists of the Jenkins activity survey (JAS) which is a questionnaire consisting of items such as the pace at which the respondent lives their life, how competitive they are and whether or not they exhibit hostile behaviours. Examples of the sorts of questions used in the JAS include: 'Do you ever set deadlines or quotas for yourself at work or at home?,' 'Has your partner or a friend ever told you that you eat too quickly?' and 'How competitive would your wife or closest friend rate you as being?'.

These two alternative ways of measuring the TABP raise a number of methodological issues arising from the fact that studies which have used the structured interview have generally yielded higher associations between TABP and coronary heart disease than studies which have used the JAS. Even more disturbing is the fact that when the same individuals are classified as Type A or Type B using both the structured interview and the JAS, there is only 60–70 per cent agreement. While this may initially seem quite high, it must be remembered that 50 per cent agreement would be expected just by chance as the classification is a dichotomous one.

of specific types of 'maladaptive appraisal'. These relate to the types of paralogical reasoning processes which were identified in earlier research as being associated with depression and include selective abstraction, over-generalization, arbitrary inference, minimization of success and maximization of failure and also involve irrational beliefs based upon flawed syllogistic reasoning processes. They suggested that these processes result in attitude statements which cohere around a central theme and that such themes may be construed as a set of metarules describing generalized patterns of belief. They provide a number of examples including the perfectionist belief system. This leads to a metarule such as 'there is a right, precise and perfect solution to human problems and it should be found' which results in attitude statements such as 'there is a right way to do everything' and 'every problem has a correct solution'. They suggested that the anger/hostility component of the TABP could result from cognitive distortions based upon such irrational belief systems which consist of absolutist beliefs about how circumstances must or should be.

Alvaro and Burgoon (1995) outlined a number of models of the way in which anger and hostility traits may exert their effects upon health including a psychological reactivity model, a physiological reactivity model, a psychosocial vulnerability model, a health behaviour model and a transactional model. They developed their own information-processing model which was similar to that of Lohr and Hamberger in that it proposed that hostility exerts its effect by heuristic processes which bias the mediating cognitions which intervene in the link between stressful events and health outcome.

There has been a great deal of research into how the TABP exerts its impact upon the stress–health link and, although the precise mechanism by which this process occurs is as yet unclear, there is a wealth of evidence which suggests that Type A individuals are more prone to suffer from stress, experiencing it more frequently and more intensely than Type B individuals and also showing a stronger association between stress and symptoms than Type B (e.g. Nakano 1989; Cinelli and Ziegler 1990).

Locus of control

In the preface to their book on the subject, Steptoe and Appels (1989) write that 'control is being increasingly recognised as a central concept in the understanding of relationships between stressful experience, behaviour and health'. Along with the TABP, locus of control (LOC) is one of the most widely studied personality variables associated with individual differences in vulnerability to stress. The notion of LOC was introduced by Rotter (1966) and was originally conceived of as a unidimensional, generalized expectancy of control over a wide variety of life domains, with control ranging along one dimension from internal, at one end, to external at the other. The nature of exactly what constitutes locus of control was subsequently expanded by researchers from various fields in psychology. For example, Abramson *et al.* (1978), in their treatment of depression, further dimensionalized control along the dimensions of generality (general–specific) and stability (stable–unstable). Other factor-analytic studies have suggested that there exist a number of independent and multidimensional control constructs such as control over personal goals, sociopolitical systems and one's own behaviour (Cox and Ferguson 1991). As the title of Wallston's (1992) article, 'Hocus-Pocus, the Focus isn't Strictly on Locus' indicates, there is some confusion over exactly how to define and therefore measure LOC.

Syme (1989) proposed three reasons why the concept of control is important to researchers in the health field: it represents a parsimonious integrating concept which links a number of ideas together, it has broad applicability having been invoked as an explanatory variable in a large number of experimental studies of humans and animals, clinical studies and epidemiological research and, finally, it deals with behaviours which are amenable to intervention.

Reviews of research into the effects of LOC on stress-related illness (e.g. Cohen and Edwards 1989; Hurrell and Murphy 1991) have reported that external beliefs about control are associated with ill health or, conversely, internal LOC acts as a buffer against the effects of stress on health. This finding has been replicated across a variety of stressors, including the minor forms of stress described in Chapter 3 (e.g. Zika and Chamberlain 1987; Kanner and Feldman 1991; Lepore *et al.* 1992). Taylor and Cooper (1989), however, suggest that it is not simply an external locus of control which is pathological, but that extremes in either direction (internal or external) are maladaptive. Folkman (1984) agrees that external control is not always necessarily maladaptive and has developed an interesting theoretical account of control within the stress and coping paradigm which considers control as a cognitive mediator of stressful transactions rather than as a personality variable *per se*.

The exact mechanism by which the effects of control on health are mediated is a topic of some dispute but Wallston (1989) offers three possible mechanisms: lack of control can itself act as a stressor, a sense of control can act as a buffer against the deleterious effects of other stressors, or those who possess an internal LOC may indulge in more effective coping behaviour than externals thereby reducing the effects of stress on health. Hamberger and Lohr (1984) also suggested that more work is needed before we can be sure of the role played by control in the mediation of the stress–health link and the LOC construct has been heavily criticized; for example, Nickels, *et al.* (1992) have pointed out that control is often confounded with prediction.

Wong (1992) suggested that the source of confusion over the role of the LOC is the proliferation of control-related concepts which have appeared in the literature and he provided a list of some examples of these differing notions of control which included locus of control beliefs, locus of causality, desired control, participatory control, primary and secondary control, contingency judgements, self-efficacy, mastery, competence, power motive, autonomy, freedom, responsibility, psychological reactance, learned helplessness, and the illusion of control, to name but a few. Burger (1992) suggests, however, that the main distinction is between desired control and perceived control and that such a distinction is supported by the research literature which indicates different patterns of results depending on whether one examines desired control (that is, the amount of control someone would like to have over a given situation) or perceived control, which refers to the amount of control they think they have. Interestingly, of least importance is the amount of control that they actually have objectively, again indicating that subjective perceptions have more proximal implications for health outcome than more objective assessments.

Hardiness

Hardiness is concerned with a variety of resistance resources available to the individual which can neutralize the otherwise debilitating effects of stress (Kobasa 1979; Kobasa *et al.* 1982). To a certain extent, the concept of hardiness is an integrative one as the resources which it includes range from genetic and other physiological constitutional strengths, through physiological reactivity and personality dispositions to social resources. The psychological components of hardiness are referred to specifically as 'cognitive hardiness' and of the personality dispositions, Kobasa found that a constellation of commitment, control and challenge (known collectively as the three C's) is a protective factor. Commitment concerns the tendency to involve oneself in, rather than experience alienation from, whatever one is doing or the encounters one experiences and also the tendency to approach life with a sense of curiosity and meaningfulness. Control relates to the LOC and refers to the disposition to feel and act as if one is influential, rather than helpless, in the face of the various contingencies of life. Challenge consists of the tendency to believe that change rather than stability is normal in life and that the anticipation of change is an interesting incentive to growth and personal development rather than a threat to security.

Again, the hardiness construct has a fairly substantial literature and, in his review, Funk (1992) concludes that hardiness moderates the stress–illness relationship by reducing cognitive appraisals of threat and reducing the use of regressive coping, although there is some argument as to whether the effects of hardiness are mediated by cognitive appraisals or influence the stress–health link directly (Nowack 1989). Cohen and Edwards (1989) argue that hardiness exerts its effect through coping, by providing increased ability or motivation to cope with events or their consequences, while others argue for a direct effect.

Funk also writes that there exist several fundamental problems with the hardiness construct, including a lack of clarity about its dimensional structure, a confounding with neuroticism and equivocal results concerning its relationship with physical illness. Funk suggests that results concerning psychological health have been more clear cut than those concerning physical health, but that there does appear to be a relationship with physical health for employed males. Overall, then, the findings concerning hardiness have been inconsistent. For example, Hills and Norvell (1991) claim that hardiness does moderate the effects of stress on physical health, whereas others (e.g. Cooper and Payne 1991) have reiterated criticisms similar to those made by Funk. There is some evidence that hardiness does moderate the effects of stress upon health. However, there is also argument about exactly which components of the hardiness construct are responsible for this effect. Some studies suggest that the commitment and control aspects have a more significant moderating effect on the stress–health link than that of challenge (e.g. Taylor and Cooper 1989; Shepperd and Kashani 1991); however, in contrast with this hypothesis, Contrada (1989), found that it was the challenge component of hardiness, as opposed to control or commitment, which correlated with blood pressure reactivity.

Sense of coherence

The sense of coherence (SOC) construct was developed by Antonovsky (1979) and has many similarities with the concept of hardiness. Like hardiness, it has three main components which may be viewed as a cognitive style or a perceptual disposition. The three components of the SOC consist of comprehensibility (the belief that the stimuli deriving from one's internal and external environments in the course of living are structured, predictable and explicable), manageability (confidence that the resources are available to meet the demands posed by these stimuli) and meaningfulness (the belief that these demands are challenges worthy of investment and engagement). These three components seem to overlap with some of the ideas embodied in the stress and coping paradigm. If the SOC is considered as a perceptual disposition, then it is concerned with how one perceives life stress and, in this sense, it is similar in its approach to the ideas put forward by Lazarus and his associates.

Antonovsky proposed that the SOC is a generalized 'resistance resource'. A resistance resource moderates the effects of stress on health by providing people with a helpful way of dealing with stressors and this resource makes them more resistant to the effects of life stress. Bishop (1993) proposed that the SOC could exert its effect in two different ways. Firstly, it could exert a direct effect on health such that people with a higher sense of coherence would experience a better general state of health. Secondly, it could interact with the ubiquitous and inescapable occurrence of life stress and exert its effect on health by buffering against this stress. Bishop tested this hypothesis using a typical quasi-experimental paradigm. He administered the Orientation to Life Questionnaire (the OLQ), which is a self-report device developed by Antonovsky specifically to measure SOC, to a group of

185 individuals and measured the amount of stress they had experienced (using both the Social Readjustment Rating Scale (SRRS) and the hassles scale) and also health outcome (by means of a self-report illness measure). The results supported the idea that the SOC acts as a moderator of stressful life experiences, rather than exerting a direct effect on health. Various other cross-sectional and prospective studies have shown that the SOC mitigates the impact of stress (e.g. Flannery and Flannery 1990). Bishop concluded that, although stress has the potential for producing illness, it is important to adopt a multidimensional and dynamic view of the process because there are other factors which moderate this relationship. Work on the SOC, together with that on other concepts such as the TABP, LOC and hardiness demonstrate that people's general orientation to life plays a significant role in the link between stress and health. This key notion constitutes one of the main arguments for the adoption of a cognitive–phenomenological approach in studying the stress–health link. The stress and coping paradigm is one attempt at cognitive–phenomenological theorizing and, while the limitations of that theory which were discussed in Chapter 3 may render that particular model less appropriate than an alternative one, it is clear that the sorts of issues addressed by the processes of appraisal and coping constitute the point at which the types of person (P) variables discussed in this chapter exert their influence.

Self-efficacy, dispositional optimism and negative affectivity

The concept of self-efficacy (S-E) was proposed by Bandura (1977) and has been referred to as the conviction that one can successfully execute the behaviour necessary to produce a desired outcome (Chwalisz *et al.* 1992) and as a general trust in one's own ability to master all kinds of environmental demands (Jerusalem and Schwarzer 1992). Bandura (1986, 1988) defines it as beliefs or judgements about one's capabilities to organize and execute courses of action and mobilize the motivation, cognitive resources and courses of action needed to exercise control over task demands or to attain designated types of performances. There is some controversy as to whether or not self-efficacy constitutes a personality variable, in the trait sense of the term, because Bandura claims that it refers to one's beliefs about the capacity to perform well in engaging in a specific task, whereas other researchers have used it as a global personality trait and developed scales to measure this general characteristic (e.g. Sherer *et al.* 1982). Bandura's work on self-efficacy took some time to diffuse into the stress literature (Antonovsky 1991), but has since become increasingly recognized as a personal resource which helps to reduce the impact of stress upon health. Conversely, low self-efficacy is seen as a vulnerability factor (Jerusalem and Schwarzer 1992).

With respect to the mechanism by which S-E exerts its influence on health, O'Leary's (1992) review of studies exploring efficacy effects on both coping behaviours and several components of the physiological stress response suggested that S-E can exert either a direct effect on health, through its influence upon health behaviours, or it can buffer the effects of stress by enhancing coping behaviour. Self-efficacy may also be considered as a cognitive mediator of the relationship between stress and health, impacting upon health through its effects upon various cognitive activities such as deciding in which ways one is best able to cope with certain types of stressor, how much time and effort to invest in attempting to cope in ways which may be effective, but in which the coper is not very skilled (i.e. has low S-E) and the level of persistence exhibited in the face of difficulties.

Self-efficacy overlaps to some extent with the concept of control as it refers to an evaluation by the individual of their ability to influence the outcome of stressful events and in this sense it would appear also to have some degree of overlap with the more generalized types of outcome expectancy such as a dispositional tendency towards optimism. The concept of dispositional optimism (DO) was formulated by Scheir and Carver (1987) and refers to a generalized expectation that good things will happen, or beliefs that the probable outcome will be positive. The concept is similar to lay conceptions of 'positive thinking' and it emphasizes the role of outcome expectancies as a determinant of the disjunction between striving to achieve a goal and giving up. In their review of the literature on the effects of DO on health, Scheir and Carver (1992) state that optimism is beneficial for both physical and psychological well-being and suggest that these effects are mediated by coping behaviour. Other researchers (e.g. Kasl and Rapp 1991) support this interpretation, but a study by Friedman et al. (1993), which employed an impressive and powerful research design consisting of a seven-decade longitudinal statistical survival analysis of longevity, reported that optimism was inversely related to longevity and the authors suggested that this highlighted a possible need for reconceptualization of its relevance to health.

Negative affectivity (NA) also constitutes a general dispositional characteristic and is defined by Watson and Clark (1984) as a mood dispositional dimension reflecting pervasive individual differences in negative emotionality and self-concept. It is conceived of as a higher-order construct which subsumes neuroticism, trait anxiety, low self-esteem and other emotion-related personality variables. It has also been considered as a confounding factor in self-report measures of stress and well-being, thereby making any observed relationship artifactual (Schaubroeck and Ganster 1991b). Because of this problem, it is difficult to demonstrate the role of NA. The measurement of NA has been undertaken using various scales such as trait anxiety and neuroticism and it has been found to correlate with stress-related somatic complaints such as, for example, the cardiovascular disorder, angina pectoris (Schaubroeck and Ganster 1991b).

The converse of NA, positive affectivity (PA), or the disposition to experience positive emotional states has correspondingly been found to be inversely related to psychological and somatic complaints (Schaubroeck and Ganster, 1991b); however, most of the research tends to suggest that evidence for the link between NA or PA is relatively weak for physical health, but stronger for mental well-being.

Other personality variables and relationships between individual difference variables implicated in the stress–health link

In addition to the main personality variables mentioned in the preceding sections, there have been a number of other personality constructs which have appeared in the stress literature. The personality dimensions of extraversion and neuroticism have been widely investigated with respect to stress and well-being (e.g. Costa and McCrae 1980; Taylor and Cooper 1989; Hills and Norvell 1991). As with most other explanatory variables which have been examined in relation to the link between stress and health, the results have been ambiguous. Some studies have suggested that those individuals high on neuroticism (N) are lower than controls on measures of well-being, while others have failed to replicate the relationship (e.g. Headey and Wearing 1989). Also, the potential for confounding has been highlighted in a thoughtful discussion by Larsen (1992), who agrees with the dominant explanation for exaggerated symptom-reporting among high-N subjects; that such individuals have an increased perception of physical sensations and are more likely to interpret such sensations as threatening. Larsen also provides data to suggest a recall effect in that when symptoms are reported, they are recalled as being worse than they really were.

Power motivation (PM) refers to the tendency to be competitive, aggressive, interested in the 'accumulation of things and memberships' and a preference for action as opposed to reflection. Studies on the effects of PM on health reviewed by Schaubroeck and Ganster (1991a) indicated that there was a positive linear relationship between PM and stress reactivity, PM and symptoms and also that PM was associated with decreased immune functioning. They also report, however, that inhibited power motivation has been associated with elevated diastolic blood pressure and physical illness.

The list of variables that have been studied in relation to their role in the stress process appears almost endless and some of the other theoretical constructs which have appeared in the literature include meaning in life (Zika and Chamberlain 1987), trait anxiety (e.g. Kohn *et al.* 1991), perfectionism (e.g. Hewitt and Flett 1993), sense of humour (e.g. Martin and Dobbin 1988), assertiveness, sex-role identification and irrationality (Braun 1989). As this ever-expanding list of personality constructs suggests, psychologists have examined a wide range of P variables in the search for an explanation of the ubiquitous observation of individual differences in susceptibility to stress. In reviewing the various personality variables which have been implicated, it is apparent that there seems to be a high degree of overlap between the various constructs. For example, Burchfield (1985)

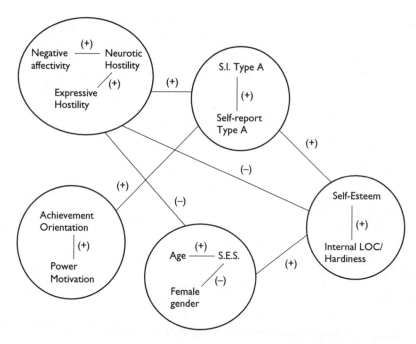

Figure 4.1   Interrelationships between some individual difference
variables which have been implicated in the stress–health link
Source: Adapted from J. Schaubrook and D.C. Ganster, Associations among
stress-related individual differences, Chapter 3 in C.L. Cooper and R. Payne
(eds) *Personality and Stress: Individual Differences in the Stress Process.* Copyright
John Wiley & Sons Limited. Reproduced with permission

suggested that there was heavy overlap between the TABP and the psychological construct of sensation-seeking and suggested that it would be
interesting to investigate the degree of correlation between the two variables.
In a study of the associations among stress-related individual differences,
Schaubroeck and Ganster (1991a) correlated various personality dimensions
including TABP, LOC, hardiness, SOC, self-esteem, PM and NA and demonstrated that there was indeed some interconstruct redundancy. This is shown
in Figure 4.1 which shows the relationships between these personality variables and also the relationship between some key demographic variables
and these personality factors.

An internal LOC, hardiness and SOC, for example, all appear to be negatively associated with trait anxiety. Similarly, Nowack (1989) found significant
correlations between coping style and cognitive hardiness, while Contrada
(1989) found a significant correlation between hardiness and TABP.

The relationships in Figure 4.1 point towards a high degree of redundancy in the field of personality and stress and in reading the literature one
is aware of the on-going battle between proponents of different constructs.
For example, in an article by Kobasa *et al.* (1983), claims that TABP and

hardiness overlapped significantly were countered with the conclusion that Type A and hardiness were found to be conceptually different and empirically independent factors. One explanation for the observed relationships is that each of the personality dimensions tap into the same overarching factor which is responsible for the relationship between stress and health. Until this hypothesized factor is identified, however, researchers are likely to continue to adopt the strategy of casting the theoretical net as widely as possible in the hope of elucidating the various mechanisms by which stress exerts its effect upon health.

Some researchers (e.g. Billings and Moos 1984; Wilson 1985; Cox and Ferguson 1991; Nakano 1991; Davey *et al.* 1993) have treated coping as an individual difference variable which moderates the stress–outcome relationship. They suggest that the various coping typologies which were described in Chapter 3 may be viewed as preferred coping styles. In a review of the literature on coping styles, Cohen and Edwards (1989) claim to have found evidence that coping flexibility (the disposition to use a wide range of coping strategies in dealing with stressful events) exerts a protective effect. They found no conclusive evidence that coping complexity (the number of different coping resources in a person's repertoire) or specific style of coping influence the effects of stress on health. In a study conducted by Kohn *et al.* (1994) which examined the effects of coping style in moderating the impact of minor forms of stress on health, coping style was found to make no predictive contribution over and above that of stress alone. They argued that coping is better conceived of in terms of ability rather than style because the most effective style will differ across circumstances. This highlights the importance of adopting an approach which takes account of both P variables and E variables in the stress process; some environmental contexts clearly make certain coping strategies more useful than others.

Environmental variables in the stress process

One of the main principles of interactional approaches such as P–E fit models is that both P variables and E variables, or personal and situational factors, interact to determine behaviour. Environmental influences impact upon behaviour in two main ways. Firstly, they act as a set of stimuli that provoke or elicit certain psychological, behavioural, biological and social responses and, secondly, they provide opportunities to engage in certain types of behaviour and fulfil particular needs or desires (or conversely act as obstacles to the fulfilment of such wants). Personality psychologists have been heavily criticized for overemphasizing the role of P variables in explaining human behaviour to the neglect of E variables and such a criticism could also be made about research and theorizing in the field of stress. One area of investigation in the stress field where E variables have been studied quite extensively is that of stress at work and the occupational stress field is reviewed in the following section.

Environmental or situational variables which exert an impact upon the stress experienced by individuals relate, at their most basic level, to the number and nature of stressors experienced. These can vary over time, with people of different ages going through different life 'epochs'. They can also vary between different groups of people, with those of lower socio-economic status (S.E.S.), for example, being more likely to experience stressful living conditions than those of higher socio-economic groups. Research has consistently demonstrated that different groups of people experience different types of stressors and this has serious methodological implications for the types of event checklists which have been employed in many studies on stress.

One of the most widely studied situational variables relates to the amount of social support available to the individual (see Chapter 5). The buffering effect of social support is, however, not exclusively a situational or environmental influence because it also involves a significant internal psychological component. Some people appear to require more support than others and what appear to be the ideal size and quality of social support for one person may be far from optimal for another. Indeed, what one person views as an essential support network in helping them to deal with stress may be viewed by another member of the same network as an unwanted and unneeded source of additional stress.

Both interactional and transactional approaches emphasize that stress phenomena arise when the person interacts with the environment and that, due to the inextricable quality of this relationship and the fact that each person is unique, there are unlikely to be more than a few purely environmental variables which can be said to exert an impact upon the levels of stress experienced by people generally. This explains why the influence of E variables has been relatively neglected by psychologists who are generally more interested in explaining individual differences in the stress process.

The dynamic equilibrium model (Headey and Wearing 1989) offers one way of handling the P–E distinction in examining the various factors influencing the stress process. This model stipulates that each person has a normal or equilibrium pattern of life events and level of subjective well-being, both of which are predictable on the basis of stable person characteristics. Stress resulting in a change in well-being occurs only when deviations in the normal pattern of life events occur. The change, however, is only usually temporary because stable personality traits, which play a crucial equilibrating function, mean that a person is likely to revert to his or her normal levels by acting in a way which moderates (either increases or decreases) the number and nature of stressors to which that person is exposed. This approach, however, still relies upon the primacy of P variables inasmuch as it asserts that it is stable personality traits which determine which E variables an individual is exposed to. Furthermore, subjective well-being may itself be viewed as a personality variable consisting of a predisposition towards either positively or negatively toned feelings, similar to negative or positive affectivity.

The most general types of environmental situations which lead to stress are those situations which challenge the individual, but once again, what is challenging for one individual is not so for another. Similarly, another type of situation which tends to be viewed as stressful is that of a highly competitive environment, but again that which one person finds highly competitive, another will find not so. Kasl (1983) adopted a psychosocial epidemiological approach and argued that it is not so much the objective characteristics of the environment which lead to the experience of stress, but rather that such environmental characteristics constitute a risk factor which is embedded in the lifestyle and life-cycle dynamics of a person. These environmental influences, along with other risk factors, including the types of P variables described above, contribute to the amount of stress one experiences and therefore to any impact that stress has on health outcomes. Thus even a stimulus-based conception of stress such as the life events approach cannot wholly separate environmental variables from person influences. One area of enquiry within the stress field which has devoted an extensive amount of research effort towards identifying those environmental characteristics which can lead to stress is that of occupational stress.

Stress at work

Psychologists have studied work stress from a number of different perspectives, including that of individual differences in susceptibility. Payne (1988) notes that the sources of such individual differences may be genetic (e.g. constitution or reactivity), acquired (e.g. social class, education) or dispositional, based upon the type of P variables discussed above including the TABP, LOC and hardiness. One of the major contributions to understanding stress at work, however, has been through the development of knowledge about how environmental factors at work impact upon health. Such knowledge derives from research in the area of ergonomics and human factors which has sought to understand and explain how people interact with the increasingly mechanized and technological working environment. The types of influence which have been studied include aspects of the physical environment such as: temperature, humidity, noise, lighting levels and exposure to risks and hazards; aspects of the tasks that people have to perform at work such as repetitiveness, strenuousness, workload and shiftwork; aspects of the types of instructions and procedures offered to the worker for performing such tasks, including the accuracy, sufficiency and readability of instructions, the simplicity of procedures and the applicability of rules and regulations and aspects of the person–machine interface such as distinguishability, compatibility and level of feedback given to the user.

Other sources of stress at work have focused less upon the strictly external components of E variables and more upon the nature of work roles, social influences at work, the organizational climate, career development issues and the work–home interface. Such influences include time pressure, level of responsibility, role conflict, role ambiguity, status incongruence, social density, leadership and management style, group pressures, career development, job security, overpromotion and underpromotion, organizational structure and organizational climate (Sutherland and Cooper 1988).

Specific interests in the field of occupational stress have varied with general trends in the pattern of working life. For example, in the early 1980s a number of studies were reported which examined the effect of poor industrial relations as a source of stress (e.g. Mundal *et al.* 1990) while the decreasing power of the unions and de-unionization over that period has seen the emergence of different influences upon workplace stress in the 1990s. The recession which followed the boom of the early 1980s meant that some of the most common workplace stressors consisted of job insecurity, performance evaluation, downsizing and ruthless cutbacks (Wong 1993), while more recent developments in the field have concentrated upon how people cope with the stress associated with organizational change. Callan (1993), for example, points out that while the work of managers has always been viewed as hectic, demanding and stressful, the very rapid increase in the pace of change that has occurred over the past decade or so means that the role of the manager seems destined to be dominated by even more chaos, change and fast-paced innovation.

In contrast to the ergonomic approach to work stress, which focuses upon designing the work environment in such a way as to limit the amount of stress workers experience, some psychologists have examined how the work setting can provide a number of positive opportunities which not only minimize stress, but seek actively to promote and enhance well-being. Warr (1987) identifies nine principal features of the working environment which can enhance well-being (or reduce stress) and these are the opportunity for control, the opportunity for skill use, the presence of externally generated goals which give the person meaning and provide some sort of structure to his or her life, the variety of experiences, environmental clarity, the availability of money, physical security, the opportunity for interpersonal contact and a valued social position. Warr has proposed what he labels the 'vitamin model' which suggests that each of these factors acts on well-being in a way which is analogous to that in which vitamins act on physical health. At low levels of these variables, vitamin deficiencies give rise to physiological impairment and ill health, while after attainment of a sufficient level, no further benefit is derived from additional quantities. In addition, some vitamins become harmful in very large quantities, while others do not and this, argues Warr, describes the way in which each of the nine factors he identifies can be involved in producing stress at work.

There are currently many different approaches to examining how both P and E variables influence well-being at work and which particular variables are of most significance. As in the stress field generally, there is a significant degree of confusion over the precise definition of occupational stress, how this concept exerts its effect on health, how it can be measured and what are the important intervening variables. Twenty-five years ago, Alan McLean wrote that 'the term "stress", and its relationship to adaptation at work, is used in such widely varying ways as to suggest we abandon the word entirely. I am reminded of the old computer concept of "garbage in, garbage out". There is a tremendous amount of garbage in the literature – a great deal of fuzzy thinking' (McLean 1972: 12). Unfortunately, not much appears to have changed in the intervening period; indeed, the increasing popularity of research into occupational stress has tended to add to the diversity of the field, thereby further muddying the waters of work-life stress. McLean is in agreement with Lazarus that stress should be considered as a general rubric for a large collection of related problems or as a collective term for an area of study, rather than as a single narrow concept.

Frankenhauser (1989) offers a useful multidisciplinary framework for explaining how environmental factors can influence health and behaviour within her biopsychosocial approach to work-life issues. This model recognizes that one of the driving forces behind the continued interest in work stress, in spite of the problems which have been outlined, is the seemingly infinite flexibility and rapid evolution of technology which drives continuing change in the socio-technical systems which define the nature of work. In contrast, Frankenhauser points out that, although the human nervous system allows for considerable plasticity, there are limits beyond which people cannot be pushed without being damaged.

About half of the working person's waking day is spent at work, usually for about five out of every seven days. Thus work is a highly salient feature of many people's lives, if not merely by virtue of the fact that a significant proportion of their waking time is taken up by it. Leisure time is therefore very valuable and the work–leisure distinction is a prominent one – even more so when the effects of a stressful work life tend to spill-over into leisure time. While some researchers have argued that this spill-over effect is greater for working women, as they have traditionally been seen as being more responsible for the smooth running of the home and welfare of the family, some recent research (e.g. Barnett and Brennan 1995) has reported that the magnitude of the relationship between job stress and well-being does not differ between the sexes.

The research evidence clearly indicates that stress at work can lead to negative changes in health status. Such stress-induced illness can be regarded as a personal injury and in a survey of personal injury solicitors in the UK, Earnshaw and Cooper (1994) found that civil actions for damages against their employers are being initiated by employees who allege that they have suffered from stress at work. Despite these research findings and the increasing threat of possible litigation, employers are still paying much less attention to psychosocial work risks than to traditional health and safety issues such as noise, machine safety and toxic agents. Kompier *et al.*

(1994) found that this is the case even in countries with well-developed health and safety framework legislation, such as the UK which, although it recognizes stress as an important health and safety policy issue, has a distinct lack of well-documented examples of prevention or good practice in the area. Employers appear reluctant to invest resources over and above those required by relevant legislation and stress interventions aimed at either the prevention of occupational stress or the management of stress in the workplace appear to be few and far between. As things currently stand, it is the employees themselves who must bear responsibility for attempting to limit the impact of stress at work, or else ignore the warning signs at their own peril.

Stress: interplay of definition, methodology, process and outcome

In examining the area of occupational stress, it becomes clear that stress arises at work not solely because of the working environment, although certain characteristics of that environment can result in a set of conditions which give rise to potentially stressful situations. Neither is stress specifiable solely in terms of the individual, although certain types of people appear to be more susceptible to stress than others. The separation of P variables and E variables in studying the stress process gives rise to a false dichotomy which has implications with respect to the definition of stress, the selection of appropriate methodologies for its assessment, the sorts of insights which may be gained into the dynamics of the stress process and the types of outcome that can be expected.

Environmental influences on the stress process imply a stimulus-based definition of stress and the types of E variables that have been identified as causing stress in the workplace certainly consist of a large number of events which may be considered as relatively objective external stimuli. On the other hand, the sorts of P variables that have been examined in relation to individual differences in the stress process imply a response-based definition of stress because, although certain events or environmental conditions have the potential to cause stress, it is only if they actually elicit a stress response in someone that stress can be said to have been generated. Obviously, neither of these approaches tell the whole story with respect to stress; however, they are useful in identifying the types of influence that need to be accounted for in an interactional or transactional analysis. Lazarus (1990a: 4) writes that:

> In a systems analysis, the question we must ask is how we can capture the changing person–environment relationship. This is a very difficult problem. Remember that I am speaking of an ideal rather than a reality, because those adopting this theoretical framework have had to

compromise with the ideal in one way or another to do research, though some compromises come closer to the ideal than others.

Many research methodologies are not sufficiently complex to account for the nature of the stress process when viewed from a transactional perspective. This criticism is particularly applicable to the types of event checklists which are so popular in stress research but which are inherently bound up in an impoverished stimulus-based conception of what stress is. Similar methodological criticisms apply to the measurement of outcome variables in stress research, which often take the form of symptom checklists or retrospective recollections of illness episodes. Such methods do retain a legitimate place within the study of how stress can influence health; however, in order to understand the phenomenon of stress fully, it is necessary to look at both structural and processual components. While the more conventional hypothetico-deductive techniques of psychological investigation are good at examining the structural elements of both person and environmental influences in the link between stress and health, they are less able to deal with the dynamics of a changing process.

It is legitimate, write Coyne and Lazarus (1980: 146), to dissect a transactional description of stress in order to make an analysis of it provisionally deterministic and therefore researchable. Relational categories of description can, they say, be partitioned into person and environment antecedent variables and an analytic model following the logic of analysis of variance be employed; the relative contribution of person aspects and environmental influences can be determined according to the amount of variance in health outcome which they explain. The problem with this approach only arises, they continue, when statistical interactions of static or structural variables are interpreted as if they represent direct observation of actual transactional processes. This fallacious interpretation, write Coyne and Lazarus (1980: 146), is the primary cause of confusion within the stress field:

> Unfortunately confusion arising from such problems dominates the field of stress. We have distinct bodies of literature focusing on antecedent environmental conditions of stress, on intervening states and traits and on responses to stress. With apologies and compromises, these conflicting definitions side-slip across each other, with little coherence and minimal integrative effort. Fractions of variance accounted for by arbitrary partitioning and sampling of person and environment variables are interpreted as if they represented proportions of causal responsibility. Linear causal relationships, dictated by the constraints of experimental design, are taken as adequate representations of what occur naturistically as mutually causative, reciprocal relationships.

With respect to the question of why experiments are so easily misinterpreted, Temoshok (1990) suggested part of the reason in writing that, although people sometimes acknowledge the existence of multiple causes, a number of psychological experiments have shown that people usually act in ways which are far more consistent with beliefs in unitary causation. She argued that this is because scientific researchers have been taught and rewarded to think this way in designing scientific experiments and that it is economic and efficient to narrow down the number of causes into single cause–effect models. When it comes to causes, writes Temoshok, people tend to embrace whatever looks like parsimony.

The types of research which are currently popular in the study of stress often fail to do justice to its intricate processual nature and this fact is often not fully acknowledged either by the researchers themselves, or by the users of this research – including me and you. The reality of the stress phenomenon demands that we move beyond the types of approaches that have previously been popular and embrace both its enormous complexity and its microscopic subtlety at the individual experiential level of analysis. Such an endeavour requires that we reconceptualize the stress process and cast it in terms which account for these varied phenomena at the multiple levels of analysis addressed in a biopsychosocial description. One such approach is developed throughout the remaining chapters of this book where a comprehensive account of the cognitive phenomenology of stress is compiled.

Further reading

Caplan, R.D. (1983) Person–environment fit: past, present and future. In C.L. Cooper (ed.) *Stress Research: Issues for the Eighties*. Chichester: John Wiley.

Cooper, C.L. and Payne, R. (eds) (1991) *Personality and Stress: Individual Differences in the Stress Process*. (Wiley Series on Occupational Stress). Chichester: John Wiley.

Cox, T. (1978) *Stress*. London: Macmillan.

Pervin, L.A. and Lewis, M. (eds) (1978) *Perspectives in Interactional Psychology*. New York: Plenum.

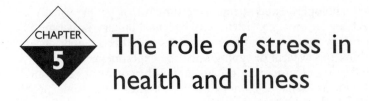

The role of stress in health and illness

Learning objectives for this chapter

This chapter begins by outlining the biological mechanisms through which stress is thought to exert its effects on health. These mechanisms are located within a biopsychosocial framework and the chapter goes on to discuss the role of social factors, the emotions and the phenomenological experience of stress and illness in order to provide an integrated overview of the stress phenomenon and how it can affect health. The final section in this chapter looks at interventions in the stress process, drawing especially on those in the field of cognitive-behavioural therapy. After reading this chapter you should be able to:

♦ describe the main biological pathways implicated in the stress–health link;
♦ appreciate that both stress and illness arise from a combination of pre-
  cipitating events in the environment, predispositions in the individual
  and the way in which these two components interact during stressful
  transactions with the environment;
♦ describe the way in which biological, psychological and social functioning may be integrated in a biopsychosocial analysis of the stress process
  by considering how each of these systems are involved in the mediating
  pathways between stress and health;
♦ identify which social factors have been implicated in the link between
  stress and health and explain some of the social psychological processes
  involved in the mediation of these influences;
♦ understand the role played by affective mechanisms in the mediation of stress;
♦ understand why it is important to consider the phenomenology of stress
  and health and how the concept of goal-directedness links phenomenological and cognitive perspectives on stress and health; and
♦ outline the main forms of intervention in the stress process.

Introduction

In considering exactly how stress exerts its influence upon health it is necessary, in a biopsychosocial analysis, to identify the various biological, psychological and social processes and mechanisms which are involved in the transmission of the stress–health link and also to explain how these systems interact with each other. Adopting a biopsychosocial approach has a number of implications for the practice of health psychology in the field of stress. Psychologists, sociologists, physiologists, immunologists and a wide range of other professionals in associated disciplines have been relatively successful at identifying some of the important influences at each of the three main levels of analysis embodied in a biopsychosocial analysis (biological, psychological and social). They have been less successful, however, at identifying and explaining interactions between these three levels. This chapter sets out some of the basic building blocks required for more integrative attempts at theorizing in the area of stress and begins by describing the main biological causal pathways which have been implicated in the stress–health link.

The biological pathways involved in the stress–health link

In attempting to identify the causal pathways through which the stress–health link is mediated, health psychologists have been interested in finding out which biological mechanisms are involved. These biological pathways can be divided into three main types: (i) those whose effects are transmitted directly from the central nervous system to the peripheral nervous system via the neurons in each of these systems (neural transmission); (ii) those which involve the production of hormones which circulate in the blood stream (hormonal transmission); and (iii) those which result from impairment of the immune system (psychoneuroimmunological transmission).

Neural pathways

The nervous system is made up of nerve cells, or neurons, and is divided into the central nervous system (CNS), consisting of the brain and spinal cord, and the peripheral nervous system (PNS) which consists of all other neurons. The peripheral nervous system is divided into the somatic nervous system, which is primarily responsible for movement (motor neurons) and senses (sensory neurons) and therefore innervates mainly the skin and voluntary muscles, and the autonomic nervous system (ANS) which serves the involuntary muscles and internal organs. The ANS is itself divided into two branches: the sympathetic division and parasympathetic division which function reciprocally. The sympathetic division of the ANS is involved with bodily excitation and the expenditure of energy, while the parasympathetic division is concerned with reducing bodily activity and restoring energy and the two systems tend to act in these opposite directions, although they do not always operate in a functionally antagonistic way.

One of the primary biological mechanisms through which stress is thought to exert its effect on health is via excitation of the sympathetic division of the ANS which becomes activated when individuals are exposed to the types of emergency situations which Cannon identified in his work on the fight or flight syndrome. When individuals are exposed to acute stressors such as these, the sympathetic division of the ANS prepares the body for action by producing bodily changes which facilitate the expenditure of energy (i.e. fighting or fleeing). The sympathetic branch of the autonomic nervous system innervates the inner part of the adrenal gland (known as the adrenal medulla and differentiated from the outer part of the adrenal gland which is known as the adrenal cortex). When activated by the sympathetic nervous system, the adrenal medulla causes the release of two chemicals; adrenaline (sometimes called epinephrine) and noradrenaline (or norepine-phrine), known collectively as catecholamines. These two neurotransmitters mobilize the body's resources by increasing the conversion of glycogen to glucose, increasing cardiovascular activity and other bodily changes which help prepare the body to either fight or run from the threat in a life or death struggle for survival. These bodily responses include: increasing cardiac output by increasing heart rate, stroke volume and force of contraction, thereby ensuring that there is adequate blood flow to supply oxygen to the active body; shunting the flow of blood away from the skin and intestines and towards the muscles, which ensures that the blood transports oxygen to where it is most needed (i.e. to the muscles being used to fight or flee); widening the airways, speeding up the rate of breathing and increasing the volume of air intake into the lungs by breathing more deeply, all of which help to oxygenate the blood; replacing the watery saliva which is used to help digest food by much more sticky saliva which will not flow into the lungs; dilating the pupils to let in more light; and changing the blood clotting mechanism by increasing the tendency of the blood to coagulate which, combined with its redirection away from the skin, reduces blood loss in case of injury.

Some of these responses will sound familiar, for example a dry mouth when one is feeling nervous or anxious; however, as we rarely have to fight or flee from a stressor, such responses are not appropriate to the types of stress we usually encounter in a civilized society and this constitutes the main argument underlying the evolutionary theory of stress discussed in Chapter 1. The repeated occurrence of these responses is one way in which stress exerts a negative impact upon health. For example, the repeated cardiovascular activation described here could lead to permanent damage to the arteries and veins and thereby cause chronically elevated blood pressure.

The central and peripheral nervous systems do not operate independently; the somatic branch of the PNS is controlled directly by neural connections to the lower part of the brain (the CNS), while the autonomic branch is regulated by a region of the brain which lies just above the roof of the mouth and which is called the hypothalamus. The hypothalamus acts as the 'head ganglion' of the ANS and is itself subject to top–down influences from other parts of the brain such as the limbic system which is involved in the experience of emotions. Thus one neural pathway through which stress exerts its effects upon health is via the hypothalamus, the sympathetic branch of the ANS and the adrenal medulla and this pathway is therefore called the sympathetic–adrenomedullary axis, or pathway (or even the limbic–hypothalamic–sympathetic–adrenomedullary axis, to extend the pathway still further into the CNS).

Hormonal transmission

Another widely studied pathway through which stress can exert its effect upon health involves hormonal transmission of the stress–health link via the endocrine system. The endocrine system consists of a number of glands located throughout the body which secrete chemicals known as hormones, in much the same way that the nervous system secretes neurotransmitters. The endocrine system is, however, much slower than the nervous system in responding to stress and for this reason it is more closely associated with chronic (longer term) stressors, while the neural transmission of stress is more closely associated with acute (shorter term) stressors. Also, hormones exert their effects by being carried through the bloodstream to the various parts of the body where they either have a direct effect on the target organ, or else cause the secretion of another hormone which in turn acts on the specialized receptors on the target tissues or organs. Neurotransmitters simply intervene across the synapse in the much more rapid neural transmission and, just as the neural system is quicker to act and quicker to desist, so hormones carried in the bloodstream are slower to act, but also slower to desist, making hormonal effects much more long-lasting.

Some glands are controlled by the nervous system and these interacting systems are referred to collectively as the neuroendocrine system. The hypothalamus, the head ganglion of the ANS, is also connected to the hormonal system via the pituitary gland which is located in the brain, just in front of the hypothalamus. The pituitary gland itself produces at least eight hormones, seven of which are produced by the anterior part of the pituitary. These hormones in turn affect many of the other glands in the endocrine system, prompting them to produce other hormones and for this reason, the pituitary is considered as the master-gland of the endocrine system, just as the hypothalamus is considered to be the head ganglion of the autonomic nervous system.

The fact that the neural and hormonal pathways are connected both to each other and to the CNS by the hypothalamus goes some way towards explaining, firstly, the complexity of the biological mechanisms thought to intervene in the stress process and, secondly, the way in which top–down, cortical activity associated with psychological processes could exert an influence upon physical health.

One major hormonal pathway through which stress exerts its effect upon health involves the hormone known as adrenocorticotropic hormone (abbreviated as ACTH). The anterior pituitary produces ACTH when it is stimulated by the hypothalamus. The hypothalamus interacts with the anterior pituitary by a very small vascular system called the hypothalamic–hypophyseal portal system. ACTH is released into the bloodstream and acts upon the outer area, or cortex, of the adrenal gland causing it to produce a group of hormones called the corticosteroids. Two subgroups of corticosteroids are the mineralocorticoids and the glucocorticoids. The mineralocorticoids regulate the balance of minerals such as sodium and potassium in the bodily fluids which surround the cells. Aldosterone, for example, regulates the concentration of sodium in bodily fluids which affects blood pressure, thereby constituting one mechanism whereby hormonally transmitted responses to stress can exert a negative health effect (hypertension). The glucocorticoids control blood sugar levels and the most important glucocorticoid is a hormone known as cortisol which produces a rapid release of glucose from the liver and inhibits the normal inflammatory response. The glucocorticoids also have a role in the regulation of blood pressure (and are thereby implicated in the onset of cardiovascular disease) and the allergic reactions involved in asthma and are also involved in the functioning of the immune system (see below). The pathway involving ACTH is that which Selye studied in his formulation of the GAS (see page 25) and it is known as the pituitary–adrenocortical axis (or the hypothalamic–pituitary–adrenocortical axis).

As discussed in Chapter 2, recent research suggests that while the pituitary–adrenocortical axis is certainly activated by a wide range of stressors, the notion of the pituitary–adrenocortical response as constituting a general arousal mechanism through which all stressors exert their effects on health is an oversimplification. Firstly, psychoendocrine research has uncovered many other hormones which are involved in the endocrine response to stress. The effects of these other hormones on their target organs are also likely to be involved in mediation of the stress–health link inasmuch as their repeated activation could result in pathology in those target organ systems. Secondly, research on response patterning has indicated that there is a top–down influence of cognitive processes which lead to differential responses according to the way in which the stressor is perceived by the individual. Such influences are mediated via the hypothalamus and limbic systems and this would suggest that the types of psychological influences discussed in previous chapters, such as the evaluative perceptions which occur during appraisal processes, can lead to differing endocrine response patterns. Thirdly, the sympathetic–adrenomedullary axis is likely to be at least equally as important as the pituitary–adrenocortical axis in producing pathology arising through exposure to stress.

Psychoneuroimmunology

The immune system is involved in protecting us from infection and illness arising from foreign microorganisms and toxins which enter the body and which are called antigens. The immune system, when functioning normally, is able to distinguish between material which is a part of the host body, and this foreign material. It consists in a complex and sophisticated series of coordinated responses to protect the body by defending it against invasion by antigens. Immune reactions involve two main types of response: cell-mediated immunity and humoral immunity. Cell-mediated immunity involves the action of a special type of white blood cell called T-cells which are secreted into the lymphatic system from the thymus gland (hence the 'T', from thymus-dependent) and which kill the invading microorganism by a number of means. Humoral immunity involves the activation of B-cells (the 'B' is from bursar or bone marrow-dependent) which release special chemicals known as antibodies, or immunoglobulins, into the bloodstream which attach themselves to the antigen and destroy it. A third type of cell involved in the immune response is known as a phagocyte which envelops and devours foreign substances. The immune response is, however, more complex than this and usually involves an integrated 'defence strategy' involving many different small-scale changes in these and other systems including a number of other accessory cells, natural killer cells and a series of proteins known as the complement system.

Psychoneuroimmunology is concerned with how these immunity mechanisms are influenced by the types of top–down cognitive processes discussed in previous chapters. The cognitive and immune systems interact via the neural and hormonal systems discussed above which, taken together, mediate the link between psychological processes and health outcomes. The activation of the sympathetic nervous system and the hypothalamic–pituitary–adrenocortical axis and the corresponding release of catecholamines and corticosteroids exert a huge variety of direct effects on immune functioning. For example, research has shown that adrenaline levels affect the balance of various kinds of T-cells, while a number of peptides and proteins which immunologists have long associated with cellular communication in the coordination of immune responses have also been shown to be influenced by the endocrine and central nervous systems (Ratcliff-Crain *et al.* 1989). Psychoneuroimmunology is a very new discipline and the precise way in which psychosocial factors impact upon these neural and hormonal mediators of immune functioning remains to be further clarified in ongoing research programmes in the area.

In a review by Schulz and Schulz (1992), it was concluded that part of the variance of immunological parameters is dependent upon psychosocial variables; however, the same authors also cautioned that the results obtained thus far are inconsistent. Similarly, Solomon *et al.* (1985: 119) in their review of the psychoneuroimmunology literature wrote that 'observations that reinforce each other are being made in different laboratories and are coalescing into a sensible, useful and exciting pattern', and continued that 'the emerging field of psychoneuroimmunology can serve to enhance a holistic understanding of the human being's intrinsically interwoven psyche and soma'. Others, however, have warned of too ready and unquestioning an acceptance of psychoneuroimmunology. An editorial which appeared in *Nature*, for example, was entitled 'Psychoimmunology: Before Its Time' (Maddox 1984). It was, however, accused of grossly misrepresenting the status of theory and research by Kiecolt-Glaser and Glaser (1988: 202) in describing researchers in the field who 'talk as if there is no state of mind which is not faithfully reflected by a state of the immune system'. Health psychologists must, none the less, exhibit some caution in accepting psychoneuroimmunology as the new panacea to the persistent mind–body problem and, in terms of stress research, we must not make the same mistake as was made with Selye's GAS or else the confusion that was generated by a similar belief about the GAS will simply be repeated in a new guise. In this connection, it is interesting to note the comments made by Kaplan (1991: 911) in his review of the area. He writes, somewhat ominously that 'the literature on the relationships between psychosocial (primarily stress-related) variables and indices of immune system responses is so heterogeneous as to seriously challenge an observer's capacity to find any order at all among these studies'. Perhaps the current state of psychoneuroimmunology research is more accurately reflected in comments from a paper by Ratcliff-Crain *et al.* (1989: 747–8) which examined a number of fundamental research issues. In it, they write that

> how the CNS and immune system interact is still a major question that needs to be answered . . . assumptions can be made by observing changes in health and behaviour and by making various measurements that reflect aspects of immunologic functioning. However, continued efforts to pinpoint the mechanisms underlying CNS and immune system interactions are needed to go beyond the state of hypotheses and assumptions.

Kiecolt-Glaser and Glaser (1995: 273) summarized the current status of the field in writing that 'there are now sufficient data to conclude that immune modulation by psychosocial stressors . . . can lead to actual health changes'. Starting with this preliminary finding, further work is needed to uncover the exact neural and endocrine mechanisms involved and how they interact with each other and with higher psychological processes to effect changes in health status.

Thus the 'conceptual hiatus' that Brown (1980) identified as existing between external psychosocial stressors and the internal psychophysiological response to stress will not disappear 'as if by magic' with the simple utterance of the word psychoneuroimmunology, but serious attempts to develop conceptual systems based on interdisciplinary collaboration between psychologists, endocrinologists and immunologists would go some way to filling the void. Viewed in this light, the search for an integrated and unified theory of stress, in which cognitively mediated psychosocial stimuli are centrally integrated and activate a system of physiological changes leading to a negative change in health status, would appear to be a valid and worthwhile enterprise.

Diathesis-stress and specificity

In the diathesis-stress paradigm (which the current author prefers to label the stress-diathesis model when referring to the stress process), the types of health outcomes which result from psychosocial stressors are dependent upon specific vulnerabilities in one or more organ systems. This approach has led to the development of a number of distinct literatures which have built up around particular illnesses, each of which have identified biological predisposing factors. For example, with respect to cardiovascular disorders, the complex system of blood-pressure regulation involving the sympathetic nervous system and hormones controlling sodium regulation and the retention of water constitute a number of possible mechanisms which may be involved in a physiological predisposition to hypertension or coronary heart disease. Other similar physiological predisposing factors have been identified for a wide array of so-called 'stress-induced' illnesses.

Physiological predisposition to certain types of illness is sometimes referred to as the somatic-weakness hypothesis, however as discussed in Chapter 1, specificity may also arise through the types of response patterning previously discussed. This is known as the specific-reaction hypothesis and research has shown that people differ markedly in the extent to which the types of biological mechanisms described above are activated by stress. This phenomenon is known as reactivity and it constitutes a second type of diathesis which may exist alongside constitutional weaknesses in certain organ systems in a stress-diathesis model.

Individual differences in response to stress are not compatible with the way in which Selye defined stress, which was as a non-specific response of the body to any demand made upon it. The argument that the very non-specificity of this response was what made the pituitary–adrenocortical axis identified with the GAS the primary mediator of the stress–health link was refuted by Mason (1974). He argued that the types of response patterning which have been discussed suggest that, even though this axis may be elicited by a wide range of stressors, specificity occurs with respect to the precise response elicited. He therefore suggested that the primary mediator of the stress–health link may lie in top–down CNS influences mediated by the limbic–hypothalamic system. This system has been closely associated with the experience of emotions and some theorists have argued that emotional arousal could therefore be the primary mediator of stress. The role of emotions in the stress–health link is considered in more detail below.

However, there is considerable debate over the extent to which emotions can be separated from cognitions. Both emotions and cognitions are of a highly experiential or phenomenological nature and the suggestion that cognitive–emotional influences could be the primary mediator of the link between stress and health would suggest that a more phenomenologically based approach to understanding stress could prove beneficial in helping to elucidate the influence of these mechanisms.

Whatever the source of specificity, the result is that people may tend towards developing specific types of illness in response to stress. These specific effects may emanate either from differences within the person in terms of vulnerabilities in organ systems and response patterning or else from differences in the environment in terms of the characteristics of different types of stressor. Different types of stressful situations (environmental, E variables) constitute specificity in that certain types of stress may lead to illnesses which are specifically associated with those particular forms of stress. As discussed in Chapter 4, however, different types of people (P variables) may expose themselves to different types of stressful situations (E variables) so that this type of specificity may not be accounted for solely in terms of the environmental characteristics of psychosocial stressors. In order to understand any stress-induced illness, it is necessary to consider both P and E factors and to understand how these factors are mediated at the biological, psychological and social levels of analysis.

A biopsychosocial perspective

The types of top–down cognitive influences which have been referred to both impact upon the biological processes described above and are themselves impacted upon by the social processes which are described below. These cognitive components of the stress process consist of the types of cognitions which accompany stressful encounters with the environment and the sorts of personality variables discussed in Chapter 4. A biopsychosocial perspective requires some mechanism which connects human functioning at these three levels of analysis and the characterization of the person embodied in a biopsychosocial account of the stress process is that of a socially situated biological organism which is conscious, sentient and volitional. This characterization of the person most closely resembles that adopted by researchers and theorists in the area of social cognition and has thus been labelled the socio-cognitive approach, or socio-cognitive theory (SCT) (Bandura 1989).

Wyer and Srull (1994) highlight the salient features of the socio-cognitive approach as involving a heavy information processing load on the individual's finite cognitive capacity which requires that we be selectively attentive to the information flowing to us from our environment. They go on to point out that this basic model of the individual as a conscious processor of information '. . . appears oppressive. It is seemingly overwhelming in the number and nature of demands upon the cognitive system. Yet humans have evolved to deal with such demands on most occasions in a near effort-less manner' (ibid.: x). Also embodied in the socio-cognitive model of the person is the idea that people evaluate stimuli in their environment either positively or negatively and go about interacting with their environment in a planful, goal-directed manner.

The socio-cognitive model of the person is useful in specifying how the types of top–down cognitive influences referred to previously, including the personality variables and coping mechanisms described in previous chap-ters, serve to mediate interactions between the social context in which the individual is located and the biological mechanisms described above. Socio-cognitive processes integrate higher-level cortical functioning (which mediates the social component of stress) with lower-level brain function-ing (which mediates the interaction between the CNS and the peripheral nervous system, thereby controlling the types of bodily responses which are exhibited in stressful situations).

The precise way in which lower brain centres such as the limbic system and hypothalamus mediate the impact of stress upon health is not yet fully understood. Certainly the role of the hypothalamus and its interaction with the pituitary gland via the hypothalamic–hypophyseal portal system is an important component of the mediating pathway. Ursin and Murison (1984) propose an integrated physiologically based system, one aspect of which is the pituitary–adrenocortical axis studied by Selye. They also assert that the integrated somatic response has other components including the sympathetic–adrenomedullary axis as studied by Cannon, the testosterone system and the parasympathetic nervous system. They suggest that this system of responses is integrated by the brainstem. Higher-order mental function-ing in the neo-cortex (i.e. psychological processes) feed, in a top–down fashion, into the brainstem which integrates a coordinated and complex set of changes mediated by the physiological components which have been discussed. This is known as the 'brainstem activation hypothesis'.

According to Brown's (1980) 'stressor processing' model, cognitive pro-cesses such as the perception of threat lead to the direct neural activation of physiological defence mechanisms and result in muscle, visceral and subjective tension. These defence mechanisms are further activated by the negatively toned emotions which often accompany a stressful transaction and a comprehensive explanation of the stress process therefore needs to encapsulate a description of the role of emotions in either generating or perpetuating biological changes in the body via the lower brain centres. A further way in which Brown proposes that the types of socio-cognitive processes involved in stressful transactions exert a top–down effect upon biological functioning is through a process known as cortical inhibition. The cortical functioning which a stressful transaction elicits exerts an inhibit-ing effect upon the normalizing actions of lower brain regulatory systems thereby sustaining physiological activation. This is because the normal homeostatic mechanisms regulating neural conduction to muscles and viscera become impaired and efferent neural signals become inactivated resulting in sustained physiological arousal. This process is analogous to the opposite of progressive relaxation and renders the homeostatic regulatory systems less effective than under normal, non-stressful conditions.

The biopsychosocial account of the stress process presented here characterizes the person as a fundamentally rational and conscious problem-solver who is, none the less, subject to many heuristic processing biases which operate as a function of the individual's innate capabilities and life history, as well as the immediate pressures of the situation. A comprehensive theory of stress needs to embrace these characteristics of people and to account for the way in which the immediate demands of a stressful situation are cognized and the way in which these cognitions mediate functioning at a biological, psychological and social level of analysis. The demand characteristics of stressful situations may derive from both the external demands of the environment and the internal demands the individual places upon him or herself. Of the internal, self-generated demands with which an individual must cope, a large majority are phenomenological in nature, concerning things such as the way in which one feels they ought to behave, the standards of behaviour to which one aspires and the type of person one wants to be. These influences concern the phenomenology of behaviour and are considered later on. Of the external demands placed upon an individual, some of the most important features of stressful situations derive from their social nature.

Social components

The social components of a biopsychosocial approach to stress and health consist of contributions from sociology, social psychology, psychosocial epidemiology and a number of other related disciplines. At one level, social influences are manifested in observations about how socio-economic and demographic variables impact upon both health and stress. The focus on these social variables has highlighted differences in stress vulnerability due to factors such as age, sex, employment status, social class and urbanization (Jenkins 1991) and indicate, for example, that females and those of lower socio-economic status tend generally to experience more stress than other groups.

There have been a large number of studies focusing upon how particular social contexts impact upon the stress process and the two most heavily studied contexts are stress in the workplace and stress at home, particularly between partners. As Moos (1992) points out, salient aspects of different social settings may amplify or moderate each other; a number of studies have reported that high work stressors are significantly correlated not only with the general stress levels in those people sampled, but also with symptoms in the spouses of these people. Stress is capable, then, of being socially transmitted and this is a familiar notion in respect of the social stress stereotypically present in inner-city ghettos. Such a notion is supported by animal experiments on overcrowding which show marked physiological responses once social density increases beyond a certain limit.

Koolhaas and Bohus (1989) report on a number of slightly different animal experiments which show that social position is strongly associated with stress pathology in terms of both adrenocortical and immunological indicators, which mirrors the findings in human studies on the relationship between socio-economic status and health. Interestingly, in the animal studies both dominant and subordinate animals tend to show little or no pathology, while those in a subdominant position in the social hierarchy or complete outcasts tend to exhibit pathology. Koolhaas and Bohus interpreted these findings as evidence for the role of social control in stress-related pathology, arguing that the amount of control both influences and is influenced by the coping strategies that are adopted.

Other approaches to examining social components of the stress process have focused upon social psychological theorizing. For example, role theory has been used to explain why working women are often reported as suffering from more stress than working men and proposes that this is due to conflicting role expectations between professional, parental and marital roles. Levo and Biggs (1989) found that women's sex-role beliefs were important cognitive variables which determined the ability of women to cope with stress. Work in the area of occupational stress has similarly identified role conflict as a significant workplace stressor (see Chapter 4).

A further social psychological influence on stress and coping concerns the role of social comparison theory. As outlined below, some of the individual motivational variables which have been studied from a self-actualization perspective may provide useful insights into the stress process; however, such a conceptualization excludes the role of social processes. In developing personal aspirations and goals, individuals inevitably compare themselves to their peer group, even more so during certain periods in the lifespan when age-graded life tasks are developed. These social comparison processes could have significant implications for the amount of stress experienced by individual groups within society.

Perhaps the most widely studied social influence on the stress process is that of social support. There is a plethora of studies which have examined the influence of social support on stress and its impact upon health; however, findings have generally been inconsistent (Schwarzer and Leppin 1989). Some studies have shown a direct influence of social support upon health, while others have indicated only an interactive effect, reporting that social support buffers the effects of stress. Still other studies have reported negative findings – that social support exerts no influence upon health. There is a variety of ways in which social support has been conceptualized and measured but it is generally taken as having two primary features: structural and functional. Structural aspects of social support include partnership status, membership of organizations and number of social networks and contacts, while functional aspects involve the nature and qualities of social relationships and include instrumental support, the provision of information and the closeness and intimacy of relationships which give the feeling that one is loved, cared for, valued and esteemed. Despite persistent controversy over exactly what constitutes social support and precisely how it is involved in the stress process, the balance of recent evidence seems to suggest that it has a buffering effect, acting as a moderating variable in the stress–health link (e.g. Greenwood *et al.* 1996).

The role of emotions

It is a widely held, but often implicit, assumption by researchers in the stress field that emotional arousal constitutes a significant influence in the stress process. This is partly due to the close association of the experience of emotion with autonomic arousal. However, there is ongoing debate about the exact relationship between the experience of emotion, cognitive processes and autonomic arousal. In particular, there is controversy over the independence of emotion and cognition and the outcome of this debate has implications for the role of affective mechanisms in the stress process. If they are viewed as distinct, then emotions must be treated as a separate influence on the stress process which occurs alongside that of cognitive mediation. If they are viewed as closely related to cognition, however, then emotions can be integrated into a single cognitive–emotional theoretical account of psychological mediation.

Zajonc (1980) argued that 'preferences need no inferences' and that the cognitive and affective systems may operate relatively independently of each other, while other researchers (e.g. Lazarus 1984a) argue for the primacy of cognition. Scherer (1995) has argued, in line with the ideas put forward by Lazarus, for emotion-antecedent appraisal and that the emotional reaction to a stressful event is the result of an automatic, unconscious and instantaneous negative appraisal. According to Zajonc (1980), however, affective reactions can precede cognitions and this is consistent with the view of Carver and Scheier (1990b) who suggested that affective reactions come quickly, while cognitive evaluations arise more slowly as a more abstract construal of the situation follows from further reflection after the event. In such a formulation, the quickly generated emotions are themselves subject to top–down cognitions generated as the event unfolds. Thus the cognitive activity which comprises the emotion-focused coping efforts of the individual shapes the experiential qualities of the emotional reaction. The issue of the antecedence of affect or cognition is not yet resolved; however, it may be the case that, as Lazarus (1982) claims, cognition and emotion are inherently fused in nature, in which case, it will not be possible to treat them as independent influences in the stress process and any comprehensive theory of stress would have to be able to account for both cognitive and emotional elements.

People are able to experience more than one emotion at a time and the changing fortunes of an individual over the course of a stressful encounter are likely to generate more than one affective reaction. These emotions are then liable to subsequent interaction and would have a moderating effect upon each other to determine one's overall level of either positive or negative affect. Furthermore, the emotions and cognitions associated with the stressful transaction cause the individual to develop strategies based upon the moderation of their affective state as they engage in emotion-focused coping. Further cognitions arise as the individual's coping efforts continue and as Carver and Scheier (1990b) note, when people stop and analyse the situation they are in, they typically bring to mind a series of possibilities regarding the situation which are briefly played through mentally as behavioural scenarios. This mental imagery relates to how people envisage being able to deal with a stressful event and therefore constitutes part of the coping process. These mental images lead to the generation of further emotions which are brought to bear in the increasingly multifarious and complex cognitive construction of experience. Such cognitive–emotional activities may exert their influence in a rapid and subconscious way, therefore making it difficult and sometimes requiring a significant amount of cognitive effort for the individual to 'work through' their phenomenological experience. Furthermore, as Schwarz and Clore (1983) point out, these activities are likely to become self-referent and exert a mutual influence upon each other as the individual contemplates their own emotional and cognitive reaction to events and begins the process of attributing these to apparent causes.

Brown (1980) described some of the cognitive activities that occur as one copes with a stressful situation. Once again, these involve the constant creation and re-creation of the social situation and stressful event as a series of mental images. Each re-creation also involves projection of various alternative solutions to the problem into both past and future imagined situations. Each of these images and projections, argues Brown, directly evoke physiological activation by generating unpleasant emotional states. Thus during the coping process, the cognitions that accompany the unfolding of an event and attempts by the individual to solve the problems created by the event can lead to a self-perpetuating cycle of arousal which is affectively mediated by negatively toned emotions such as anxiety. Certain habitual ways of coping may involve the imaginal evocation of 'worst-case' scenarios and this style of coping, sometimes referred to as 'catastrophizing', is likely to lead to greater emotional responses and subsequent physiological arousal than other types of coping response. These emotions, in turn, cause further physiological arousal leading to the experience of more anxiety, muscular and visceral responses and the subjective experience of stress. A transactional conceptualization of the stress process which takes account of the dynamic nature of these processes is able to account for the various directions that emotional reactions to a stressful event may take and how those reactions change over time in both quality and intensity.

Emotions change with the unfolding of an event and the cognitive interpretations that follow it, ranging from the initial and almost instantaneous affective reaction, through longer term (in the range of minutes to hours) changes in general mood to subsequent affective reactions which may be experienced over a period of days as the event is remembered and contemplated. An initially negative affective response such as anger or annoyance may change its quality over time through a feeling of challenge and possibly satisfaction in response to success in the face of adversity, or humour as the initial response is remembered several days later.

The affective reaction can be analysed in terms of two primary dimensions: quality and intensity. Each of these may vary relatively independently over the course of a stressful event. Which type of emotion is produced during a stress episode and how strong that reaction is depends largely upon the way in which the situation is construed by the individual. In particular, the beliefs and commitments involved in the appraisal processes described by Lazarus and the ways in which the individual copes with the event serve as particularly powerful determinants of the sorts of emotions a stressful episode generates, as do the on-going cognitive activities which provide the context within which the autonomic arousal associated with emotional experience is interpreted.

The assignment of meaning that occurs during stressful transactions is highly contextually embedded within the interpretive framework of the individual. This framework is largely based upon an individual's life history and it is therefore experiential–phenomenological in nature. The interpretive framework consists partly of the beliefs and commitments of the individual which influence the appraisal process by determining what is salient for that person, shaping their understanding of the event and, in consequence, their emotions and coping efforts and, finally by providing the basis for evaluating outcomes (Lazarus and Folkman 1984a). These appraisal and coping mechanisms, despite being thoroughly grounded in the life experience and personal agenda of the individual, also contain several more nomothetic components which determine the emotional impact of stressful events. Two such components are the processes of outcome expectancy judgements and the assignment of causal attributions and Weiner (1982) has provided evidence that both outcome expectancies and causal attributions contribute independently to the affective reactions to stressful events.

Consider, firstly, the role of the attribution process. The types of attributions that are made following a stressful event are dependent upon both the personal agenda of the individual and the objective environmental characteristics of the event. Thus it would seem likely that individuals would vary both in the relative contribution of internal–external contributions to the attributive process and in the overall flexibility of their attributional styles. To take an example, one individual may respond to a particular event with a series of attributions involving their own incompetence and inability to think things through in an intelligent and realistic way, while another may respond with attributions concerning the high standards they set and the incompetence of others who are unable to match such perfectly reasonable expectations. Obviously the quality and intensity of the emotions generated would be affected by each of these respective cognitions and the subsequent chains of thought and sequences of action which they initiate as the event unfolds.

With respect to the effect of outcome expectancy judgements, a negative expectancy would increase the intensity of the initial negative reaction while a positive one may reduce the intensity of the negative reaction or change its quality to one of a more positive valence (Carver and Scheier 1981, 1990b). Also important here is the role of efficacy beliefs which play a significant part in the determination of outcome-expectancy judgements. According to Bandura (1989), positive efficacy beliefs result in positive affect and increased motivation, whereas negative efficacy beliefs result in depression. Indeed, within the literature on depression, it has been noted that there are affective benefits of optimistic self-efficacy beliefs and that those who suffer from depression actually make more realistic efficacy judgements, a phenomenon known as 'depressive realism' (Kendall 1992).

The role of the commitments and beliefs of an individual in determining the emotional reaction to stress draws together a number of other necessary components which need to be considered in a comprehensive theory of how stress impacts upon health. Commitments are described as expressing what is important to a person and thereby determine what stressful transactions mean for that person in terms of their significance to valued ideals and personal goals. Beliefs are described as notions about reality which serve as a perceptual lens and which enable people to create meaning out of life and may be existential in nature, referring to a god, or some natural order in the universe. Lazarus and Folkman (1984a) view the role of an individual's beliefs and commitments as related to broader personality concepts related to the 'self' and the influence of self-related psychological constructs such as self-efficacy and the self-concept in the stress process must also be examined.

The work of Markus and Ruvolvo (1989) on the relationship between what they refer to as 'possible selves' and the genesis of emotional states suggests a way in which the self-concept may be involved in the stress process. They outline the affective and somatic consequences of the activation of possible selves which may be evoked during an individual's efforts to cope with stressful transactions. For example, an event which jeopardizes the actualization of a possible self-concept or calls into question the self-efficacy of individuals in particular striving domains is likely to result in the elicitation of negatively toned emotions, whereas the successful coping and consequent activation of positive self-efficacy evaluations is likely to result in the elicitation of positive affect (Bandura 1989). Similarly, Strauman and Higgins (1987) provide empirical evidence that discrepancies between actual-self and ideal-self or ought-self produce automatic activation of distinct types of emotional discomfort which depend upon the cognitive context within which autonomic arousal occurs, a phenomenon known as 'contextual priming' as it primes, or prepares, our cognitive–emotional apparatus to experience certain sorts of emotions.

Markus and Ruvolvo (1989: 233) also present evidence that the elicitation of either positive or negative possible-selves has physiological effects in terms of changes in ANS arousal: 'it is possible that a keenly experienced possible-self may function to focus or coordinate the autonomic, neural or sensorimotor systems, or some aspects of these systems. In contrast, the presence of negative possible selves may disrupt the synchronous functioning of these systems'. Linville (1987) presented evidence that self-complexity acts as a cognitive buffer against stress-related illness. Self-complexity is defined as the organization of self-knowledge in terms of a greater number of distinctive self-aspects. Stressful events involving a threat to one particular self-aspect or possible self have a relatively lower impact upon the overall psychological functioning of the individual if that person has a large number of other self-aspects upon which they can draw. Stressful events would therefore lead to a lower level of affective and physiological arousal in such individuals and this proposition has received empirical support in the literature (e.g. Dixon and Baumeister 1991; Niedenthal *et al.* 1992). The role of the self-concept in the stress process is described in further detail in Chapter 5.

The phenomenology of stress and health

A biopsychosocial perspective upon the stress process is holistic in nature and takes as its primary unit of analysis the whole person in their social context. As the preceding discussion about the involvement of emotions demonstrates by its reference to terms such as 'mental imagery', 'the cognitive–emotional apparatus' and cognitive processes such as attribution and outcome expectancies, such a perspective needs to assign greater importance to the subjective, experiential and phenomenological aspects of mental functioning than socio-cognitive models of mental life. Phenomenological approaches in psychology incorporate a conceptualization of the person as reflexively aware of his or her own existence and therefore contemplative of their relationship to the external world, which is particularly appropriate in relation to the study of stress within a transactional framework.

Phenomenology is a widely used, but ill-defined term and there are several schools of phenomenological inquiry that exist in psychological research

(Cohen and Omery 1994). Within psychology, the word phenomenology tends to be used in the way suggested by Apter (1981: 2); that is:

> ... phenomenological in the rather wide and loose sense that it is concerned to a great extent with experience rather than with just behaviour ... it says that in order to have a full understanding of at least some kinds of behaviour, you have to know how the person who is performing the behaviour interprets and understands his behaviour. Unless this is done, your understanding may be rather superficial, and you may even be misled about the significance and meaning of the behaviour.

Phenomenological approaches, such as that of Abraham Maslow and Carl Rogers, recognize the primacy of the self-concept and the life-world of individuals and emphasize the striving of individuals to become their ideal-self, a process known an self-actualization (e.g. Rogers 1951, 1963; Maslow 1970). Self-actualization is of supreme motivational importance and is therefore intimately connected with a person's commitments and agenda which Lazarus described as having such an important influence in the stress process.

As long ago as 1960, Haward called for psychologists to pay greater attention to the phenomenological qualities of the experience of stress and argued that by focusing upon how stress is subjectively experienced, we were likely to develop a greater understanding of how stress comes to exert its influence upon health. He reported that the way in which stress is subjectively experienced fundamentally alters the physiological response to stressful situations and suggested that it may even be possible that different health outcomes or diseases may be associated with particular patterns of phenomenological experience. Despite Haward's proposition nearly forty years ago, there have been very few attempts by psychologists to study the phenomenology of stress. The work of Lazarus and his colleagues in their development of the stress and coping paradigm goes furthest in describing the importance of personal agendas, commitments and beliefs. Unfortunately, the usefulness of this approach has been reduced by too narrow a focus upon the significance of the appraisal process (in particular, appraisals of harm, loss, threat or challenge) and the assignment of many of the processes involved in appraisal to the unconscious.

Just as the way in which a stressful transaction is phenomenologically experienced may have implications for how it impacts upon health, the way in which health itself is subjectively experienced could have reciprocal implications for stress. For example, Salovey and Birnbaum (1989) examined the influence of mood on health-relevant cognitions and found that those people who experienced negative mood states thought differently about their illnesses than those who experienced positive mood states. Furthermore, they found that these differences in illness cognitions could play an important role in determining care-seeking behaviour, adherence and therefore recovery from illness which is, of course, itself a stressful experience.

Research on health cognitions has shown that people often think about health in terms of the way it makes them feel subjectively, the behavioural consequences of their illness in terms of what they can or cannot do and the time for which they expect to be affected by the illness. Such cognitions constitute a schema which people use to make sense of their illness and help them cope with it (e.g. Leventhal and Nerenz 1985). Such schemata are used to guide behaviour during transactions with the environment and the way in which the phenomenology of both stress and health interact during stressful transactions may have a role in explaining how the individual reacts psychologically, behaviourally and possibly, therefore, physiologically to stressful events. This is an area of enquiry which remains almost completely unexplored in the stress field, perhaps partly due to the lack of a suitably comprehensive phenomenologically based theoretical framework from which research questions and hypotheses could be derived. The cognitive–phenomenological approach outlined in Chapter 6 constitutes one attempt at the development of such a framework.

The motivational aspects of the two main phenomenological theories of self-actualization, which were proposed by Maslow and Rogers respectively, arise from a discrepancy between the self-concept of a person as it is currently perceived by that individual and that which the person holds as being their ideal-self. The precise explanation of human motivation that each of these theories embodies, however, is somewhat different. Rogers (1951: 487) postulated the single drive or tendency of self-actualization: 'The organism has one basic tendency and striving, to actualise, maintain and enhance the experiencing organism'. In contrast, Maslow (1970) postulated a hierarchy of needs, arguing that individuals progress up the hierarchy and that in order to strive for higher levels, lower needs must have been met. While Maslow's hierarchy has been criticized for being ethnocentric and class-biased and his claims of both universality and sequential invariance have been challenged, these features of the model can, none the less, be amended while leaving some of the main principles intact.

Maslow (1970: xii–xiii) writes, in his preface to the second edition of *Motivation and Personality* that

> human life will never be understood unless its highest aspirations are taken into account. Growth, self-actualization, the striving toward health, the quest for identity and autonomy, the yearning for excellence (and other ways of phrasing the striving upward) must by now be accepted beyond question as a widespread and perhaps universal human tendency.

This quotation is very telling for two reasons. Firstly, it highlights that it is possible to think of motivation in terms of a single striving, the striving upwards towards self-actualization. Secondly, it says that such a conceptualization is only perhaps, rather than is for certain, universal; it may not be. Indeed, Maslow (ibid.: xiii–xiv) goes on to state that the hierarchy of needs . . . serves as a kind of smorgasbord table from which people can choose in accordance with their own tastes and appetites.

Thus the differences between Maslow's and Rogers' theories may, at a fundamental level, be only superficial ones and they may both be reducible to one basic striving – that of self-actualization.

Goal-directedness

The notion of a sole striving towards self-actualization institutes the concept of goal-directed behaviour, with self-actualization as the most abstract of a series of goals and residing at the top of Maslow's hierarchy. Goal-directed behaviour accounts for human motivation by viewing human activity as being associated with the fulfilment of particular goals which the person wishes to achieve and which constitute the commitments referred to by Lazarus in his formulation of the stress and coping paradigm. Phenomenological writers consider the ultimate human goal to be that of self-actualization and that all other goals relate to this superordinate goal. These lower-level goals mediate between the abstract hopes and aspirations of an individual and the perceived concrete limitations and realities of the world and they determine the types of things people strive towards in terms of their career, personal lives and how one chooses to spend one's life generally. They therefore relate to the types of situations to which people choose to expose themselves and in this way determine the types of transactions a person has with the environment on a day-to-day basis. It is in this way that the formal phenomenological writings of Maslow, Rogers and others are connected with the rather less formal phenomenological approach in psychology which involves focusing upon the subjective experience of, in this case, stress and health. Such an approach seems to be currently lacking in mainstream health psychology, but would appear to be essential in the development of a convincing biopsychosocial account of the stress process.

Interventions in the stress process

Intervention in the stress process has generally taken one of two forms: either direct intervention in the biological pathways thought to mediate the stress process, primarily through either biofeedback or drug therapies, or else psychotherapeutic interventions which generally fall under the rubric of stress management therapy. Commonly prescribed pharmacological interventions include beta-blockers which serve to lessen some of the physiological effects of sympathetic arousal and psychoactive drugs such as anxiolytics and antidepressants which serve to dampen some of the psychological distress which often accompanies stressful periods. Biofeedback techniques involve bringing normally involuntary biological functions such as cardiovascular regulation under voluntary control. This is achieved by providing the person with feedback about the activity of the biological mechanisms involved in the stress process, usually consisting of indices of autonomic arousal such as skin conductance responses, heart rate or blood pressure and helping them to develop psychological techniques to moderate these responses.

Of the psychotherapeutic interventions, the most commonly used methods are based upon cognitive–behavioural therapies which are based on the idea that self-generated cognitions mediate and moderate the impact of stressors. Techniques include cognitive restructuring which aims to help individuals recognize stress, gain insight into negative self-statements which contribute to the stress process and modify irrational attitudes, beliefs and thought processes. For example, commonly modified cognitions include lowering the need for approval, reducing perfectionism and changing attitudes towards the nature of life's unfairness. Other cognitive techniques involve helping the individual to cope with the consequences of stressful transactions and include anxiety management, anger control and equipping the person with new coping techniques.

One popular cognitive–behavioural intervention in the stress process consists of an approach known as 'stress inoculation training'. This consists of a systematic programme of training people in various strategies and techniques aimed at helping them cope with stressful transactions. The first phase of stress inoculation training consists in educating the individual about the way in which emotional and physiological responses to stress arise. The importance of this phase of therapy is that it provides a basis for the person to understand subsequent intervention strategies; the efficacy of the particular 'theories' of stress responding is often not considered as crucial in the process. This is one area where a clearer theoretical understanding of the stress process, especially one which is grounded in the phenomenological experience of the individual could serve to improve the success of intervention techniques by making patients more adequately equipped with a fuller knowledge of exactly how stress exerts its effects, which would thereby facilitate the development of more sophisticated and comprehensive strategies for intervening in that process.

The second stage of stress inoculation training consists in helping the person to become aware of the types of situations in which stress is likely to arise and also of their maladaptive patterns of responding to such situations. The person is encouraged to engage in self-observation to identify specific examples of stress episodes and, in conjunction with the therapist, he or she is then helped to develop a range of coping skills. The person then rehearses these coping skills with the therapist. The therapist trains the individual in particular techniques such as progressive relaxation to help control the physiological components of their response and behavioural or interpersonal skills in which they may have particular deficits. The bulk of training is concerned with the development of a package of self-statements which help the person prepare for confronting and dealing with stress and which often address individual efficacy and control beliefs. These serve to direct attention to particular environmental cues, appraise potentially stressful situations, direct action and coping during stressful encounters and rein-force positive self-statements after having successfully coped with stressful episodes. After these strategies have been developed and rehearsed, the therapeutic process moves on to the stage of their application in the person's day-to-day life which generally involves gradually increasing the level of exposure to stressful situations and environments.

As Hamberger and Lohr (1984) have pointed out, stress inoculation train-ing has considerable intuitive appeal, it appears to be generalizable across a variety of situations and is therefore economical to apply as people do not need to have repeated treatments and it also appears to have a number of clinical applications ranging from coping with pain and surgery to improv-ing functioning at work. There remain a number of questions, however, about the necessity and sufficiency of the initial education phase and although research has generally supported the efficacy of stress inoculation procedures, there is a lack of good quality studies which have attempted to evaluate both the process and outcome of the technique.

Aside from interventions aimed at the individual level, a further approach to intervention in the stress process concerns interventions at the group level. Most interventions of this kind involve efforts to reduce the stress levels of particular groups of people, often at work. Group-level interven-tions at work usually consist in attempts to change the environment by reducing the number of stressful events to which group members are ex-posed and they rely upon the ergonomic literature around job design which was discussed in Chapter 4. The ergonomic approach tends to focus almost exclusively upon environmental factors, while more comprehensive inter-ventions include individual techniques such as stress inoculation training being applied to each member of the group. Outside of the work context and despite the existence of community health workers, there is a distinct lack of evidence concerning the prevalence of stress interventions, from which it may be safe to conclude that there is not a great deal of stress intervention occurring in community settings. Again, as with individually based techniques, evidence for the efficacy of group interventions is poor. This is not to say that such interventions do not work, but merely that there is a lack of high-quality studies in the area.

The problem of a lack of good quality evaluation studies examining the impact of stress interventions is compounded by debate over exactly which components of the intervention process are beneficial. Reynolds *et al.* (1993), for example, demonstrated that although stress management training pro-grammes proved to be effective in decreasing psychological distress, they were not related to either job satisfaction or satisfaction in spheres outside of work. Furthermore, it appeared that such benefits were attributable more to non-specific factors than to the specific technical components of stress management training. Clearly, more research needs to be done on the development and assessment of interventions in the stress process and such work clearly needs to be founded upon sound theories of exactly how stress impacts upon well-being. Theories which are of practical use and significance with respect to intervention therefore need to provide a good understanding of how those dimensions which are subject to therapeutic influence impact upon both the generation of stress and how it is subsequently coped with. Chapter 6 outlines a cognitive–phenomenological approach within which practically relevant and useful theories of stress may be developed.

Further reading

Hamberger, L.K. and Lohr, J.M. (1984) *Stress and Stress Management: Research and Applications.* New York: Springer.

Kaplan, H.B. (1991) Social psychology of the immune system: a conceptual framework and review of the literature. *Social Science and Medicine*, 33(8): 909–23.

Steptoe, A. (1991) The links between stress and illness. *Journal of Psychosomatic Research*, 35(6): 633–44.

A cognitive–phenomenological perspective

Learning objectives for this chapter

This chapter expands upon some of the ideas presented in Chapter 5 and develops a cognitive–phenomenological perspective on stress. The chapter explains how this perspective adds to our understanding of the stress process and identifies the main components of this approach. The chapter elaborates upon the role of goal-directed behaviour and describes how self-regulation theory can help explain both the genesis of stressful encounters and how they are coped with. The chapter explains how some of these theoretical ideas relate to more conventional socio-cognitive analyses of person–environment (P–E) transactions which involve cognitive planning, scripts and expectations. It also explains how some forms of stress may be viewed as expectancy violations which take the form of script inconsistencies. Throughout the chapter, attention is paid to ensuring that the various theoretical strands which have been developed in earlier chapters are integrated into a cognitive–phenomenological theory of stress which is, itself, located within a transactional biopsychosocial framework. After reading this chapter, you should be able to:

♦ understand why a cognitive–phenomenological perspective on stress aids our understanding of the stress process and facilitates the development of integrated and practically useful stress theory;
♦ describe the main elements of the stress process emphasized by a cognitive–phenomenological account;
♦ describe how the concept of goal-directed behaviour unites cognitive and phenomenological perspectives and understand the role of goal-directed behaviour in the genesis of stressful transactions;
♦ understand the role of the self-concept in the stress process and explain how the knowledge structures which have been developed throughout

one's previous life history impact upon the way in which transactions with the environment are perceived and coped with;

♦ understand the role of cybernetic and self-regulation theory in explaining person–environment interactions and how this relates to the phenomenon of stress;

♦ understand how, from this perspective, stress may be viewed as arising from a perceived discrepancy or expectancy violation and be able to describe the script inconsistency theory of stress; and

♦ explain how the cognitive–phenomenological equivalent of the coping process, which is labelled as 'rumination', relates to phenomenological concepts such as the world view and self-concept and to theories of goal-directed behaviour, planning and self-regulation.

Why a cognitive–phenomenological perspective?

Chapter 5 provided some indication of why a cognitive–phenomenological perspective can aid our understanding of the stress process. Firstly, one of the unifying elements in a biopsychosocial analysis of the stress process consists of the role assigned to cognitive and emotional processes in the psychological mediation of stress. The highly experiential nature of both emotions and cognitions would suggest that a more phenomenologically based approach to understanding stress could prove beneficial in helping to elucidate the mediating role of these cognitive–emotional influences.

A second reason for focusing upon the cognitive–phenomenology of stress concerns the role played by internal, self-generated demands which come into play during stressful encounters. Some of these demands are considered in more depth below, but they are fundamentally concerned with the type of person one wants to be and are therefore phenomenological in nature.

The processes involved in the assignment of meaning that occurs during stressful transactions with the environment provides a third reason for focusing upon the cognitive–phenomenology of stress. Such processes are contextually embedded within the interpretive framework of the individual which is dependent upon their life history. The focus upon the life world of the individual in phenomenological approaches is therefore particularly useful in helping to explain the role of these processes in the genesis of stress and how it is subsequently coped with.

The locus of intervention in the stress process

The usefulness of a phenomenologically based theoretical framework with respect to intervention in the stress process was mentioned in Chapter 5, as was the need to understand the way in which the subjective experience of stress influences how the individual reacts psychologically, behaviourally and physiologically to stressful events. Also, the self-actualization process which is of motivational importance in phenomenological theorizing, is intimately connected with a person's commitments, aspirations and personal agenda which Lazarus described as having such an important influence in the stress and coping process.

Lazarus argues that the commitments and belief systems held by an individual influence the subjective situation as perceived by that person. He proposes that the extent to which an encounter between the person and the environment is stressful depends upon the meaning or significance of that encounter which, in turn is based upon the personal agendas and coping resources the person brings to it (Lazarus 1984b). Because of the focus on individual subjectivity and personal meaning, Lazarus claims that his stress and coping theory is a cognitive–phenomenological one. As outlined in Chapter 5, however, the usefulness of the stress and coping paradigm is limited by the assignment of many of the processes involved in appraisal to the unconscious. The development of useful cognitive–behavioural strategies of intervention in the stress process requires that we develop a better understanding of how conscious processes can be manipulated in order to moderate the impact of stressful events. The fact that the locus of intervention in this process is at the level of consciousness means that only theories which explain how conscious functioning mediates the stress–health link are likely to yield significant benefits with respect to the development of suitable strategies aimed at preventing or ameliorating the effects of stress. Phenomenological approaches assign a central role to the phenomenon of consciousness in human functioning. Furthermore, they incorporate a conceptualization of the person as reflexively aware of his or her own existence and therefore contemplative of their relationship to the external world. This is particularly appropriate in relation to the study of stress within a transactional framework because it is precisely here, at the P–E interface that stressful transactions occur.

In cognitive theories of stress, consciousness is identified with the central processing unit (CPU) in the computer metaphor, or else with short-term memory, working memory, or attention. Socio-cognitive theories also take into account the various types of subjective biases which occur in the form of processing heuristics. In order to account fully for top–down influences in the stress process, however, it is also necessary to consider the way in which higher level cognitive functioning mediates social influences. Such higher-level functioning is concerned with the influence of conscious processes, as opposed to the often unconscious types of heuristics which are emphasized within a socio-cognitive framework. Thus we require some theoretical framework within which these conscious influences may be located.

Unlike many theoretical perspectives in psychology, which still refuse to consider the life world of the individual as the essential psychological datum, the biopsychosocial approach focuses upon the whole person and concerns the realm of that person's conscious existence in the situated context of everyday life. Historically, psychology has neglected the life world of the individual, a fact which is amusingly illustrated by Miller (1991: 109) who, personifying and describing the hapless life story of psychology, writes 'Poor Psychology! First she lost her soul, then she lost her mind, and finally, she lost consciousness!'. While there has indeed been something of a 'conative revolution' (Karoly 1993) in recent times, there is still a long way to go before the life world, consisting of contextually embedded cognitive structures such as the self-concept and world view, asserts itself as the psychological sovereign. The more recent upsurge of interest in things such as personal biographies which have come about with the dawning of discursive psychology go some way towards remedying this situation.

As McGuire and McGuire (1991) point out, the organ of thought, the brain constitutes only 2 per cent of body weight but accounts for 25 per cent of the resting person's total oxygen consumption and also for an overwhelmingly large proportion of all body cells. A system this costly is unlikely to have evolved unless it contributes substantially to the individual's and the species' survival and, given that a large part of this capacity is devoted to conscious activity, consciousness must therefore be of considerable evolutionary significance. Other evolutionary arguments concerning the significance of consciousness have been offered by Bargh (1994) who argued that the automatization of routine thought processes frees one's limited attentional resources for non-routine matters and enables us to reduce the massive amount of stimulation and information with which we would otherwise be bombarded to a more manageable subset of important objects, events and appraisals. Once again, the requirement that we consider consciousness as a fundamental quality of psychological functioning, means that it should be incorporated into the psychological component of a biopsychosocial analysis and this, in turn, requires that we adopt a cognitive–phenomenological approach.

Components of a cognitive–phenomenological account: goal-directedness

The goal-directed aspect of phenomenological theorizing is highly compatible with the type of transactional perspective described in Chapter 3. People are constantly doing something and P–E interaction tends to be continuous inasmuch as, unless people are actually asleep, they are always interacting in some way or another with the environment and the potential for a stressful event, even a minor one such as the types of daily hassles discussed in Chapter 3, is therefore ever present.

The notion that human behaviour consists of P–E interactions and can be explained largely in terms of goal-directed behaviour is certainly not new in psychology. Pervin (1989) traces its roots back to the work of James and

Wundt at the end of the nineteenth century. Of course, there have been many developments since then as the concept of motivation has fallen in and out of favour in psychology and psychologists have shifted their focus from behaviour to cognition.

The field of motivation is a massive area in psychology. Ford (1992) describes 32 different theoretical approaches in his 'brief' review of the area. Pervin (1989) highlights the advantages of a goal conception of motivation over previously popular 'stick and carrot' notions of internal drives or instincts and external environmental incentives. In so doing, he partitions the problem of motivation into two essential elements: firstly, the existence of a hierarchically organized goal system and, secondly, the distinction between the goals themselves, which are 'the end points the organism seeks to achieve' and plans which are 'the means through which goals are achieved' (p. 7). This distinction highlights the overlap between phenomenological approaches and more conventional socio-cognitive theorizing. For example, Bandura's (1989) social cognitive theory and, in particular, his cognitively based description of motivation consists of the setting of goals, the anticipation of the likely outcomes of prospective actions and the planning of courses of action designed to realize valued futures. Bandura (1989) suggests that goals that operate as the proximal regulators of motivation and action subserve broader goals reflecting matters of personal import and value. Such broader goals may be seen as akin to that of self-actualization, as described in the phenomenological theories of human motivation. Indeed, Bandura theorized that cognitive motivators are mediated by three types of self-influence: affective self-evaluation, perceived self-efficacy and the adjustment of personal standards. He proposed that we may sometimes strive to be successful at particular lower-level goals because, through the engagement of the self-system, proximal goals invest activities with personal significance.

Other approaches to human motivation have combined notions of both personal significance and goal-directed behaviour and one such approach is that developed by Klinger (1977) who developed the concept of the 'current concern' which is a hypothetical motivational state that exists between two points in time – when a person identifies a goal and when that goal is either achieved or abandoned. This state relates to relatively short-term goals and sequences of action and it guides a person's ongoing thoughts and behaviour during their everyday interactions with the environment. The types of current concerns that an individual possesses are highly idiographic and are therefore explicable in terms of the life world of the individual; however other researchers (e.g. Harlow and Cantor 1994) have noted that some concerns or goals may be more nomothetic, relating to whole groups of people.

Nomothetic goals constitute the age-graded expectations referred to in Chapter 5 and act as a source of consensual goals which are reminiscent of Erikson's stages of psychosocial development. This approach has been adopted in the study of goals such as 'providing for the next generation' in older adults (McAdams *et al.* 1993) which relates to Erikson's concept of generativity. This research used a typical paradigm which related a particular aspect of the goal (in this case, commitment to it) to a well-being outcome measure (in this case, life satisfaction) and showed that high commitment to the goal was associated with a higher life satisfaction. Other research looking at goal attributes (e.g. Brunstein 1993) has shown that attributes such as commitment to, attainability of and progress towards goals are predictive of well-being. Such findings accord well with the theoretical treatment of stress described here and highlight the importance of considering a person's goals, which form part of their personal agenda, in looking at the effects of stressful transactions upon health outcomes.

The study of personal goals in relation to personality and well-being has undergone something of a renaissance in recent times (Karoly and Lecci 1993; Brunstein 1993) and this has led to a blossoming of the number of terms used to describe these goals. Gaeddert and Facteau (1990), for example, use the term 'achievement strivings', while the more popular concept of the 'life task' has been developed by Nancy Cantor (e.g. Cantor and Langston 1989; Harlow and Cantor 1994). Cantor *et al.* (1991) proposed that the goals on which an individual works structure the experiences of daily life and are therefore likely to impact upon the sorts of stressors to which people are exposed, how the person reacts to these stressors and the impact that they subsequently have on health. Again, Cantor views goals as inherently intertwined with self-dynamics and their treatment in the life-task literature is strongly related to the concept of self-actualization: 'Goals are instantiated for individuals in the life tasks that are currently time consuming, self-relevant and self-defined as important and in the set of contexts in which those particular self-ideals can be realised or lost' (Cantor and Langston 1989: 129).

There have been other approaches which share much in common with that of the life task. For example, the personal projects approach (e.g. Little 1983; Lecci *et al.* 1994). Little (1983) identified the personal project as an interrelated sequence of actions intended to achieve a personal goal. The personal project concept has been used in empirical studies in the field of health and well-being on, for example, life satisfaction (Little 1983), hypochondriasis (Karoly and Lecci 1993) and depression (Lecci *et al.* 1994), but has not been applied to the study of the effects of stress upon health.

Perhaps the most popular recent approach to personal goals is that of 'personal strivings' proposed by Robert Emmons (1986, 1989; King and Emmons 1991; Emmons and McAdams 1991). Emmons (1986: 1058) defined personal strivings as 'the characteristic types of goals that individuals try to achieve through their everyday behaviour' and asserted that they serve to organize and integrate an individual's goals. Emmons contrasts his approach with others which, he claims, focus on individual goals. Personal strivings are both idiographic and nomothetic; they represent 'individualised instantiations of nomothetic motives' (Emmons 1989: 95). There have been several empirical findings in relation to personal strivings and their significance in the stress process in relation to both physical and emotional well-being (see Box 6.1).

In the literature on personal strivings, life tasks and other similar concepts, such as achievement goals (e.g. Gaeddert and Facteau 1990), life aspirations (e.g. Kasser and Ryan 1993) and personal goals (e.g. Brunstein 1993), a recurrent issue is the level of abstraction that constitutes the goal-oriented unit of analysis. These vary from very concrete and idiographic to very abstract and nomothetic, but in all cases the units used represent ways of describing the manifestation or instantiation of a particular goal in a particular context. While most of the approaches which have been outlined above concur that there is a degree of distinctiveness to an individual's goal system, there have been several attempts to derive a nomothetic typology of goals. In discussing the origins of personal strivings, Emmons (1989) has proposed a genotypical constitution which is common to all individuals and which consists of three main goals which are: (i) a desire for safety, predictability and control; (ii) a desire for social approval, intimacy and belongingness; and (iii) the desire for self-esteem, competence and mastery. He points out that a number of personality theories converge on these three main goals, for example Maslow's (1970) hierarchy of needs (Figure 6.1) contains these three goals as the three middle levels of the hierarchy.

Box 6.1   Personal strivings, stress and health

Emmons (1986) encouraged subjects to generate lists of strivings and rate each one using Striving Assessment Scales (SAS) which include measures of the striving's subjective value, the degree of commitment to it and the degree of fulfilment obtained from it in the past. Using experience sampling methodology, he found that different aspects of the strivings generated by participants were predictive of positive affect, negative affect and life satisfaction. In a replication and extension of this work, Emmons (1991) found that power strivings were correlated with Global Severity Index (GSI) scores which measure both physical and psychological well-being and also that individuals experience positive and negative affect in their lives as a function of the association of stressful minor life events with their personal strivings. These findings are consistent with the published work on the concept of centrality (e.g. Gruen et al. 1988; Santiago-Rivera et al. 1995) and confirm the importance of developing theory which is able to incorporate and explain the role of goals, personal attributes and their interaction in the stress process.

Other findings by Emmons (1989) have demonstrated that conflict between and ambivalence about personal strivings were correlated with psychological well-being (anxiety and depression) and physical well-being (somatization, number of visits to the health centre and number of illnesses), respectively. These findings were accounted for in terms of an 'inhibition model' which postulates that a lack of expressive emotion causes increased autonomic arousal which leads to a negative change in both physical and psychological well-being and this interpretation was supported by correlational data which showed that participants spent more time thinking about conflictual and ambivalent strivings (which are likely to elicit negative affective status) in comparison with other strivings, but less time acting on them (which means they remain unresolved and therefore cause sustained autonomic arousal). In a further study, they suggested that it was not lack of emotional expression *per se* which had deleterious consequences for health, but rather that it was ambivalence over expressing emotion which led to these consequences and thus the focus should be on the role of individual goals and attitudes that underlie expressive or inhibitory behaviour in causing physical and psychological distress. Recent evidence has, however, suggested that such effects may be limited to psychological well-being only (e.g. Katz and Campbell 1994), but whatever the extent of such influences, they are consistent with an alternative explanation to that offered by Emmons. Such an explanation may focus upon the role of strivings in the stress process and, in particular, upon the notion that stress may arise when progress towards those goals is in some way blocked or impeded. Also, the role of goal dynamics and the relationship between the types of goals one holds, how realistic such goals are and the opportunities for their fulfilment afforded by the environment may turn out to be significant influences in the genesis, transmission and maintenance of stress.

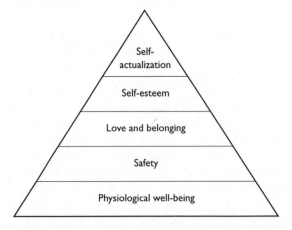

Figure 6.1 Maslow's hierarchy of needs

Ultimately, then, all of a person's strivings can be linked to the types of goals which they strive towards which are, in turn, closely related to the phenomenological notion of self-actualization. They therefore concern the person that an individual wants to become, their aspirations, and how to go about achieving these given their current situation. The notion of self-actualization is therefore of considerable importance in a cognitive–phenomenological account of the stress process. The types of goals that phenomenological theories of self-actualization describe are of an abstract nature, but the processes that are used to achieve them are generalizable to much lower-level goals which are generally associated with goal-directed behaviour. This is due to the hierarchical nature of a goal systems perspective.

It would appear that goals may usefully be viewed as both idiographic and nomothetic in nature and, in this connection, a phenomenological goal systems approach is able to account for individual differences in the stress process in two ways. Firstly, there are differences in exactly how the individual views their ideal-self and the sort of personal qualities which they view as desirable. Secondly, there are differences in the potentialities of individuals (owing to the biological injustice of which Maslow writes) and the opportunity of individuals to achieve their own potential (owing to social injustice).

The self-concept

The involvement of the self-concept in the stress process has already been alluded to, both in previous chapters which have described the role of personality variables and a number of other self-related constructs, and in relation to the types of goals a person strives towards. Lazarus views the role of the self in the stress process as stemming from the relationship between the self-concept and the beliefs and commitments which shape an individual's personal agenda, in turn shaping the types of appraisals and coping efforts which particular encounters with the environment are likely to generate.

Despite the apparent significance of the self-concept for the stress phenomenon, there are relatively few theoretical treatments of its precise involvement. This is, perhaps a little curious; however, Epstein (1973: 404) suggests one possible reason as to why this should be the case:

> One can neither see a self-concept, nor touch it, and no one has succeeded as yet in adequately defining it as a hypothetical construct. . . .
> Some authors, apparently having despaired of providing an adequate definition, dispense with the matter by an appeal to common sense and by asserting that everyone knows he has a self as surely as he knows what belongs to him and what does not.

The empirical difficulties which Epstein describes mean that it is often difficult to obtain reliable 'measures' of the self-concept which, given the current emphasis within psychology upon empiricism in research, may explain the relative decline in its popularity.

Kihlstrom and Klein (1994) discuss several possible formats for the self-knowledge structure. Firstly, the self may be viewed as a proper set of objects whose features are singly necessary and jointly sufficient to identify an object as an instance of the set. Secondly, the self may be viewed as a probabilistic category, whose members consist of those elements which lean towards the central tendency of certain prototypical features or dimensions. Thirdly, the self may be a collection of various context-specific selves, organized into some sort of hierarchy of varying degrees of abstraction. Fourthly, the exemplar view contrasts with the prototype view by asserting that the self is a collection of concrete exemplars or instances of how we perceive ourselves at various times and in various situations. Finally, according to the theory-based view, concepts are organized by the theories we possess about the domain to which they relate. Thus, the self-concept is represented by a group of intercorrelated attributes of the self and is defined according to some organizing principle or theory of the self which explains why we act, feel and think the way we do. Such conceptions of the self-concept do relatively little to inform us of the actual structure of the self, which may be for example a schema, a semantic associative network or some sort of personal narrative, perhaps consisting of a number of elaborate, concrete and autobiographical episodic units, and as Kihlstrom and Klein point out, there exists evidence for each of these formulations.

The self-concept is conceived of as a fundamental psychological structure and Schlenker and Weigold (1989) present a compelling argument for this assertion. They suggest that as individuals, we are deeply culturally embedded in the social practices that constitute our society and as a result of this, it is necessary to have a self-identification process which allows us to distinguish the self from others and construct and express our self-concept. With respect to the discussion in the previous section of the relationship between the self-concept and some sort of motivational goal hierarchy, several researchers (e.g. Bandura 1989; Lee *et al.* 1989) have highlighted the self-efficacy component of the self-concept as a crucial mediator between goals and action. The self-concept represents a critical evaluative context for personal interpretations of prototypical age-graded goals and it has been suggested by Cantor and Langston (1989: 151) that 'individuals frame specific versions of commonly held life tasks and select strategies based on their readings of personal experience, capacities and efficacy in relevant domains'. Conversely, Emmons (1989) has proposed that the self-concept has important motivational elements which he labels 'ego tasks'.

With respect to the role of the self-concept in stress and health, it has been suggested that the number of possible or actual selves (self-complexity) mediates and/or moderates both performance, in terms of the success of one's strivings, and affective reactions to feedback about the success or failure of one's strivings and can therefore be conceived of as a buffering variable against stress (e.g. Linville 1987; Strauman and Higgins 1987; Dixon and Baumeister 1991; Niedenthal *et al.* 1992). Other researchers, however, have reported negative results concerning the buffering effects of self-complexity (e.g. Woolfolk 1995). In any case, the inclusion of the self-concept in a cognitive–phenomenological account of the stress process permits the integration of relevant self-concept research into a transactional conception of person–environment interaction and therefore goes some way towards rectifying the problem identified by Shibutani (1991: 59):

> Several thousand empirical studies have been reported – disclosing interesting observations, provocative insights and surprising associations. To date, however, the findings have not been organised into anything resembling an empirically grounded account of the manner in which self-concepts are involved in the organisation and execution of voluntary conduct.

The world view

The world view contains an individual's values, attitudes, beliefs and ideas about the world and how it works and therefore constitutes an important influence upon how the individual perceives and reacts to potentially stressful events. The world view may be considered as the static abstraction of the more interactive and personally involved life world about which phenomenological theorists have written. It is the knowledge structure which constitutes the background context from which an individual creates meaning in their world and thereby determines how they experience their dynamic interactions which constitute their perceived life world. The world view consists of the residue of one's life experiences and history. The term 'assumptive worlds' has been used by some researchers (e.g. Marshall *et al.* 1985; Janoff-Bulman 1989: 114) who have described it as a perceptual screen, or set of schemata and defined it as

> a basic conceptual system, developed over time, that provides us with expectations about ourselves and the world so that we might function effectively. This conceptual system is best represented by a set of assumptions, or theories, that generally prove viable in interactions with the world.

According to this definition, assumptive worlds constitute the knowledge-based schemas which act as a source of the type of biases, or heuristic processing effects, that are described in socio-cognitive accounts of information processing. Furthermore, as they are, themselves, a particular form of cognitive structure (a schema) they are also subject to the sorts of cognitive biases thought to operate on schemata including resistance to change, perceived consistency, and accessibility effects (e.g. Wyer and Srull 1994). Of course, the world view is a very complex and idiographic cognitive structure which contains information relating to many domains and which, from a social learning perspective, consists of the accumulated knowledge that an individual holds about the universe and which has been acquired both through direct experience and vicariously.

Janoff-Bulman has proposed several key assumptions which may, to a greater or lesser degree, be present in a general world view shared by individuals within a Western culture and these are the perceived benevolence of the world, or belief in a 'just world' (e.g. Lerner 1971), the meaningfulness of the world and the worthiness of the self. Such components of the world view overlap heavily with the types of cognitions which cognitive–behavioural interventions in the stress process aim to manipulate and therefore constitute the type of cognitive mediators which require comprehensive theoretical treatment if we are to develop better applications of health psychology in the stress field.

The degree to which individuals share a world view is, of course, open to debate; for example, Marshall et al. (1985) refer to the assumptive worlds of a particular group of individuals – education policymakers – in their research, while Ware and Kleinman (1992), in their study of the influence of culture on neurasthenia, refer to the shared local worlds of interpersonal experience constituted by particular neighbourhoods, villages or social networks which determine the experiential quality of the activities of daily living. Similarly, the age-graded tasks of Cantor et al. (1991) are reflections of the expectations of individuals within particular subcultures. While these tasks are shared by members of the subculture, there are probably differences in the importance assigned to them by individuals and these differences manifest themselves in terms of the emotional involvement associated with each task and the degree of affect induced by stressful transactions involving these particular components of the world view.

Some social psychological theories are clearly predicated upon the assumption of some degree of commonality in world views. Equity theory, for example, assumes that an individual believes that the world should operate in a just and fair way and that individuals are therefore motivated to restore equity whenever a perceived inequity is encountered. While this may certainly hold true for a large number of individuals, it is certainly not the case that everyone holds this initial fundamental assumption. Thus an approach which incorporates a phenomenological construct like the world view would seem better able to account for such between-person variation than some social psychological theories. The consequences of these individual differences for the nature and degree of stress response to events which seem to contradict fundamental assumptions such as the belief in a just world are therefore more explicable from such a perspective.

Wortman et al. (1992) proposed that an individual's philosophical perspective on life or their view of the world can have important influences upon subsequent appraisals of and reactions to stressful events. They described one such, particularly obvious, influence thus (p. 229):

Events that can be incorporated into a person's view of the world may cause little disequilibrium and resultant distress; those that shatter a person's view of the world may cause intense distress and result in subsequent health problems.

Other researchers have also looked at the way in which very generalized attitudes or beliefs impact upon the stress process. For example, the work of Scheier and Carver (1987) showed that optimism can moderate the effects of stress on physical well being in such a way that optimists (who, presumably, have a more optimistic world view than pessimists) fare better than pessimists in stressful situations. Also, Petrie *et al.* (1995) showed that certain beliefs exert an influence on the maintenance and course of specific illnesses, with those individuals who possess catastrophic beliefs faring worse than non-catastrophizers. The concept of the world view is therefore able to integrate a number of relatively diverse strands within the literature on the stress–health link and in this way it adds significantly to our overall understanding of stress as a biopsychosocial phenomenon.

Self-regulation, action and planning

A cognitive–phenomenological theory of the stress process requires an account of the types of cognitive mechanisms which mediate the link between goal-directed behaviour and the experience of stress resulting from certain types of transactions with the environment. It is likely that the self-regulation mechanisms identified by Karoly (1993) in his excellent review of mechanisms of the control of action fulfil such a function. Self-regulation is defined by Karoly (1993: 24) thus:

Self-regulation refers to those processes . . . that enable an individual to guide his/her goal-directed activities over time and across changing circumstances (contexts). Regulation implies modulation of thought, affect and behavior, or attention via deliberate or automated use of specific mechanisms and supportive metaskills . . . [and] . . . may be said to encompass up to five interrelated and iterative component phases: 1. goal selection, 2. goal cognition, 3. directional maintenance, 4. directional change or reprioritization, and 5. goal termination.

Descriptions such as this bring to mind familiar criticisms of cognitivistic accounts of human functioning which remain unconvincing due the their reliance upon a disconnected source of agency which acts as a 'person inside the head' who decides when and when not to act. Such accounts neglect the ongoing nature of person–environment interaction which, as Feather (1982c: 396) points out, views behaviour as '. . . an extended and continuing stream rather than as a succession of discrete episodic events that involve a reactive rather than a continually active organism'. Cognitive theories which leave the organism 'buried in thought' neglect the primacy of action, a criticism to which a cognitive–phenomenological account of the stress process located within a transactional framework is not subject due to its incorporation of the dynamics of time and the phenomenological assertion that individuals are reflexively aware of their own existence.

One model of goal selection has been provided by Feather (1982b) in his theory of achievement motivation. He proposed that the level of difficulty of achieving a goal is a factor which makes one goal preferable over another, along with the motive strength an individual has in a particular striving domain, an appraisal of the likelihood of success in achieving the goal and the importance, or incentive value of the goal. The appraised likelihood of success is referred to as the expectancy of goal attainment, while the incentive value is referred to as the value and models such as these are therefore known as 'expectancy-value' theories. Static accounts of goal-selection fail, however, to capture the dynamic nature of the P–E relationship; an individual is constantly engaged in a stream of P–E interactions which form the context of future goal-selection processes and the theory of achievement motivation does not really account for this. To analyse goal selection in this highly 'computational' framework fails to capture the dynamic interaction between the constituent structures of a cognitive–phenomenological account such as that presented here.

How do people attempt to realize the goals contained in their goal hierarchies when engaging in goal-directed behaviour? The answer is through the cognitive process of planning. Planning involves identifying and appraising possible courses of action which aim to achieve the particular goal under consideration at the time. During the process of planning, the cognitive activities in which an individual engages resemble those of an expectancy-value model. As Feather (1982a: ix) writes, expectancy-value theory

> . . . relates action to the perceived attractiveness or aversiveness of expected consequences. A person's behaviour is seen to bear some relation to the expectations the person holds and the subjective value of the consequences that might occur following the action.

This model has also been characterized by behavioural decision theorists as a decision rule which aims to maximize the subjective expected utility (SEU) in a choice situation. Fischhoff *et al.* (1982: 315) provide a comprehensive description of the processes through which an individual progresses in making a decision and this description may be applied to the planning process:

> A simple and comprehensive rule for making decisions is the following. List all feasible courses of action. For each action, enumerate all possible consequences. For each consequence, assess the attractiveness

or aversiveness of its occurrence, as well as the probability that it will be incurred should the action be taken. Compute the expected worth of each consequence by multiplying its worth by its probability of occurrence. The expected worth of an action is the sum of the expected worths of all possible consequences. Once the calculations are completed, choose the action with the greatest expected worth.

This neatly describes the perfectly rational operation of an information processing system during the planning process, but as previously outlined, such descriptions have very limited ecological validity as they fail to take account of the heuristic processes to which human information processing is subject. Mann and Janis (1982) propose that, because the alternatives and their potential to achieve a desired outcome are uncertain, such decisions are necessarily conflictual in nature and this conflict results in 'decisional stress' and a number of habitual coping patterns which allow for individual differences in the actual processing strategies adopted by individuals. Such differences represent the manifestation of the types of heuristic influences which socio-cognitive theorists have elaborated, such as the choice of a low effort strategy in circumstances of information overload or the biasing and discounting influences of particular attitudes or beliefs. This issue highlights the importance of taking account of the life world of the individual in constructing ecologically valid theory and illustrates why a cognitive–phenomenological theory is superior to a strictly cognitive one; its emphasis on subjective perception and the world view means that it is consequently able to offer a much more realistic description of the actual cognitive functioning of people in the real world. The enormous range of possible variation in structures such as the self-concept or world view, which are residues of our experiential life history, allows for individuality in the general model of cognition which the cognitive–phenomenological framework presented here describes.

The process of planning bridges the gap between motivation and action and thereby animates the otherwise static description of goal-directed behaviour implied in an expectancy-value conceptualization of self-regulatory behaviour. In a transactional formulation, the planning process occurs not in isolation from the demands placed upon an individual by the environment, but in the situated context of that environment. The stimuli which impinge upon our central nervous systems via our perceptual apparatus push us towards action, encouraging us to interact with the environment in the ongoing flow of activity. This special quality of the environment is unique to an ecological psychological perspective upon person–environment interaction and refers to the 'affordance' of the environment; particular stimulus arrays from the environment 'afford' certain interactions with the environment. The affordances of the environment and the cognitive process of planning in response to those affordances mediate between the person and the environment in the cognitive–phenomenological perspective presented here.

The planning process is of relevance not only in determining the types of transactions in which individuals regularly engage, but also in explaining the problem-solving activities which occur as part of the coping process. In relation to a goal-based theory of P–E interaction, planning may be conceived of as a special type of problem-solving. Kahney (1993: 15) writes that 'whenever you have a goal which is blocked for any reason – lack of resources, lack of information, and so on – you have a problem. Whatever you do in order to achieve your goal is problem solving'. Plans may therefore be viewed as goal-based structures and, as Read and Miller (1989) have argued, person–situation interactions can be analysed as the interplay between the goals, plans, resources and beliefs of the person and the parallel structures in the environment. Aside from the expectancy-value conceptualization of the cognitive activities in which individuals engage in regulating their interactions with the environment, other problem-solving strategies which are of relevance include analysing the ends one wishes to achieve and evaluating the possible means by which these ends may be realized (means-ends analysis) and also weighing up the relative pros and cons of possible courses of action, which may be termed 'cost-benefit analysis' and which has been applied to the stress process by Mann and Janis (1982) in what they refer to as their 'balance sheet schema'.

Cantor and Langston (1989: 127) also examined goal-directed activity from within a problem-solving framework. They introduced the concept of 'social intelligence' which they defined as 'a multifaceted repertoire of social knowledge, developed within . . . personal, social and cultural life contexts'. The problems which social intelligence is brought to bear in solving are characterized as real-world problems, life problems or life tasks and are grounded in the subjective experience, or life world, of the individual, as is the expertise which constitutes social intelligence. Life tasks are the result of differences between the current state of an individual and a desired end state, or goal, and are often related to the self-concept in terms of a difference between a current perception of the self on a particular dimension and that of some future ideal-self. They relate clearly, therefore, to the process of self-actualization. Social intelligence is, then, strongly grounded in the phenomenological experience of the individual, which makes it a particularly useful device for conceptualizing the role of knowledge structures such as the world view in a cognitive–phenomenological account of the stress process. Furthermore, the approach accords special importance to the social aspects of the planning process and accounts for the social dimension of situations in which individuals find themselves during previous, current and future transactions with the environment. It is therefore particularly useful in mediating between the social and psychological levels of analysis in a biopsychosocial framework.

The subjectively interpreted context in which problems are solved constitutes an interpretive framework within which coping occurs and this phenomenological context, argue Cantor and Langston (1989: 132), has significant implications for the selection and appraisal of task-relevant aspects of stressful encounters, the choice of problem-solving or coping strategies one adopts and the resultant plans an individual chooses when faced with a stressor:

> we tend to think of people as having quite consistent, generalised styles of problem solving . . . yet, to the extent that strategies are intimately linked, at least in principle, to particular life-task goals and domains of life task activity, individuals should be able to vary their strategic orientations in line with their different readings of their self-in-situations.

The situated self constitutes the fundamental unit of analysis in both cognitive–phenomenological and biopsychosocial analyses of the stress process.

Interpretive frameworks were defined by Cantor and Langston (1989: 146) as

> the background set of messages, ideas, feelings and memories that come to mind for the individual as they approach . . . particular domains of life-task activity . . . [which] . . . derive, often fairly directly, from experiences with the values, demands and tasks encouraged by familial, sub-cultural and socio-institutional life settings.

They identified three especially powerful aspects of interpretive frameworks: a normative influence; the influence of self-perceptions and self-ideals; and an autobiographical context of goal-relevant experiences. These influences, claim Cantor and Langston, serve to permit the framing of life tasks or goals in particular ways and influence the selection of particular strategies or plans based on previous experience and personal efficacies. These 'strategic orientations' constitute a heuristic influence which operates during planning activity and which relates to the individual's cognitive construction of the task and their thoughts, feelings and judgements about past, present and possible selves. One issue raised by Cantor and Langston (1989: 161) is that of the strategic flexibility or rigidity of an individual:

> for life-task problem-solving to be intelligent it should be highly discriminative, reflecting the individual's sensitive reading or the demands in each important life situation.

The overgeneralization or habitual and inflexible use of a limited range of strategies, particularly those that might be labelled 'pathological' (i.e. those that are unsuccessful or result in the production of more, or more difficult, problems or tasks) can have negative effects in those life-task domains for which more appropriate strategies exist but, through habit, are rejected in favour of a preferred strategy. Harlow and Cantor (1994), for example, showed how 'spillover' effects (i.e. the use of strategies developed for one particular life-task domain being used in a different and inappropriate domain) lead to decreased satisfaction in domains other than those to which the habitually used strategy corresponds. Cantor and Langston (1989) have identified particular generalized strategies, such as defensive pessimism and social constraint, which are used in life-task problem-solving and which may

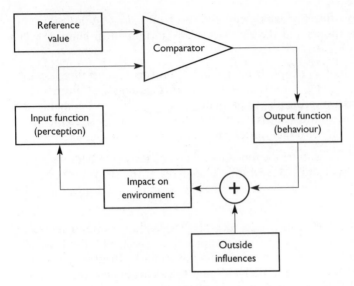

Figure 6.2 The negative-feedback loop
Source: Reproduced from C.S. Carver and M.F. Scheier, Origins and functions of positive and negative affect: A control process view, *Psychological Review*, 1990, 97(1), 19–35. Copyright © 1990 by the American Psychological Association. Reprinted with permission

be considered to be habitual coping responses when applied to the study of stressful person–environment transactions.

Karoly (1993) describes the process of planning as the ability to envision vividly an intended outcome, to create a possible future that connects with the present as well as the past, and to anticipate obstacles. Thus planning is an 'off-line' process in that it relates to future events and is not, therefore, constrained to operate in real time. It is proposed that the individual engages in such off-line planning activity in order to guide intended behaviour, thereby maximizing the amount of free cognitive capacity available for on-line processing during interactions with the environment. In terms of control theory, planning may be viewed as a feedback control mechanism which is used to guide behaviour.

Control, or cybernetic, theory has been used, most notably by Carver and Scheier (1981, 1982, 1990a,b) to explain how people's moment-to-moment actions are determined. The basic unit of cybernetic control is the negative-feedback loop (see Figure 6.2).

According to the cybernetic theory of Carver and Scheier, actual (as opposed to planned or intended) behaviour is controlled by a series of hierarchically connected feedback loops and this approach is, therefore, highly compatible with the general systems theory upon which the biopsychosocial framework is based (see Chapter 1). Cybernetic theory constitutes the psychological equivalent of physiological homeostasis and thus self-regulation theory in the psychological domain is of a similar nature to physiological self-regulation. Given this similarity and the way in which social aspects are mediated psychologically, the cognitive–phenomenological perspective described here offers the theoretical overlap across the various levels of analysis which are necessary in the formulation of truly integrated bio-psychosocial theorizing.

Script inconsistency and rumination

Ford (1992), in his description of the living systems framework as an explanatory account of the organized flow of behaviour, uses the concept of the behaviour episode which is very similar to that of a 'script' developed by Schank and Abelson (1979). A behaviour episode is a 'slice of life' and is defined as a context-specific goal-directed pattern of behaviour that unfolds over time until either the goal is accomplished or attention is diverted towards another goal or the goal is evaluated as unattainable and the individual gives up. The behavioural episode schema, or BES, is the result of a frequently experienced behavioural episode that becomes integrated into a stable, internal, stereotypical representation – a script. Ford proposes that individuals possess a repertoire of BESs and that they are used to guide behaviour during transactions with the environment. As Trzebinski (1989) points out, the action-oriented schemata an individual brings to a problem may determine the cognitive procedures one uses to construct and interpret a problem and thus there is something of a reciprocal influence between planning activity and the repertoire of scripts with which an individual is familiar. Planning may be conceptualized as the derivation of a course of action which is designed to realize particular goals and which individuals use to guide their behaviour during goal-directed interactions with the environment. Such courses of action may take the form of a causally connected sequence of scripts.

As Trzebinski (1989: 364) points out:

> in everyday contexts, the processes of understanding social reality have an inter-subjective character: they include different forms of social negotiations on the meaning of ongoing events and facts. A process of understanding is embedded within a given social action network. Fundamentally, we are not 'thinkers', but 'doers', and this action-rooted character of our mental activity should have an impact on the structure of cognitive processes and knowledge systems that emerge from them.

This is accounted for in the cognitive–phenomenological theory presented here by invoking the script concept, which links thought with behaviour by assigning to each the same unifying knowledge structure which is based directly upon intended and actual interaction between the organism and the environment. In the words of Emmons (1989: 365):

if social action is a natural framework for our everyday cognitions and evaluations, the structure of knowledge that emerges out of such experiences should in some sense be isomorphic to the structure of the action as it is understood by participants.

The script concept fulfils this criterion and research conducted by the current author (Bartlett 1996) has indicated that certain types of stressful events, particularly those minor sorts of events known as daily hassles, may be conceptualized as expectancy violations which take the form of script inconsistencies.

The scriptual expectations which are developed during the planning process are based upon the person's accumulated knowledge about the world and the various contingencies which they have learnt, either from direct experience, or else vicariously – that is, their world view. The planning process which constitutes one component of the self-regulatory cycle may, therefore, be seen as the development of scriptual expectations based upon the knowledge contained in the world view. Stress, or at least some forms of stress, may then be conceptualized as script inconsistency. Script inconsistencies are more likely to occur in situations where the person's world view is, in some way, not sufficient to account for the actuality of the world and is therefore likely to cause a state of script inconsistency when it is acted upon. Indeed, Schank and Abelson (1979: 4) developed the script concept in order to elaborate the understanding of knowledge structures such as the world view:

> our knowledge systems will embody what has been called 'naive psychology' – the common sense (though perhaps wrong) assumptions which people make about the motives and behaviour of themselves and others – and also a kind of naive physics, or primitive intuition about physical reality.

In Carver and Scheier's (1981) cybernetic formulation of self-regulation, they propose that the focus of attention constantly shifts back and forth between the environment and the self. This shifting of the focus of attention is what facilitates the recognition of script inconsistences in a script-inconsistency theory of stress. A more general notion of monitoring activity was proposed by Karoly (1993) which is referred to as 'metamonitoring'. It is the flow of consciousness and is directed by both purposive shifts in attentional focus and by stimuli that impinge upon the organism, both environmental stimuli and internal psychological or physiological stimuli such as hunger, wants or desires.

The self-monitoring function of consciousness serves the purpose of maintaining the desired sequence of events during transactions with the environment, as depicted in the particular series of scripts being used to guide behaviour at any given moment. If no script inconsistency occurs, the event unfolds according to the script and no corrective actions to maintain the sequence of events is necessary. Minor deviations from script-guided transactions inevitably arise during the on-going stream of interaction. However, they do not usually represent deviations significant enough to constitute a script-inconsistent event and can therefore be rectified by small and relatively automatized changes in behaviour; the more insignificant and mundane, the more automatized. This type of regulation may be referred to as 'directional maintenance' and an example may help clarify the distinction between this type of regulation and that which becomes necessary following a script-inconsistent, and therefore stressful, event.

Consider an individual who is thirsty and wants a drink of water and has therefore invoked a script which consists of picking up a clean glass from the side of the sink, filling it with water, raising it to the mouth and drinking. This script is compared to the events as they unfold, not in an active way, but reflexively as the stream of events pass through consciousness. As the individual picks up the glass and turns on the tap and water comes out, all is well and as predicted and a state of script inconsistency has not thus far arisen. If, however, the water that comes out of the tap is a little warmer than the individual was expecting, they may wait for a few seconds until the fresher, cooler water begins to emerge and then fill up the glass. Now, this event was script inconsistent, but not inconsistent enough to constitute a script-inconsistent event as such and it is 'coped' with in a relatively automatic fashion. Similarly, as one raises the glass to one's lips, the successive approximations as the glass moves closer to the lips is under an even higher degree of automatic (and therefore unconscious) negative-feedback control. Consider what would happen, however, if when the tap was turned on, a gurgling rumbling sound was heard and the tap shot out of its seating in the sink, causing a jet of water to shoot out of the pipe, hit the ceiling and spray all over the kitchen. Such an event would be very discrepant with expectations – so much so as to constitute a script-inconsistent stressful event and initiate the process of coping.

Coping is referred to in the cognitive–phenomenological perspective developed here as a particular type of cognitive process called 'rumination'. In a script-inconsistency conceptualization of the stress process, rumination arises as a result of particular expectancy violations which take the form of script inconsistencies. However, the process can be generalized to other types of expectancy violation which may constitute stressful transactions more generally. This is in line with Fisher's (1986) proposition that stress may be generally conceived of as a mismatch, or perceived discrepancy, between intentions (or expectations) and reality.

A script-inconsistency theory of stress raises the issue of exactly how discrepant (or script inconsistent) an event has to be in order for it to result in the experience of stress. Many treatments of this issue invoke the concept of control and suggest that those discrepancies which are easily controllable, or rectifiable, result in little or no stress, whereas those which are less easily controlled are experienced as more stressful. It is likely that perceptions of control, plus the individual level of tolerance, or what Hyland (1988) refers to as 'error sensitivity', varies both between individuals (the perfectionist versus the slap-dash person) and within individuals (the task that requires very minute attention to detail versus the more relaxed approximations for which we sometimes aim). The determinant of the 'trigger level' for the experience of stress is therefore partly dependent upon both the perceived nature of the specific task (e.g. exacting versus approximation, important versus unimportant, etc.) and upon the characteristics of the person (e.g. an uptight perfectionist, or Type A individual versus a more laid-back casual type of person) and such parameters are themselves dependent upon entities such as the valence of the goal, the level of motivation, the level of effort invested and the self-efficacy in that particular striving domain.

A perceived discrepancy, or script-inconsistency, conceptualization of stress is supported by biological research which has identified possible physiological substrates of a 'comparator' or 'servomechanism' which recognizes inconsistencies when they arise (e.g. Stadler and Wehner 1985) and by research on the orienting reflex or OR (e.g. Siddle 1983). The OR is defined as a reflex response to any novel stimulus and is characterized by an increase in arousal of the autonomic nervous system signified by cardiovascular changes and skin-conductance responses. While there are several competing theories of OR elicitation, the majority of them view the novelty of a stimulus as the necessary and sufficient condition and this novelty arises as a result of discrepancy detected by a 'comparator unit' between the incoming stimulus and a stored neural model of the expected stimulus (i.e. an expectation). The stored neuronal model constitutes an expectancy which operates to prime the comparator. This accords very well with the idea that bodily stress responses occur following perceived discrepancies between intended actions or expectations and perceptions of events as they unfold during transactions with the environment. The stored mental model, which could conceivably take the form of a script, primes the monitoring function of self-regulatory consciousness to expect a certain sequence of events and when there is a discrepancy an OR is produced which increases arousal and directs attention towards the source of the discrepancy.

The initial increase in arousal generated by a script inconsistency is interpreted to become an emotion and such a formulation is consistent with current theories of emotion which argue that the source of general arousal is a discrepancy and that this is interpreted by the available cognitions, in line with Schacter and Singer's (1962) cognitive theory of emotion. This interpretive process carries on throughout the unfolding sequence of events and thus determines the genesis and evolution of an emotional reaction to a stressful encounter.

Rumination involves interpreting and assigning meaning to script-inconsistent events, working out exactly what went wrong and why, planning how to go about rectifying the problem and initiating instrumental and cognitive–emotion focused coping strategies. The assigning of meaning to a stressful event involves assessing how and why the event happened and appraising its implications for the achievement of the goal. One primary cognitive process by which meaning is assigned to inconsistent events is that of causal attribution and research by Weiner (1985) and Hastie (1984) has shown that people spontaneously engage in causal thinking when they encounter an expectancy violation. Attribution theory is based on Heider's assumption that individuals are motivated to identify the necessary and sufficient conditions for an event to have occurred in order to construct a causal explanation as to why the event happened. Such explanations are the result of assessments made by the individual along the dimensions, or personal constructs, that seem relevant or salient to the individual at that particular time.

The particular dimensions that an individual chooses to adopt in seeking a causal explanation depend upon both the nature of the event itself and upon the interpretive framework the individual has adopted in assigning meaning to the event which is, in turn, a function of their world view. Eiser (1986) provides a review of the attribution dimensions that have been popularly studied and these include internality and responsibility, both of which could have affective implications for the type and intensity of affective reaction a discrepant event produces. Similarly Johnson (1995) reports that event-specific attributions interact with daily hassles to predict depression.

With respect to the appraisal of the implications for the achievement of the goal, according to Carver and Scheier, individuals firstly determine if the goal at which they were striving is still accomplishable, given the new environmental configuration. If it is not, people generally give up striving for the goal whereas if there is a chance that the original goal can still be achieved, it is proposed that individuals engage in the type of planning activity described above. Such judgements are highly heuristic, depending upon the instant availability of a number of available coping options which are, in turn, dependent upon the knowledge base held by an individual (their world view).

This 'quick-and-easy' judgement may be conceptualized as an outcome-expectancy judgement and Carver and Scheier (1981) propose that such judgements are made when progress towards a goal is impeded. They describe the consequences of outcome expectancy judgements following an interruption of the expected sequence of events. If an initial judgement indicates that the outcome is unattainable, the individual withdraws from any further attempts, either mentally or, if appropriate, physically. Under these conditions the individual must abandon the goal, whereas if the outcome is possible, the individual is more likely to either retain the current goal or engage in reprioritization activity. During such activity, expectancy-value and cost-benefit processes determine whether or not the individual decides to proceed with the striving. In these cases, such courses of action constitute what have previously been termed 'instrumental coping' attempts. It is likely, however, that because many of the cognitions associated with this goal would already have been produced during initial planning activity, cognitive functioning is likely to be subject to a large number of top–down, heuristic interferences under these conditions. Such influences are likely to make the type of planning that occurs during rumination rather different from that which happens during 'off-line' planning activity which occurs before the individual actually engages with the environment. In contrast, the type of planning that occurs during rumination involves 'on-line' activity and the individual is therefore more influenced by the real-time constraints of the environment; unfortunately, the world does not stop turning when a stressful event happens and the individual therefore has to make much more immediate decisions to guide behaviour. The need for speed under these circumstances predisposes the individual to heuristic functioning as they cannot afford to become 'lost in thought' during their everyday transactions with the environment.

Bargh (1994) proposes that we have an innate need for efficiency in our everyday cognitive activities and this corresponds to the principle of cognitive conservatism in socio-cognitive theory and characterization of the person as a cognitive miser. Even if a more rational analysis could yield a better solution, such analysis requires both time and cognitive effort and the individual prefers to conserve such resources and settle for a possibly suboptimal solution. In a script-inconsistency conceptualization of stress, this may be conceived of as 'script inertia' – where possible, the individual attempts to revert to as close an approximation of the original script as is possible, rather than completely abandoning the current script. This is a special type of planning activity which may be thought of as a 'damage limitation' exercise in that the individual is motivated to preserve the integrity of the original script to as great an extent as possible, even if a more rational (but therefore more time-consuming) analysis would indicate that alternative courses of action would be preferable.

The phenomenon of script inertia does not propose that the individual considers alternatives and then rejects them in favour of the original script, but that the individual does not even consider any fundamentally different alternative scripts (unless they are motivated to do so by some particularly salient piece of information) and opts instead to adopt the strategy of re-invoking the original script with as few and minor modifications as possible, because this requires less processing capacity. It also requires less effort because of the hierarchically nested quality of the behavioural episodes that constitute a script, as modification takes place only at the lowest necessary level of the hierarchy. Only if circumstances demand, or under conditions of increased cost over and above that of investing the cognitive effort required to generate a new alternative script, would an existing script be ditched in favour of a new one and this in turn is dependent upon the number, accessibility and degree of preconstruction of alternative scripts.

Thus script inertia is a result of two factors: real-time environmental demands and more general cognitive conservatism. Superimposed upon these general influences are a host of personality differences that determine the 'cognitive style' of individuals and which exert a direct effect upon the amount of time individuals devote to formulating problem solutions (Weinman *et al.* 1985). Given equal time pressure, it is likely that there would be individual differences in the extent to which individuals consider alternative scripts and these differences are reminiscent of Langer's distinction between 'mindful' and 'mindless' behaviour; it would appear likely that some people (or the same person at different times) are more 'cognitively lazy' than others and this may in turn have a reciprocal relationship with the concept of social, or even general, intelligence.

With respect to their social intelligence framework, Cantor and Langston (1989: 127) write that

> intelligence can be viewed as a multifaceted repertoire of social knowledge, developed within, and fine tuned to meet the demands of personal, social and cultural life contexts. Individuals bring their social intelligence to bear in the hopes of solving their currently pressing life tasks (i.e. to reach their desired self-goals).

Those who are more socially intelligent would therefore find it easier and have to expend less effort (and time) in considering alternatives than others who are less intelligent, because their world views present more and better operators to solve the problem. Such a formulation is in agreement with results reported by Paterson and Neufeld (1995) which indicated that the larger the number of options available and the lower the cognitive load under conditions of time pressure, the less stressful participants rated an event. Those endowed with a high level of intelligence are more likely to adopt optimal courses of action than their less well-endowed counterparts and this is consistent with empirical evidence (e.g. Weinman and Cooper 1981; Weinman *et al.* 1985) and provides one example of the way in which intelligence may have conferred evolutionary survival advantages, thereby leading to evolution of the neo-cortex.

Some types of script-inconsistent events will not permit the whole or partial re-invocation of a script. In the exploding tap example, the individual is unlikely to, for example, search for another tap to get her drink and then re-invoke the original script, but would be more likely to attempt to stop the flow of water by, say, searching for and turning off the stopcock. This is known as 'reprioritization' and it occurs when unpredicted or unplanned events interrupt the on-going stream of behaviour and result in a situation which takes precedence in being dealt with over the goals for which the individual was previously striving before the event happened.

The process of reprioritization is largely dependent upon the new priority becoming self-evident as a pressing need requiring immediate action. Of course, this is not a quality of the event itself, but instead, based upon the goal and value systems held by individuals, certain events will be interpreted or perceived as pressing needs. An example of the subjectivity apparent in individual interpretations of what type of situation constitutes an emergency requiring immediate action comes from the phenomenon of bystander apathy; the decision about whether to act in such circumstances depends, at least partially, upon the nature and strength of commitment to the values held by individual passers by.

Under conditions that may be labelled an 'emergency', the individual focuses their attention upon the pressing problems created by the event, that of limiting flood damage in the tap example. Although attention is narrowly focused on this problem, because of the pressing need for immediate action, the individual has less time to deliberate in the performance of detailed processing strategies such as cost-benefit analyses, for example. The need for very quick decisions results in the dominance of heuristic, as opposed to rational, processing strategies and these are liable to severely interfere with the type of planning activity that occurs during rumination. Depending upon the urgency of the situation and how much it disturbs them, the individual may do the 'first thing that comes to mind' (e.g. run out of the house rather than turn off the stopcock). Doing 'the first thing that comes to mind' is a prime example of highly heuristic processing and obviously the actual actions carried out by different people under the same circumstances would vary enormously depending upon a wide array of parameters, for example their previous experience with similar incidents (e.g. an experienced plumber would search for the stopcock versus a young child who may run out of the kitchen) or their most salient goals (e.g. 'stay dry and avoid damaging my clothes' versus 'save the house from flood damage'). Decision-making processes under such 'emergency' conditions have been of great interest to ergonomists in the study of human factors contributing to disasters.

Dealing with this type of emergency situation constitutes a rather specialized form of coping: one which requires quick thinking and action on the part of the person experiencing this sort of stressful encounter. Such events may therefore be likely to elicit certain types of ruminative process, such as instrumental forms of coping, as an immediate response. The rumination process is, however, posited to occur over a longer period of time than simply the length of duration of the stressor or its immediate aftermath. Making immediate sense of a stressful encounter and deciding what to do next is the first of a series of outcomes of the rumination process and the cognitive-phenomenological theory presented in this chapter explains how these activities relate to the scriptual expectations held by individuals as they go about their everyday interactions with the world. The rumination process continues for some time after these immediate concerns have been dealt with and subsequent elements are likely to resemble the types of coping processes outlined in Chapter 3. In this connection, the script-inconsistency theory of stress presented here tends to focus upon the genesis of stress, emphasizing its 'front-end' determinants to a slightly greater extent than the subsequent coping activities which occur after a stressful transaction has been generated. In this respect, it is perhaps more a theory of stress than a theory of coping, which is advantageous given the relatively weak status of theorizing in the area of stress in comparison to the more theoretically elaborate accounts of coping which have been presented by Lazarus and others. Despite the emphasis of the script-inconsistency theory upon the genesis of stress as opposed to how it is subsequently dealt with, the cognitive-phenomenological framework within which the theory is located appears to offer a particularly rich set of concepts which are of fundamental importance in the study of human functioning and upon which theorizing in the area of coping, as well as that of intervention in the stress process, is able to draw in the development of an integrated biopsychosocial account of the stress process.

The importance of accounting for the dynamic nature of the stress process has been emphasized throughout this book. While the temporal dimensions of the rumination process consist largely of changes over time as the sequence of events unfolds, there is also another important temporal influence which has not yet been discussed. This concerns the temporal quality of the stressful events themselves. The types of processes elicited by ongoing strains or chronic stressors are likely to be somewhat different in quality to those involved in more acute types of stress such as emergencies or more commonly occurring daily hassles. While the broad components of the rumination process, such as the element of sense-making and the instrumental and emotion-focused coping processes described in Chapter 3, are likely to be common across different types of stressor, there is perhaps some divergence in the cognitive micro-processes which accompany these differing types of events. The precise nature of these differences is a topic which has not been addressed in the current research literature. This has tended to focus upon differences in outcome between the two types of stressor, as opposed to differences in process. Despite the prodigious amount of research which has been conducted in the stress field, it would appear that some important questions remain unanswered. As suggested in Chapter 2, any further research in the area needs to be sharply focused if it is to be of any significant benefit in furthering our understanding of the stress process.

Conclusion

This chapter has outlined the various components of a cognitive–phenomenological perspective on stress and shown how these may be integrated with the theoretical material presented in earlier chapters to derive an integrated, transactional, biopsychosocial account of the stress process. Despite the appealing features of this approach which have been described in this chapter, the cognitive–phenomenological perspective has not been developed much beyond the seminal work of Lazarus and his colleagues. Both the cognitive appraisal theory of stress propounded by Lazarus and the script-inconsistency theory presented here adopt a transactional approach to P–E interaction and both claim to be cognitive–phenomenological theories. The script-inconsistency theory of stress is, however, of a much more tentative status than that of Lazarus but it does address some of the problems with the stress and coping paradigm by assigning its main cognitive components to conscious, as opposed to unconscious, processes. The chapter has devoted much attention to the functional significance of consciousness and has argued that, as it constitutes the primary locus of psychological intervention in the stress process, cognitive–phenomenological theories of stress should take account of the significance of conscious processing if they are to be of any practical significance.

Further reading

Cantor, N., Norem, J., Langston, C., Zirkel, S., Fleeson, W. and Cook-Flannagan, C. (1991) Life tasks and daily life experiences. *Journal of Personality*, 59(3): 425–51.

Carver, C.S. and Scheier, M.F. (1982) Control theory: a useful conceptual framework for personality – social, clinical and health psychology. *Psychological Bulletin*, 92(1): 111–35.

Giorgi, A. (ed.) (1985) *Phenomenology and Psychological Research*. Pittsburgh, PA: Duquesne University Press.

Pervin, L.A. (ed.) (1989) *Goal Concepts in Personality and Social Psychology*. Hove: Lawrence Erlbaum Associates.

Conclusions

Learning objectives for this chapter

This concluding chapter summarizes and draws together the main themes that have been presented in this volume, focusing on the current status of the stress field and outlining some of the remaining problems. As we have seen, no simple solution to those problems is likely to provide an adequate understanding of the many and varied influences on the stress process. The cognitive–phenomenological conceptualization of stress which has been described in this volume provides a useful integrative transactional definition of stress which helps overcome some of these problems and which is considered in greater detail in this chapter. The mechanisms by which stress impacts upon health are summarized and special attention is given to the role of cognitive processes in mediating between biological, psychological and social levels of analysis in a biopsychosocial formulation. The possibility of unified stress theory is considered and the chapter concludes by returning to a number of phenomenological issues which arise when stress is considered from a truly transactional perspective. After reading this chapter you should be able to:

- outline current perspectives on the stress phenomenon;
- summarize the biopsychosocial mediating pathways through which stress can exert a negative influence upon health;
- explain why the search for a unified theory of stress has been so problematic and outline the form that such a theory may take;
- describe both the practical and theoretical problems which remain in the study of stress and how it impacts upon health;
- explain how a cognitive–phenomenological perspective illuminates our understanding of the stress process and also acts as a window upon a

number of other important issues of significance in the study of human functioning; and

◆ give a cognitive–phenomenological definition of stress.

Current perspectives on the stress phenomenon

The earlier chapters of this volume identified one of the main problems in the study of stress – the conceptual and definitional confusion surrounding exactly what stress is. Many currently popular definitions are bound up in either stimulus-based or response-based events that either happen to a passive person or which the person actively creates him or herself. The fact that these issues should be so persistent is one indication that the concept of stress taps into issues of importance in human inquiry. However, it has meant that the field has been plagued by seemingly incessant argument and debate. This book has presented a number of perspectives on the stress phenomenon, each of which highlight particular aspects of stress, but none of which seem to account fully for the nature of stressful 'commerce' with the environment or explain precisely how stress can lead to ill health.

The critical historical analysis of the development of the stress concept which was presented in Chapter 2 highlighted the fact that there are a number of distinct strands of work which have shaped the face of the stress field as it stands today. These strands have each stemmed from their own particular traditions and have resulted in an extremely varied and rich discourse about the stress process. This has, however, resulted in a chaotic array of disparate findings in the literature. It has therefore been difficult to specify the precise extent to which stress can exert a negative impact on health status, although the balance of research findings suggests that it does have a negative impact. Unfortunately, the precise mechanisms, processes and pathways by which these negative health changes are induced are not yet well understood. This is due, at least partly, to a lack of sufficiently comprehensive theoretical accounts of stress: ones which adopt transactional conceptualizations of the stress process and which are located within an integrative biopsychosocial framework.

A wide array of environmental influences and person factors have been implicated in the stress process, although they explain little when taken in isolation from one another. In order to understand fully the mechanisms which link stress and health, it is necessary to adopt a process perspective and analyse the person factors and environmental influences from a transactional point of view. The most popular transactional theories of stress consist of those describing certain forms of cognitive appraisal in the mould of Lazarus and Folkman's stress and coping theory. A number of problems with the concept of cognitive appraisal have, however, been identified. These relate to its inferred status as a cognitive process, the lack of any theoretical correspondence between cognitive appraisals and the biological mechanisms implicated in the stress–health link and the precise role assigned to emotions. The concept of coping is also problematic with respect to its relation to the process of secondary appraisal, its extremely wide-ranging description of almost anything someone could do and, consequently, its inability to provide a detailed account of precisely which aspects of stress and particular ways of reacting to it are pathological.

The work of Lazarus and his associates resulted in what is possibly the most currently accepted and widely convincing account of the stress process. This is owing perhaps to its location within a transactional metatheoretical framework, its appeal to cognitive–phenomenological aspects of stress and its ability to account for individual differences and the role of subjective perceptions. The stress and coping paradigm has furthered greatly our understanding of the psychological aspects of stress, but it extends insufficiently across to other levels of analysis. The theory is also limited within the realm of psychological analysis owing to its narrow focus upon a single hypothesized intervening process, that of cognitive appraisal. Lazarus and Folkman (1984a) argue that the appraisal process is a necessary intervening psychological process. However, they have presented only indirect evidence of this, owing to their assertion that such appraisals may be unconscious. Lazarus' treatment of this issue has been severely criticized by Scherer (1995) who has pointed out that the evidence that has been presented by Lazarus in support of his assertions regarding the primacy of appraisal is limited by the methods used and the assignment of unconscious appraisal to Freudian processes. Other theoretical treatments of the stress process have also emphasized the perception of threat and the affective consequences of this in order to explain the link between cognition, emotion and arousal. However, not all of them invoke the concept of appraisal.

In line with other researchers (e.g. Meeks et al. 1986), the cognitive–phenomenological perspective developed in this volume invokes a generalized concept of cognitive evaluation which may be labelled 'appraisal', but it does not appeal to the specific appraisals of harm/loss, threat or challenge. The more general evaluations described in previous chapters occur in response to the independent existence of stressful environmental transactions, rather than stress being defined in terms of a specific type of appraisal or resulting directly from it. Furthermore, even if some sort of appraisal-type cognitive evaluation is a necessary component of the stress process, then the particular outcomes of the appraisal process which are hypothesized to lead to stress are not sufficiently described by the limited subset specified by Lazarus (i.e. by appraisals of harm/loss, threat or challenge). Other types of outcome of an appraisal-like process, indeed other types of process, are likely to be required. The cognitive appraisal theory of stress has highlighted the importance of considering the individual's interpretive framework or personal agenda. Furthermore, it has suggested that such influences may be accounted for in terms of perceptual and evaluative cognitive processes. However, it is necessary to avoid an overdependence upon the concept of appraisal as an explanatory construct if further progress is to be made. The stress process most certainly derives from, and consists of, a more complex and protracted series of cognitive mediating processes and contexts of life history.

The cognitive–phenomenological conceptualization of stress which is presented in the latter chapters of the current volume would suggest that the genesis of a stressful event may be traced much further back in the self-regulatory cycle than the time at which a particular stressful stimulus impinges upon our senses or some habitual way of responding to adversity is somehow 'activated' by our current situation. It suggests that when we take into account the phenomenological and reflexive nature of human consciousness and the goal-directed nature of human strivings, stress may be traced as far back as the cognitions that take place when people decide what sort of life they want to lead, the sort of person they want to become, the types of goals they want to work towards and exactly how they plan to achieve those goals. Stress arises, then, when a conscious and volitional, reflexively self-aware person actively engages with the environment and, in particular, when those transactions with the environment do not go quite as that person had hoped, planned or expected.

The influence of stress upon health

There is a considerable quantity of empirical support for the notion that stress can have a negative influence on physical and psychological health. However, the quality of this literature is difficult to evaluate and it is internally inconsistent. In a biopsychosocial analysis of the stress–health link, it is necessary to adopt an interdisciplinary perspective upon mediating processes and mechanisms and the influence of stress upon health must therefore be seen as dependent upon its impact on the biopsychosocial system. This system may be specified in terms of biological, psychological and social variables and processes which interact in complex ways and which, as a system, interact with the broader environment. The extent to which stress influences health depends, therefore, upon what changes in the biopsychosocial system a stressor evokes and the magnitude of those changes. The level of impact a stressor has on the system is especially dependent upon the significance of the stressor for the individual which, in turn, depends upon its subjective meaning for that individual. Extending this analysis logically backwards, the subjective meaning of an event derives from the way in which people perceive, conceptualize and interpret the event which, in turn, result from complex, dynamic and bidirectional interactions between the person and the environment. Within a transactional conceptualization of the stress process, psychological structures and processes which determine the subjective meaning of events and hence how they are phenomenologically experienced act as the primary mediators between stressors and changes in the biological mechanisms implicated in the stress process. Stressors are not, therefore, external stimuli or events which occur in the environment, but are partly the result of pretransactional cognitive activity which determines the interpretive framework with which one approaches a transaction.

The cognitive mediation of stress is explained, then, by the interpretive framework with which an individual engages with the environment. If these interpretive processes result in the transactional generation of stress, further cognitions which have been labelled 'rumination' mediate emotional and physiological changes in the person which themselves interact and result in the further activation of neural and hormonal mechanisms. These mechanisms include the sympathetic–adrenomedullary axis, the pituitary–adrenocortical axis, various other psychoendocrine pathways and psychoneuroimmunological mediation, all of which were described in Chapter 4.

The psychological mediation of the link between stress and health therefore has two main elements. The first involves the influence of psychological processes in determining the interpretive frameworks or personal agendas with which a person approaches an encounter, while the second consists of the psychological processes involved in the understanding and resolution of stressful encounters. The first of these psychological elements of the stress process requires phenomenological description, goal-directed accounts of motivation and specification of the mechanisms of self-regulation. The latter element consists of the collection of processes referred to as rumination and which include emotion-focused and instrumental coping, planning and the mental imagery which results in brainstem activation, cortical inhibition and the subjective experience of stress.

Rumination either serves to resolve a stressful transaction in which case the individual may be said to have successfully coped with the encounter, or else it results in continued physiological activation. This is cognitively mediated through the process of mental imagery where the situation is created and re-created mentally and also by the experience of associated negative affective states. These processes serve to integrate social, emotional, cognitive and biological aspects of stress because they occur, particularly in the case of social stressors, with inadequate and unrealistic information due to the heuristic processes which operate during transactions with the environment. This can lead to the generation of 'worst case' scenarios and thereby result in further apprehension, uncertainty and physiological arousal which leads to greater heuristic processing, perceptual distortions and continued cognitive, emotional and physiological sequelae.

Frankenhauser (1989) has outlined the way in which a cognitive mediational theory of stress may be integrated within a biopsychosocial framework, theorizing that when a situation is appraised as stressful, there is top–down communication between the cortex and hypothalamus in the

CNS. The hypothalamus then activates the sympathetic-adreno medullary axis and the pituitary adrenocortical response. A similar case may be made for the role of those mechanisms identified in both psychoneuroimmunology research and the neural and pscyhoendocrine mechanisms involved in brain-stem activation, involving the transmission of information from the cor-tex, via the hypothalamus and brainstem to the various biological pathways thought to mediate the stress–health link. Thus we have a conceptual basis for describing the integration of human functioning on a cognitive level, providing cortical input which mediates self and social influences in the stress process via the individual's interpretive framework, and which generates the types of biological changes which were described in Chapter 4.

Towards integrated stress theory?

The earlier chapters of this book outlined a number of firmly entrenched problems with the stress concept. Multiple perspectives and piecemeal theo-rizing have led to immense diversity in the stress field. The diversity of the field as it currently stands constitutes a threat to the very existence of stress as a unified concept. However, there is another view on current contro-versy in the area. As Montefiore (1989: 14) has written, 'no clue to the understanding of what are complex and controversial matters can be itself uncontroversial. Often, no doubt, the controversiality of a matter may be taken as one measure of its importance'. Also, as discussed in Chapter 2, Mason (1975a) argues that the persistent durability and widespread usage of the stress concept, despite almost chaotic disagreement over its definition, is indicative of its intuitive appeal and scientific usefulness.

A continued search for a unified theory of stress is therefore a worthy quest and although the tentative hypotheses of cognitive or emotional mediation have not yet been subject to rigorous empirical validation, they are none the less plausible hypotheses which may at some stage be convinc-ingly tied, either neurally or hormonally, to physiological mechanisms which in turn effect the changes in health status which have been reported in the literature. These reasons, plus the ubiquitous and increasing presence of stress in our society and the potential to reduce human suffering through theoretically informed intervention in the stress process means that the possibility of integrated stress theory is not only plausible, but highly de-sirable. As Elliot and Eisdorfer have argued, the study of stress seeks to answer questions which lie close to the heart of the human condition.

One of the most pressing problems facing workers in the stress field is, therefore, the lack of attempts at integrative theorizing across the various levels of analysis which are necessary to produce a unified biopsychosocial explanatory framework. In this connection, Lazarus *et al.* (1980: 107) write that:

The three levels of stress analysis [physiological, psychological and social] are to a degree independent and they refer to different conditions, concepts and mechanisms. If one level led automatically to another, we would not need coordinated interdisciplinary research, but could reduce stress to the lowest usable common denominator of explanation . . . however the links between these levels are largely unexplored, tenuous and complex, primarily because they have not been studied within the same research design . . . the most thorough research must be designed to access all three levels concurrently.

Other researchers agree that the links between these various levels of analysis are not yet understood and need further research (e.g. Steptoe 1991; Kaplan 1996) and popular accounts of stress which emphasize integrated functioning (e.g. Maier and Laudenslanger 1985), are generally a little overoptimistic in their evaluation of the links between cognitive and biological mechanisms involved in the stress process. The 'conceptual hiatus' that exists between psychological and biological functioning is, however, not a new problem; it is the spectre of Cartesian dualism which has plagued psychology since its inception and philosophy before then. It is in the context of a recent convergence of psychology and medicine in the field of health psychology that, in areas such as stress, this age old problem is brought into sharp focus.

The reductionism of the natural sciences has tended to result in the reduction of stress phenomena to a solely physiological level, thereby neglecting important processes at higher levels of explanation and limiting the biological parameters within which stress is studied to particular physiological axes. Selye (1983a: v) described how a colleague introduced him to electron microscopy by developing the world's first electron microscope:

One day, in his laboratory, he showed me an object that had been magnified two million times. Can you imagine? . . . two million times! Up to then, no one had ever seen molecules . . . but once I had calmed down, I said to myself: 'This great genius has spent all these years narrowing his field of vision two million times!' . . . The more we narrow our field, the less we will see of . . . things on the periphery.

This anecdote is to be found in the preface to his book on stress research, the purpose of which was specifically to facilitate coordination and cooperation among specialists and encourage interdisciplinary research. It is precisely this sort of interdisciplinary collaboration which is required in the development of unified stress theory. This is prevented by the lack of comprehensive theorizing which addresses all of the levels required in a biopsychosocial analysis. Kellam (1979: 207) characterized the quality of interdisciplinary research in the field of stress by referring to the distinction made by Isiah Berlin in his essay on Tolstoy's view of history:

Isiah Berlin [in 1953] once made the distinction between people called hedgehogs – who are temperamentally disposed to look for connections between things, and are content only with a unified theory explaining reality – and people called foxes – who are content to examine in detail individual aspects of life and have no need to search for the interrelationships among such aspects. Investigators in the broad domain called mental health can be spread along a dimension extending from those concerned with rich (some would say florid) theoretical frameworks tying everything into a comprehensive theory to those who prefer to remain strict empiricists, cautiously using only minimal theoretical development in an effort to avoid drawing inferences prematurely and erroneously. The latter might be said to be a somewhat exaggerated characterisation of many investigators in the field of stressful life events and illness.

Kellam contrasted himself with many other stress researchers in that he thought of himself as more of a hedgehog than a fox and he also went on to subdivide hedgehogs and foxes into Alices and Mables. Alices were those hedgehogs and foxes who needed to do something about the world, however they saw it, and Mables were those who were content to merely observe the world but do nothing about it. Kellam thought of himself as an 'Alice tending toward hedghoginess' and one reason that the age-old controversies described towards the earlier sections of this book are so persistent is that there are, perhaps, not enough hedgehogs called Alice working in the field of stress!

The stress field is in need of conceptual development which makes it necessary to examine previous work in all its breadth in order to survey the ground that has already been covered. Only by doing this can one identify areas of ground that remain uncovered and tease out links between the various patches of ground which have previously been identified as important. Research into stress and coping is particularly broad-ranging, but there are relatively few attempts at linking what sometimes appear to be disparate sets of theoretical ideas. Such an enterprise is essential if real progress is to be made in the development of stress theory. As Staats (1991) has noted, there are many common concepts and principles in psychology which, because they are described in different languages and are parts of different theories, are not seen as being related. This magnifies psychology's diversity immensely and, in order to create a unified science, it is necessary to recognize this commonality through thickets of superficial difference.

The current volume, by adopting a transactional approach to the stress phenomenon, locating it within a biopsychosocial framework and developing the notion of cognitive mediation from a socio-cognitive and phenomenological perspective, offers a tentative approach towards formulating an integrated theory of stress. The cognitive–phenomenological perspective recognizes that the reductionistic practices of the natural sciences which are particularly well suited to the study of that which is mechanistic and objective are perhaps less well suited to the human sciences. The fundamental nature of people is not mechanistic and objective, but creative and subjective, living in an embedded context of meaning which depends on the intentional relationship of people with their environment. The cognitive–phenomenological perspective is couched in the terms of socio-cognitive theory. Clark (1989) argues that this is an attractive property of theorizing about stress because the focus of stress and coping research on environmental demands, motivation, goal-directed behaviour and the self is served well, in terms of both methodological techniques and theoretical constructs, by a socio-cognitive perspective. To the extent that the socio-cognitive approach may be called cognitive, so may the cognitive–phenomenological perspective presented in Chapter 6, while the phenomenological aspects of it stem from the way in which it is grounded in the biographical context of the individual which constitutes the residue of the everyday lived experience of that person.

The nature of a unified theory of stress necessarily cuts across different levels of analysis ranging from the physiological, through the cognitive and experiential, to the social level of analysis and explanation. Such a broad range of coverage is symptomatic of the numerous approaches that have been adopted in the investigation of stress. The hierarchical infrastructures of systems theory, the biopsychosocial approach and the self-regulatory mechanisms of goal-directed behaviour which have been adopted in the cognitive–phenomenological framework presented here facilitate the sort of broadly integrative theorizing which is needed in the field. Such theorizing permits the development of a common framework that serves to bridge the philosophical gap between different theoretical perspectives and different levels of analysis and provides a common language with which researchers from various relevant disciplines can communicate.

Remaining problems

The nascent field of psychoneuroimmunology goes some way towards the development of the types of conceptual systems based on interdisciplinary empirical findings which are necessary in the search for an integrated and unified theory of stress. Such a theory would explain how cognitively mediated psychosocial stimuli are centrally integrated and activate a system of physiological changes leading to a negative change in health status. The development of such an interdisciplinary conceptual framework in the field of stress requires that the current inundation of empirical research literature be supplemented by conceptual and theoretical development. Selye (1983a) argued that there is an unwarranted overemphasis upon fact-finding, accompanied by what often amounts to an actual disdain for theories in the field of stress and MacKay (1988) suggested that this is applicable in areas of psychology outside the stress field as well. In relation to the abundance of empirical articles and relative scarcity of those of a more theoretical nature, he wrote that many of the research literatures have been primarily gathering facts, and largely for the sake of fact gathering, adding that 'even the best psychologists sometimes seem to assume . . . that experiments can proceed in the absence of theory . . .' (ibid.: 562). The article was a response to Greenwald *et al.* (1986) who suggested that theory obstructs research because of the ego involvement of the researcher in the research enterprise and the resulting confirmation bias to which she or he is subject. This article initiated a lively and instructive debate which appeared later on the pages of the *Psychological Bulletin* (Moser *et al.* 1988; Greenwald and Pratkanis 1988; Greenberg *et al.* 1988; MacKay 1988).

Greenwald *et al.* (1986) suggested that the prevailing paradigm of theory-centred research often results in a disconfirmation dilemma whereby a theory tester 'explains away' disconfirming results in terms of faulty data analysis or data collection procedures or else simply tests another part of the theory, as opposed to publishing the disconfirmatory results as evidence against the theory and suggesting its abandonment. This, claim Greenwald *et al.* results in 'avoidable overgeneralisations' which use the existing theory to explain the newly modified data. When faced with the disconfirmation dilemma, they argue, researchers tend to exhibit confirmatory biases which lead them to believe that the theory is true and there must therefore be something wrong with the procedures used to test the theory.

Owing to the poor state of theorizing in the stress field, the suggestion that theory impedes research progress does not apply. Indeed Moser *et al.* (1988) argued that, generally, the opposite may apply. They refuted the suggestion of Greenwald *et al.* (1986) that researchers are subject to a confirmatory bias, arguing from a Popperian critical rationalist perspective that the procedures associated with the hypothetico-deductive experimental research paradigm used in psychology prevent this effect. In contradistinction to the view of Greenwald *et al.* (1986), Greenberg *et al.* (1988: 570) outlined the conditions under which the reverse of their thesis is true:

Under what conditions does research obstruct theory progress? It does so when

(a) researchers are more interested in their own careers than with assessing theoretical ideas,

(b) research is directed toward producing results rather than advancing understanding through theory testing,

(c) theories are assessed by research findings in a *post hoc* rather than an *a priori* fashion,

(d) existing research is the primary determinant of what are considered to be the important questions for a field,

(e) laboratory research is treated as the sole or primary basis for theory generation, and

(f) currently available research methods and technologies dictate the form and content of new theories.

In the light of Selye's (1983a) incisive observations, this list of conditions certainly seems characteristic of research in the area of stress. Montefiore and Noble (1989) have argued that because the sorts of observations that are made during experimentation and theory testing are bound up in the very theoretical perspective that spawned the experiment, the 'reality' of what we are trying to identify, to understand and to explain is often of secondary importance. They wrote (ibid.: 8) that it may also follow that 'philosophers, as they work primarily on their analyses of concepts, and scientists, as they work primarily on their investigations of "reality", have more regular and thoroughgoing need of each other's participation than present institutional habits and arrangements can easily provide for'. One of the primary remaining problems in the field of stress concerns the lack of attempts at integrated theorizing due to both an overemphasis upon hypothetico-deductive theory testing and the lack of interdisciplinary collaboration.

A second, but related, problem which follows on from this is the lack of suitably sophisticated methodologies to study transactional processes. The compromise that has been used by Lazarus and his colleagues consists of the dissection of the transactional process into an interactional framework as described in Chapter 3 and the adoption of what Lazarus refers to as the ipsative–normative research strategy (Lazarus 1981; Lazarus and Folkman 1984a; Lazarus 1990b). The ipsative–normative strategy consists of an examining process using a within-subject, intraindividual or idiographic approach by observing the same person over and over again in different situations (ipsative), while at the same time determining the generality of cognitive processes by using between-subject, interindividual or nomothetic approaches by making comparisons across subjects (normative). This method involves partitioning variance in outcome variables such as health status into person and environment antecedent variables. However, these statistical interactions are interpreted as if they represent direct observation of actual transactional processes. This fallacious interpretation, they argue, is the primary cause of confusion within the stress field.

Further methodological problems arise in the use of various 'stress scales' to measure the amount of stress that an individual has experienced over a given period. As well as being criticized for confounding predictor with outcome (e.g. Holm and Holroyd 1992), the association of high scores on stress scales with high-trait anxiety (e.g. Russell and Davey 1993) has led to criticism of such scales on the grounds of a global contamination due to the effects of neuroticism (e.g. Pearlstone *et al.* 1994). Others, however, have reported data which refute the neuroticism hypothesis (e.g. DeLongis 1985; Johal 1995) and Lazarus has argued that, even if such effects do exist, they may represent the manifestation of a complex system of variables that are inherently fused in nature and that to abandon the approach purely on the grounds of this confound would be tantamount to 'distorting nature to fit a simpler, mythical metatheory of separable antecedent and consequent variables' (Lazarus 1990a: 10). The cognitive–phenomenological perspective on stress which has been outlined in the current volume would suggest that it is not really possible to operationalize the complex transactional phenomenon of stress in the form of a simple checklist.

To accept this argument is to acknowledge the inherent complexity of the stress process and the difficulty of performing transactional research. Facing up to such difficulties does not, however, preclude the sorts of research designs and methods that attempt to account for them. The crux of the matter lies in the operationalization of the theoretical concepts employed to provide an indication of the presence of stress and, in relation to the use of the hassles scale in stress research, Lazarus (1990a: 11) writes that

> it should be obvious that even a heavily revised hassles scale, which would reflect individual vulnerability and the psychodynamics of the stress process better than the present scales, must fall short of the mark if we do not also measure the many variables contributing to the stress process.

Although other, less popular, scales have been developed to measure similar minor life events including the Perceived Stress Scale (e.g. Pbert *et al.* 1992), the Derogatis Stress Profile (e.g. Dobkin *et al.* 1991), the Daily Stress Inventory (Brantley *et al.* 1987), the Inventory of College Students Recent Life Experience (e.g. Kohn and Gurevich 1993; Osman *et al.* 1994) and the Survey of Recent Life Experiences (e.g. Kohn and MacDonald 1992b), such scales are far less popular than the widely used hassles scale and none succeed in faithfully capturing and operationalizing the transactional approach described by Lazarus and his colleagues.

Many of the remaining problems in the stress field exist as a result of the reluctance to embrace a fully transactional conception of the stress process, the impracticality of conducting interdisciplinary research and a simple lack of awareness of many of the problems which have been described throughout the course of this book. The cognitive–phenomenological perspective presented in the latter chapters of the current work is based upon a transactional metatheoretical framework and has thereby overcome some of these problems. However, this perspective is a relatively new one. Previous attempts at cognitive–phenomenological theorizing, such as that of Lazarus and his colleagues, have been met with a near-complete disregard of the phenomenological components and an immediate seizing upon, and rather poor operationalization of, the cognitive element of appraisal. The phenomenological elements of the perspective outlined in Chapter 6 are therefore re-emphasized here as an essential component of a cognitive–phenomenological conceptualization of stress which cannot be ignored if we are to capture the true nature of the stress process.

Stress and the human condition

In considering the motivational aspects of stress in Chapter 6, the relationship between the individual goals towards which a person works and the more general human strivings, which we share in common and which are reflected in our cultures, was described in terms of a hierarchy of individual contextually-embedded instantiations of more general abstract goals. Such a description begs the question of what constitutes the uppermost goal in the hierarchy, or the end-point of human striving. Of course, this question concerns the very essence of reflexive human awareness – the meaning of life itself – and it is one which has occupied generations of philosophers for many centuries. This penultimate section considers how a cognitive–phenomenological perspective on stress contributes to these philosophical concerns and, in so doing, it illuminates an understanding of a recently emerging lay concept, the Western ideal of a 'happy, stress-free existence'.

If a theory of stress is to be useful in this regard, it must capture the currently pressing issues of our time and in this respect the cognitive–phenomenological perspective, with its focus upon the personal strivings which people aim to achieve, is attuned to the social, political and economic forces which have, over the past few decades, supported the Western ideals and values of free will and individualism, but it also recognizes the limitations of this movement. A generation of Thatcherism in the UK and the persistence of the American Dream on the other side of the Atlantic have encouraged people to strive towards and fully actualize their potentialities, achieve a higher standard of living and a fulfilled and satisfied life. At their most extreme, such accounts may even suggest that people are limited only by their aspirations. Such a viewpoint is hopeful and optimistic about the future. However, recent experiences and social currents on both sides of the Atlantic have shown that such individualistic aspirations can also have their downside in a capitalistic society. An article by Kasser and Ryan (1993) entitled 'A Dark Side of the American Dream: Correlates of Financial Success as a Central Life Aspiration' provided evidence that materialistic world views can have deleterious effects on adjustment and well-being. The recent phenomenon of 'down-shifting' (which describes the decision taken by well-paid but overworked professionals to change their career down a gear in order to restore a balance in their life between work and leisure) also reflects this, as does a move towards socially inclusive government in the UK. The phenomenological approaches, such as that of Maslow and Rogers, advocate the motivational importance of self-actualization, but at the same time, engender a non-individualistic philosophy.

The conservation of resources perspective on stress (Hobfall 1988, 1989) emphasizes the primary motivator of the protection and enhancement of self, arguing that people are motivated to seek firstly physical resources, then social resources and finally psychological resources in a hierarchical manner similar to that proposed by Maslow. The main human striving, according to the model, is that of actively seeking to create a world that will provide pleasure and success. Hobfall argues that stress arises as a result of the actual or threatened net loss of resources or the lack of resource gain following the investment of resources. The model would seem to suggest that a primary motivator in a capitalist society is the striving for financial success. This would appear to go against recent social and political trends which have de-emphasized financial success in favour of personal happiness and fulfilment and have seen a shift away from excessive individualism and towards social inclusion.

The principle of self-actualization is, despite its name, not one of inherent selfishness. Phenomenological theorists recognize that there are differences in both the potentialities of individuals and the opportunity of individuals to achieve their own potential. The notion that we are not all born equal goes against the individualistic ideals of capitalism and entrepreneurship that underlie both Thatcherism and the American Dream and such ideals cannot, according to the more humanistic perspective on life, be the basis from which a path to enduring human happiness could be constructed. In fact, Maslow (1970: xv) states that

> the human hope for eternal happiness can never be fulfilled . . . happiness does come and is obtainable . . . but we must accept its intrinsic transience . . . peak experiences do not last and cannot last. Intense happiness is episodic, not continuous.

Ford (1992) accepts similar arguments that enduring happiness is the result of change, but suggests that it is permanently achievable under certain conditions, and that it is often undermined by social demands, pressures and expectations that promote negative context beliefs. Similarly, Maslow writes (1970: xiv) that the downlevelling of the motivations of others is the result of the tendency of people to attribute purely materialistic motivations to the behaviour of individuals, rather than social or metamotivational ones: 'It is a form of paranoid-like suspicion, a form of devaluation of human nature'.

Ford argues that this way of being and its resultant cynicism is avoidable by the mental conversion of problems and constraints into opportunities and challenges and the adoption of an everyday 'motivational lifestyle' characterized by a proactive, dynamic repertoire of behavioural episode schemata, a rich mix of short- and long-term goals (what might be labelled goal complexity) and a philosophy of flexible optimism (constituting a particular world view). The cognitive–phenomenological perspective described here provides a theoretical framework in which issues such as these can be studied and it therefore appears to offer the possibility of psychotherapeutic intervention aimed, not only at reducing the deleterious effects of stress, but also at promoting well-being more generally.

Enduring happiness is, according to Maslow (1970: 163), dependent upon change and in his description of the self-actualizing person he writes that:

Self-actualising people have the wonderful capacity to appreciate again and again, freshly and naively, the basic goods of life, with awe, pleasure, wonder and even ecstasy, however stale these experiences may have become to others . . . For such people, even the casual workaday, moment-to-moment business of living can be thrilling, exciting and ecstatic . . . they derive ecstasy, inspiration, and strength from the basic experiences of life. No one of them, for instance, will get this same sort of reaction from going to a nightclub or getting a lot of money or having a good time at a party.

Maslow's (1970) description of the self-actualizing person is that of an almost god-like individual as the title of a recent article by Landsman and Landsman (1991) suggests: 'The Beautiful and Noble Person'. Maslow also states, however, that there is no such thing as the perfect human being and even those individuals who are fully actualized suffer occasionally from internal strife and conflict and can be 'boring, irritating, petulant, selfish, angry or depressed' (ibid.: 176). He continues that, 'to avoid disillusionment with human nature, we must first give up our illusions of it' (ibid.: 176).

In most goal-directed theories of human functioning, happiness is said to derive from the successful attainment of valued goals, but this is contrary to both folk wisdom and the formulation offered by Maslow. As Feather (1982d: 413) points out,

there could be a discrepancy between the reality of goal attainment and the perceived attractiveness or aversiveness of the goal as perceived from a distance. The sweet that looks attractive to the child may turn out to have an unpleasant flavour.

Thus, one aspect of the perceived unattainability of happiness relates to the goal-directed, future orientation that the cognitive–phenomenological perspective encompasses: how do you know what you really want unless you already have it? A possible solution to this remaining problem may be found in social learning theory in that one could aim to learn vicariously and develop an empathic appreciation by investigating role models which resemble the ideal towards which one aspires.

Even if someone is sure of her or his most abstract goals, if the logical end state of an individual's goal hierarchy does not provide enduring happiness, which is what Maslow appears to be suggesting, then one is led to question the prudence of investing time and effort in striving to achieve self-actualization. Surely one would be better off adopting a hedonistic philosophy and such a view has been put forward by some who are sympathetic to Maslow's theoretical ideas. Ellis (1991: 5), for example, points out that the ultimate end point of self-actualization is the peak experience, or altered state of consciousness that resembles the Zen state of egolessness, no-mind or desirelessness and that, 'even if that state helped them to give up depressed, panicked and damning feelings, they would then throw away the baby with the bath water, probably achieve little or no pleasure and therefore be dubiously self-actualised'. In any case, if an individual were to achieve such a state which is viewed by Maslow as one of ultimate psychological health, they would, paradoxically and in all likelihood, be perceived by others within our society as suffering from some form of psychotic disorder, the precise opposite of psychological health. Ellis suggests that self-actualization is a worthy goal, but proposes, from a rational–emotive therapeutic perspective, that the mode in which it should be striven for is one of hedonism, albeit long-range hedonism, and that the life task of self-actualization will never be completed. The alternative strategy of short-range hedonism is also unlikely to lead to enduring happiness because of its lack of long-term viability; in order to have a good time, one needs the means to sustain oneself and these can be gained only by forfeiting the time that one would rather be spending having fun.

The solution to the problem of enduring human happiness is unlikely to be found, at least not within the pages of this book, however the consideration of the most abstract, and therefore the most universal, human goals certainly provides a more thorough cognitive–phenomenological treatment of the stress concept than is often the case. In Chapter 1, it was suggested that the study of stress is likely to concern issues which lie close to the heart of the human condition and the issues that have been raised in this concluding chapter are surely remaining problems for a unified cognitive–phenomenological theory of stress, just as they remain problems for humanity.

Conclusion

As this concluding chapter has outlined, the stress concept currently faces a number of fundamental problems which must be addressed by the field of health psychology if progress is to be made in developing our understanding of stress and devising effective interventions in the stress process. In the search for solutions to these problems, health psychologists are faced with two options. The first of these is to clarify and make explicit the diverse and often implicit definitions of stress used by various researchers and practitioners working within the field. This would lead to a fracturation of the stress area into many different branches according to the particular definition being used and corresponding aspect of stress being investigated by each worker. This would, in turn, necessitate the abandonment of efforts to integrate what would be seen as essentially different phenomena and a rejection of the concept of stress as it is currently understood. The interpretation and application of research findings based upon one conception of stress which utilized, for example, a stimulus-based definition of stress would be incompatible with those from studies based on a different conception of stress which used, for example, a response-based definition.

The second option would be to retain the hypothesis of a unified explanatory concept labelled 'stress', but this concept would remain of hypothetical status until an integrated theory of stress was developed and empirically confirmed. This would necessitate either a drastic refocusing, or possibly even a suspension, of the enormous amount of empirical work which is currently being conducted, in favour of the conceptual and theoretical development of such a model of stress which would, in turn, yield a new paradigm within which to conduct empirical and applied work.

The title of this book, *Stress: Perspectives and Processes*, highlights two of the main features of the stress phenomenon that must be recognized and addressed if we are to progress our understanding beyond current levels. The first of these is that there are currently multiple theoretical perspectives on stress, some of which provide more adequate description and explanation than others. The second is that, whichever theoretical perspective is taken, stress must be considered as a process – not as a static feature of the environment, nor as a stable personality disposition, but as a transactional phenomenon which arises through certain types of person–environment (P–E) dynamics.

The cognitive–phenomenological perspective, with its focus upon goal-directed behaviour, the self-involvement of human life and the conscious quality of human striving, offers a new conceptualization of stress. A person's life consists of the totality of their transactions with the environment and stress consists of 'those transactions with the environment which have not gone quite as that person wanted, planned and expected'. By thinking about stress in this way, we move far beyond the stimulus or response-based definitional arguments and embrace a truly transactional conceptualization of stress. When incorporated into the theoretical framework that constitutes the cognitive–phenomenological perspective presented here, such a conceptualization takes account of the ongoing processual nature of P–E interaction. This approach therefore manages to isolate a genuinely transactional conception of stress in that it is nothing about the environmental event on its own, or about the person in isolation from the environmental context, that makes an event stressful; it is where the two meet and result in some type of mismatch or inconsistency during P–E interactions that the real locus of stress is to be found.

Many researchers agree with the fundamental principles of transactional accounts of stress phenomena. Some have elaborated further, for example Lepore *et al.* (1991) who articulated the conception of stress as a hierarchy of stressors, those at different levels each exerting a differential impact upon health. However, suggestions as to the biopsychosocial mechanisms by which such a wide array of stimuli may exhibit these effects have been lacking. The work presented in this volume provides an account of the cognitive mediation of stress which is located within a biopsychosocial framework, explaining how events that may be labelled as 'stressors', but which do not in themselves constitute stress, may exert their effects. The cognitive–phenomenological perspective on stress is offered as a potential account of the stress process, one which suggests particular ways of formulating research problems and which implies certain approaches to the collection and analysis of data and to clinical intervention. Of course, further work is needed in this area, work which seeks to address some of the remaining problems that have been outlined in this concluding chapter. It is hoped, however, that this book will go at least some way towards bringing about some of the changes that are required to progress towards a deeper understanding of the stress process and, more importantly, the potential benefits that such an understanding could bring.

Further reading

Karoly, P. (1993) Mechanisms of self-regulation. *Annual Review of Psychology*, 44: 23–52.
Klinger, E. (1977) *Meaning and Void: Inner Experience and the Incentives in People's Lives*. Minneapolis, MI: University of Minnesota Press.

References

Abramson, L.Y., Seligman, M.E.P. and Teasdale, J.D. (1978) Learned helplessness in humans: critique and reformulation. *Journal of Abnormal Psychology*, 87: 49–74.

Ader, R. (1980) Psychosomatic and psychoimmunological research. Presidential Address. *Psychosomatic Medicine*, 42: 307–21.

Ader, R. (ed.) (1981) *Psychoneuroimmunology*. London: Academic Press.

Allen, R.E. (1985) *The Oxford Dictionary of Current English*. Oxford: Oxford University Press.

Alvaro, E.M. and Burgoon, M. (1995) Individual differences in responses to social influence attempts: theory and research on the effects of misanthropy. *Communication Research*, 22(3): 347–84.

Antonovsky, A. (1979) *Health, Stress and Coping*. San Francisco: Jossey-Bass.

Antonovsky, A. (1991) The structural sources of salutinogenic strengths. In C.L. Cooper and R. Payne *Personality and Stress: Individual Differences in the Stress Process*. Chichester: John Wiley.

Appley, R. and Trumbull, M.H. (1967) *Psychological Stress: Issues in Research*. New York: Appleton-Century-Crofts.

Apter, M.J. (1981) An introduction to reversal theory. In M.J. Apter and C. Rushton *Reversal Theory and Personality*. Wiltshire: South-West Inter-Clinic Conference.

Bandura, A. (1977) Self-efficacy: toward a unifying theory of behavioral change. *Psychological Review*, 84: 191–215.

Bandura, A. (1986) *Social Foundations of Thought and Action: A Social Cognitive Theory*. Englewood Cliffs, NJ: Prentice-Hall.

Bandura, A. (1988) Reflections on non-ability determinants of competence. In *Competence Considered: Perceptions of Competence and Incompetence across the Life-Span*. New Haven, CT: Yale University Press.

Bandura, A. (1989) Self-regulation of motivation and action through internal standards and goal systems. In L.A. Pervin *Goal Concepts in Personality and Social Psychology*. Hove: Lawrence Erlbaum Associates.

Bargh, J.A. (1994) The four horsemen of automaticity: awareness, intention, efficiency and control in social cognition. In R.S. Wyer and T.K. Srull *Handbook of Social Cognition. Volume 1: Basic Processes*. Hove: Lawrence Erlbaum Associates.

Barnett, R.C. and Brennan, R.T. (1995) The relationship between job experiences and psychological distress – a structural equation approach. *Journal of Organizational Behavior*, 16(3): 259–76.

Bartlett, D.T. (1996) The development of a new theory of microstress. Doctoral thesis, Department of Psychology, University of Southampton.

Billings, A.G. and Moos, R.H. (1984) Coping, stress and social resources among adults with unipolar depression. *Journal of Personality and Social Psychology*, 46(4): 877–91.

Bishop, G.D. (1993) The sense of coherence as a resource in dealing with stress. *Psychologia*, 36: 259–63.

Brantley, P.J., Waggoner, C.D., Jones, G.N. and Rappaport, N.B. (1987) A daily stress inventory: development, reliability and validity. *Journal of Behavioral Medicine*, 10(1): 61–74.

Braun, L.M. (1989) Predicting adaptational outcomes from hassles and other measures. *Journal of Social Behavior and Personality*, 4(4): 363–76.

Briner, R. (1994) Stress: The Creation of a Modern Myth. Paper presented at the Annual Conference of the British Psychological Society, Brighton, March 1994.

Brosschot, J.F., Benschop, R.J., Godaert, G.L.R., Olff, M., DeSmet, M., Heijnen, C.J. and Ballieux, R.E. (1994) Influence of life stress on immunological reactivity to mild psychological stress. *Psychosomatic Medicine*, 56: 216–24.

Brown, B.B. (1980) Perspectives on social stress. In H. Selye (ed.) *Selye's Guide To Stress Research, Volume 1*. New York City, NY: Van Nostrand Reinhold.

Brown, G.W. and Harris, T.O. (1989) *Life Events and Illness*. London: Unwin Hyman.

Brunstein, J.C. (1993) Personal goals and subjective well-being: a longitudinal study. *Journal of Personality and Social Psychology*, 65(5): 1061–70.

Buell, J.C. and Eliot, R.S. (1979) Stress and cardiovascular disease. *Modern Concepts of Cardiovascular Disease*, 48(4): 19–24.

Burchfield, S.R. (1979) The stress response: a new perspective. *Psychosomatic Medicine*, 41: 661–72.

Burchfield, S.R. (1985) *Stress: Psychological and Physiological Interactions*. London: Hemisphere.

Burger, J.M. (1992) Desire for control and academic performance. *Canadian Journal of Behavioural Science*, 24(2): 143–6.

Callan, V.J. (1993) Individual and organizational strategies for coping with organizational change. *Work and Stress*, 7(1): 63–75.

Cantor, N. and Langston, C.A. (1989) Ups and downs of life tasks in a life transition. In L.A. Pervin (ed.) *Goal Concepts in Personality and Social Psychology*. Hove: Lawrence Erlbaum Associates.

Cantor, N., Norem, J., Langston, C., Zirkel, S. Fleeson, W. and Cook-Flannagan, C. (1991) Life tasks and daily life experiences. *Journal of Personality*, 59(3): 425–51.

Caplan, R.D. (1983) Person-environment fit: past, present and future. In C.L. Cooper (ed.) *Stress Research: Issues for the Eighties*. Chichester: John Wiley.

Carver, C.S. and Scheier, M.F. (1981) *Attention and Self-Regulation: A Control Theory Approach to Human Behaviour*. New York: Springer-Verlag.

Carver, C.S. and Scheier, M.F. (1982) Control theory: a useful conceptual framework for personality–social, clinical and health psychology. *Psychological Bulletin*, 92(1): 111–35.

Carver, C.S. and Scheier, M.F. (1990a) Principles of self-regulation: action and emotion. In E.T. Higgins and R.M. Sorentino *Handbook of Motivation and Cognition*. London: The Guilford Press.

Carver, C.S. and Scheier, M.F. (1990b) Origins and functions of positive and negative affect: a control process view. *Psychological Review*, 97(1): 19–35.

Carver, C.S., Scheier, M.F. and Weintraub, J. (1989) Assessing coping strategies: a theoretically-based approach. *Journal of Personality and Social Psychology*, 56: 267–83.

Chamberlain, K. and Zika, S. (1990) The minor events approach to stress: support for the use of daily hassles. *British Journal of Psychology*, 81: 469–81.

Chwalisz, K., Altmaier, E.M. and Russell, D.W. (1992) Causal attributions, self-efficacy and coping with stress. *Journal of Social and Clinical Psychology*, 11(4): 377–400.

Cinelli, L.A. and Ziegler, D.J. (1990) Cognitive appraisal of daily hassles in college students showing type A or type B behavior patterns. *Psychological Reports*, 67: 83–8.

Clark, L.F. (1989) Approaching stress and coping from a social cognition perspective: a two-way street. *Social Cognition*, 7(2): 79–91.

Cohen, E. and Lazarus, R.S. (1983) Coping and adaptation in health and illness. In D. Mechanic (ed.) *Handbook of Health, Health Care and the Health Professions*. New York: The Free Press.

Cohen, S. and Edwards, J.R. (1989) Personality characteristics as moderators of the relationship between stress and disorder. In R.W.J. Neufeld (ed.) *Advances in the Investigation of Psychological Stress*. Chichester: Wiley Interscience.

Cohen, M.Z. and Omery, A. (1994) Schools of phenomenology: implications for research. In J.M. Morse (ed.) *Critical Issues in Qualitative Research Methods*. London: Sage.

Contrada, R.J. (1989) Type A behaviour. Personality hardiness and cardiovascular responses to stress. *Journal of Personality and Social Psychology*, 57(5): 895–903.

Cooper, C.L. and Payne, R. (eds) (1991) *Personality and Stress: Individual Differences in the Stress Process* (Wiley Series on Occupational Stress). Chichester: John Wiley.

Costa, P.T. and McCrae, R.R. (1980) Influence of extraversion and neuroticism on subjective well-being: happy and unhappy people. *Journal of Personality and Social Psychology*, 38(4): 668–78.

Cox, T. (1978) *Stress*. London: Macmillan.

Cox, T. and Ferguson, E. (1991) Individual differences in stress and coping. In C.L. Cooper and R. Payne *Personality and Stress: Individual Differences in the Stress Process*. Chichester: John Wiley.

Coyne, J.C. and Lazarus, R.S. (1980) Cognitive style, stress perception and coping. In I.L. Kutash, L.B. Schlesinger and associates. *Handbook on Stress and Anxiety*. London: Jossey-Bass.

Crandall, J.E. and Lehman, R.E. (1977) Relationship of stressful life events to social interest and locus of control. *Journal of Consulting and Clinical Psychology*, 45(6): 1208.

Croyle, R.T. (1992) Appraisal of health threats: cognition, motivation and social comparison. *Cognitive Therapy and Research*, 16(2): 165–82.

Davey, G.C.L., Tallis, F. and Hodgson, S. (1993) The relationship between information-seeking and information-avoiding coping styles and the reporting of psychological symptoms. *Journal of Psychometric Research*, 37(4): 333–44.

De Benedittis, G. and Lorenzetti, A. (1992) The role of stressful life events in the persistence of primary headache: major events vs. daily hassles. *Pain*, 51: 35–42.

DeLongis, A.M. (1985) The Relationship of Everyday Stress to Health and Well-Being: Inter- and Intraindividual Approaches. Unpublished Doctoral Dissertation. University of California in Berkeley.

DeLongis, A., Coyne, J.C., Dakof, G., Folkman, S. and Lazarus, R.S. (1982) Relationship of daily hassles, uplifts and major life events to health status. *Health Psychology*, 1(2): 119–36.

Deutsch, F. (1986) Calling a freeze on stress wars: there is hope for adaptational outcomes. *American Psychologist*, 41(6): 713–14.

Dixon, T.M. and Baumeister, R.F. (1991) Escaping the self: the moderating effect of self-complexity. *Personality and Social Psychology Bulletin*, 17(4): 363–8.

Dobkin, PL., Pihl, R.O. and Breault, C. (1991) Validation of the Derogatis Stress Profile using laboratory and real world data. *Psychotherapy and Psychosomatics*, 56: 185–96.

Dohrenwend, B.P. and Shrout, P.E. (1985) 'Hassles' in the conceptualisation and measurement of life stress variables. *American Psychologist*, 40: 780–85.

Dohrenwend, B.P. and Shrout, P.E. (1986) Reply to Green and Deutsch. *American Psychologist*, 41: 716.

Dohrenwend, B.S. and Dohrenwend, B.P. (1979) *Stressful Life Events: Their Nature and Effects*. London: John Wiley.

Dohrenwend, B.S., Dohrenwend, B.P., Dodson, M. and Shrout, P.E. (1984) Symptoms, hassles, social supports and life events: problem of confounded measures. *Journal of Abnormal Psychology*, 93(2): 222–30.

Earnshaw, J. and Cooper, C. (1994) Employee stress litigation – the UK experience. *Work and Stress*, 8(4): 287–95.

Edwards, J.R. (1991) The measurement of type A behaviour pattern: an assessment of criterion-oriented validity, content validity and construct validity. In C.L. Cooper and R. Payne *Personality and Stress: Individual Differences in the Stress Process*. Chichester: John Wiley.

Eisdorfer, C. (1981) Critique of the stress and coping paradigm. In C. Eisdorfer, D. Cohen, A. Kleinman and P. Maxim *Models for Clinical Psychopathology*. Lancaster: MTP Press.

Eiser, J.R. (1986) *Social Psychology: Attitudes, Cognition and Social Behaviour*. Cambridge: Cambridge University Press.

Elliot, G.R. and Eisdorfer, C. (eds) (1982) *Stress and Human Health: Analysis and Implications of Research*. A Study by the Institute of Medicine/National Academy of Sciences. New York: Springer.

Ellis, A. (1991) Achieving self-actualization: the rational–emotive approach. In Handbook of Self-Actualization. Special edition of the *Journal of Social Behavior and Personality*, 6(5): 1–18.

Emmons, R.A. (1986) Personal strivings: an approach to personality and subjective well-being. *Journal of Personality and Social Psychology*, 51(5): 1058–68.

Emmons, R.A. (1989) The personal striving approach to personality. In L.A. Pervin (ed.) *Goal Concepts in Personality and Social Psychology*. Hove: Lawrence Erlbaum Associates.

Emmons, R.A. (1991) Personal strivings, daily life events, and psychological and physical well-being. *Journal of Personality*, 59(3): 453–72.

Emmons, R.A. and McAdams, D.P. (1991) Personal strivings and motive dispositions: exploring the links. *Personality and Social Psychology Bulletin*, 17(6): 648–54.

Engel, G.L. (1977) The need for a new medical model: a challenge for biomedicine. *Science*, 196: 129–36.

Epstein, S. (1973) The self-concept revisited: or a theory of a theory. *American Psychologist*, 28: 404–16.

Feather, T. (ed.) (1982a) *Expectations and Actions: Expectancy–Value Models in Psychology*. Hillsdale, NJ: Lawrence Erlbaum Associates.

Feather, T. (1982b) Actions in relation to expected consequences: an overview of a research program. In T. Feather (ed.) *Expectations and Actions: Expectancy–Value Models in Psychology*. Hillsdale, NJ: Lawrence Erlbaum Associates.

Feather, T. (1982c) Expectancy–value approaches: present status and future directions. In T. Feather (ed.) *Expectations and Actions: Expectancy–Value Models in Psychology*. Hillsdale, NJ: Lawrence Erlbaum Associates.

Feather, T. (1982d) Human values and the prediction of action: an expectancy-valence analysis. In T. Feather (ed.) *Expectations and Actions: Expectancy–Value Models in Psychology*. Hillsdale, NJ: Lawrence Erlbaum Associates.

Fischhoff, B., Goitein, B. and Shapira, Z. (1982) The experienced utility of expected utility approaches. In T. Feather (ed.) *Expectations and Actions: Expectancy–Value Models in Psychology*. Hillsdale, NJ: Lawrence Erlbaum Associates.

Fisher, S. (1986) *Stress and Strategy*. London: Lawrence Erlbaum.

Flannery, R.B. and Flannery, G.F. (1990) Sense of coherence, life stress and psychological distress: a prospective methodological enquiry. *Journal of Clinical Psychology*, 46(4): 415–20.

Fleming, R., Baum, A. and Singer, J.E. (1984) Toward an integrative approach to the study of stress. *Journal of Personality and Social Psychology*, 46(4): 939–49.

Folkman, S. (1984) Personal control and stress and coping processes: a theoretical analysis. *Journal of Personality and Social Psychology*, 46(4): 839–52.

Folkman, S. and Lazarus, R.S. (1985) If It changes, it must be a process: study of emotion and coping during three stages of a college examination. *Journal of Personality and Social Psychology*, 48(1): 150–70.

Folkman, S. and Lazarus, R.S. (1986) Stress processes and depressive symptomatology. *Journal of Abnormal Psychology*, 95(2): 107–13.

Folkman, S. and Lazarus, R.S. (1988a) The relationship between coping and emotion. *Social Science and Medicine*, 26(3): 309–17.

Folkman, S. and Lazarus, R.S. (1988b) Coping as a mediator of emotion. *Journal of Personality and Social Psychology*, 54(3): 466–75.

Folkman, S., Lazarus, R.S., Dunkel-Schetter, C., DeLongis, A. and Gruen, R.J. (1986) Dynamics of a stressful encounter: cognitive appraisal, coping and encounter outcomes. *Journal of Personality and Social Psychology*, 50(5): 992–1003.

Ford, M.E. (1992) *Motivating Humans: Goals, Emotions and Personal Agency Beliefs*. London: Sage.

Frankenhauser, M. (1980) Psychoneuroendocrine approaches to the study of stressful person–environment transactions. In H. Selye (ed.) *Selye's Guide to Stress Research, Volume 1*. New York: Van Nostrand Reinhold.

Frankenhauser, M. (1984) Psychology as a means of reducing stress and promoting health. In K.M.J. Lagerspetz and P. Niemi (eds) *Psychology in the 1990s*. North Holland: Elsevier Science Publishers B.V.

Frankenhauser, M. (1989) A biopsychosocial approach to work life stress. *International Journal of Health Services*, 19(4): 747–58.

Frese, M. and Zapf, D. (1988) Methodological issues in the study of work stress: objective vs subjective measurement of work stress and the question of longitudinal studies. In C.L. Cooper and R. Payne *Causes, Coping and Consequences of Stress at Work*. Chichester: John Wiley.

Friedman, H.S., Tucker, J.S., Tomlinson-Keasey, C., Schwartz, J.E., Wingard, D.L. and Criqui, M.H. (1993) Does childhood personality predict longevity? *Journal of Personality and Social Psychology*, 65(1): 176–85.

Funk, S.C. (1992) Hardiness: a review of theory and research. *Health Psychology*, 11(5): 335–45.

Gaeddert, W.P. and Facteau, J.D. (1990) The effects of gender and achievement domain on two cognitive indices of strivings in personal accomplishments. *Journal of Research in Personality*, 24: 522–35.

Garrity, T.F. and Marx, M.B. (1985) Effects of moderator variables on the response to stress. In S. Burchfield (ed.) *Stress: Psychological and Physiological Interactions*. London: Hemisphere.

Greenberg, J., Solomon, S., Pyszczynski, T. and Steinberg, L. (1988) A reaction to Greenwald, Pratkanis, Leippe and Baumgardner (1986): under what conditions does research obstruct theory progress? *Psychological Review*, 95(4): 566–71.

Greenwald, A.G. and Pratkanis, A.R. (1988) On the use of 'theory' and the usefulness of theory. *Psychological Review*, 95(4): 575–9.

Greenwald, A.G., Pratkanis, A.R., Leippe, M.R. and Baumgardner, M.H. (1986) Under what conditions does theory obstruct research progress? *Psychological Review*, 93(2): 216–29.

Greenwood, D.C., Muir, K.R., Packham, C.J. and Madeley, R.J. (1996) Coronary heart disease: a review of the role of psychosocial stress and social support. *Journal of Public Health Medicine*, 18(2): 221–31.

Grinker, R.R. and Spiegel, J.P. (1945) *Men Under Stress*. New York: McGraw-Hill.

Gruen, R.J., Folkman, S. and Lazarus, S. (1988) Centrality and individual differences in the meaning of daily hassles. *Journal of Personality*, 56(4): 743–62.

Hamberger, L.K. and Lohr, J.M. (1984) *Stress and Stress Management: Research and Applications*. New York: Springer.

Hamilton, V. and Warburton, D.M. (eds) (1979) *Human Stress and Cognition: An Information Processing Approach*. Chichester: John Wiley.

Haney, T.L. and Blumenthal, J.A. (1985) Stress and the type A behaviour pattern. In S.R. Burchfield *Stress: Psychological and Physiological Interactions*. London: Hemisphere.

Harlow, R.E. and Cantor, N. (1994) Social pursuit of academics: side-effects and spillover of strategic reassurance seeking. *Journal of Personality and Social Psychology*, 66(2): 386–97.

Harris, W., Mackie, R.R. and Wilson, C.R. (1956) *Performance under stress: a review and critique of recent studies*. Technical Reports *VI* (July) (ASTIA AD No. 103779) Los Angeles, CA: Human Factors Research Corp.

Hastie, R. (1984) Causes and effects of causal attribution. *Journal of Personality and Social Psychology*, 46: 44–56.

Haward, L.R.C. (1960) The subjective meaning of stress. *British Journal of Medical Psychology*, 33: 185–94.

Headey, B. and Wearing, A. (1989) Personality, life events and subjective well-being: toward a dynamic equilibrium model. *Journal of Personality and Social Psychology*, 57(4): 731–9.

Hewitt, P.L. and Flett, G. (1993) Dimensions of perfectionism, daily stress and depression: a test of the specific vulnerability hypothesis. *Journal of Abnormal Psychology*, 102(1): 58–65.

Hills, H. and Norvell, N. (1991) An examination of hardiness and neuroticism as potential moderators of stress outcomes. *Behavioural Medicine*, 17(1): 31–8.

Hinkle, L.E. (1977) The concept of stress in the biological and social sciences. In Z.J. Lipowski, D.R. Lipsitt and P.C. Whybrow (eds) *Psychosomatic Medicine: Current Trends and Clinical Applications*. New York: Oxford University Press.

Hobfall, S.E. (1988) *The Ecology of Stress*. London: Taylor and Francis.

Hobfall, S.E. (1989) Conservation of resources: a new attempt at conceptualising stress. *American Psychologist*, 44(3): 513–24.

Holm, J.E. and Holroyd, K.A. (1992) The daily hassles scale (revised): does it measure stress or symptoms? *Behavioral Assessment*, 14: 465–82.

Holm, J.E., Holroyd, K.A., Hursey, K.G. and Penzien, D.B. (1986) The role of stress in recurrent tension headache. *Headache*, 26(4): 160–7.

Holmes, T.H. and Rahe, R.H. (1967) The Social Readjustment Rating scale. *Journal of Psychosomatic Research*, 11: 213–18.

Hurrell, J.J. and Murphy, L.R. (1991) Locus of control, job demands and health. In C.L. Cooper and R. Payne *Personality and Stress: Individual Differences in the Stress Process*. Chichester: John Wiley.

Hyland, M.E. (1988) Motivational control theory: an integrative framework. *Journal of Personality and Social Psychology*, 55(4): 642–51.

Ivancevich, J.M. (1986) Life events and hassles as predictors of health symptoms, job performance and absenteeism. *Journal of Occupational Behaviour*, 7: 39–51.

Janoff-Bulman, R. (1989) Assumptive worlds and the stress of traumatic events: applications of the schema construct. *Social Cognition*, 7(2): 113–36.

Jenkins, R. (1991) Demographic aspects of stress. In C.L. Cooper and R. Payne (eds) *Personality and Stress: Individual Differences in the Stress Process* (Wiley Series on Occupational Stress). Chichester: John Wiley.

Jerusalem, M. and Schwarzer, R. (1992) Self-efficacy as a resource factor in stress appraisal processes. In R. Schwarzer (ed.) *Self-Efficacy: Thought Control of Action*. London: Hemisphere.

Johal, S. (1995) Stability of hassles over time: negative affectivity strikes again? *Proceedings of the British Psychological Society*, 3(2): 123.

Johnson, J.G. (1995) Event-specific attributions and daily life events as predictors of depression symptom change. *Journal of Psychopathology and Behavioral Assessment*, 17(1): 39–49.

Johnson, J.G. and Bornstein, R.F. (1991) Does daily stress independently predict psychopathology? *Journal of Social and Clinical Psychology*, 19(1): 58–74.

Johnson, J.G. and Bornstein, R.F. (1993) The revised Hassles scale predicts psychopathology symptoms when pre-existing psychopathology is accounted for. *Journal of Social Behavior and Personality*, 8(6): 123–8.

Julius, M., Harburg, E., Cottington, E.M. and Johnson, E.H. (1986) Anger-coping types, blood pressure and all-cause mortality: a follow-up in Tecumseh, Michigan (1971–1983). *American Journal of Epidemiology*, 124(2): 220–33.

Kahney, H. (1993) *Problem Solving: Current Issues (2nd edn.)*. Milton Keynes: Open University Press.

Kanner, A.D. and Feldman, S.S. (1991) Control over uplifts and hassles and its relationship to adaptational outcomes. *Journal of Behavioral Medicine*, 14(2): 187–201.

Kanner, A.D., Coyne, J.C., Schaefer, C. and Lazarus, R.S. (1981) Comparison of two modes of stress measurement: daily hassles and uplifts versus major life events. *Journal of Behavioral Medicine*, 4(1): 1–39.

Kaplan, H.B. (1990a) Measurement and the stress process. *Stress Medicine*, 6: 249–55.

Kaplan, H.B. (1990b) Measurement problems in estimating theoretically informed models of stress: a sociological perspective. *Stress Medicine*, 6: 81–91.

Kaplan, H.B. (1991) Social psychology of the immune system: a conceptual framework and review of the literature. *Social Science and Medicine*, 33(8): 909–23.

Kaplan, H.B. (1996) Themes, lacunae and directions in research on psychosocial stress. In H.B. Kaplan (ed.) *Psychosocial Stress: Perspectives on Structure, Theory, Life-course and Methods*. San Diego, CA: Academic Press.

Karoly, P. (1993) Mechanisms of self-regulation. *Annual Review of Psychology*, 44: 23–52.

Karoly, P. and Lecci, L. (1993) Hypochondriasis and somatisation in college women: a personal projects analysis. *Health Psychology*, 12(2): 103–9.

Kasl, S.V. (1983) Pursuing the links between stressful life experiences and disease: a time for reappraisal. In C.L. Cooper (ed.) *Stress Research: Issues for the Eighties*. Chichester: John Wiley.

Kasl, S.V. and Rapp, S.R. (1991) Stress, health and well-being: the role of individual differences. In C.L. Cooper and R. Payne *Personality and Stress: Individual Differences in the Stress Process*. Chichester: John Wiley.

Kasser, T. and Ryan, R.M. (1993) A dark side of the American dream: correlates of financial success as a central life aspiration. *Journal of Personality and Social Psychology*, 65(2): 410–22.

Katz, I.M. and Campbell, J.D. (1994) Ambivalence over emotional expression and well-being: nomothetic and idiographic of the stress-buffering hypothesis. *Journal of Personality and Social Psychology*, 67(3): 513–24.

Kellam, S.G. (1979) Stressful life events and illness: a research area in need of conceptual development. In B.S. Dohrenwend and B.P. Dohrenwend *Stressful Life Events: Their Nature and Effects*. London: John Wiley.

Kendall, P.C. (1992) Healthy thinking. *Behaviour Therapy*, 23: 1–11.

Kiecolt-Glaser, J.K. and Glaser, R. (1998) Immune function: evidence for the interplay between stress and health. In T. Field, P.M. McCabe and N. Schneiderman (eds) *Stress and Coping Across Development*. Hove: Lawrence Erlbaum Associates.

Kiecolt-Glaser, J.K. and Glaser, R. (1995) Psychoneuroimmunology and health consequences: data and shared mechanisms. *Psychosomatic Medicine*, 57: 269–74.

Kihlstrom, J.F. and Klein, S.B. (1994) The self as a knowledge structure. In R.S. Wyer and T.K. Srull (eds) *Handbook of Social Cognition. Volume 1: Basic Processes*. Hove: Lawrence Erlbaum Associates.

King, L.A. and Emmons, R.A. (1991) Psychological, physical, and interpersonal correlates of emotional expressiveness, conflict, and control. *European Journal of Personality*, 5: 131–50.

Klinger, E. (1977) *Meaning and Void: Inner Experience and the Incentives in People's Lives*. Minneapolis, MI: University of Minnesota Press.

Kobasa, S.C. (1979) Stressful life events, personality and hardiness: an inquiry into hardiness. *Journal of Personality and Social Psychology*, 37: 1–11.

Kobasa, S.C., Maddi, S.R. and Kahn, S. (1982) Hardiness and health: a prospective study. *Journal of Personality and Social Psychology*, 42(1): 168–77.

Kobasa, S.C., Maddi, S.R. and Zola, M.A. (1983) Type A and hardiness. *Journal of Behavioral Medicine*, 6(1): 41–51.

Kohn, P.M. and MacDonald, J.E. (1992a) Hassles, anxiety and negative well-being. *Anxiety, Stress and Coping*, 5: 151–63.

Kohn, P.M. and MacDonald, J.E. (1992b) The survey of recent life experiences: a decontaminated hassles scale for adults. *Journal of Behavioral Medicine*, 15(2): 221–36.

Kohn, P.M. and Gurevich, M. (1993) On the adequacy of the indirect method of measuring the primary appraisal of hassles-based stress. *Personality and Individual Differences*, 14(5): 679–84.

Kohn, P.M., Hay, B.D. and Legere, J.J. (1994) Hassles, coping styles and negative well-being. *Personality and Individual Differences*, 17(2): 169–79.

Kohn, P.M., Lafreniere, K. and Gurevich, M. (1991) Hassles, health and personality. *Journal of Personality and Social Psychology*, 61(3): 478–82.

Kompier, M., Degier, E. and Draaisma, D. (1994) Regulations, policies, and practices concerning work stress in 5 European countries. *Work and Stress*, 8(4): 296–318.

Koolhaas, J. and Bohus, B. (1989) Social control in relation to neuroendocrine and immunological responses. In A. Steptoe and A. Appels (eds) *Stress, Personal Control and Health*. Chichester: John Wiley.

Landreville, P. (1992) A comparison between daily hassles and major life events as correlates of well-being in older adults. *Canadian Journal on Aging*, 11(2): 137–49.

Landsman, T. and Landsman, M.S. (1991) The beautiful and noble person. *Journal of Special Behavior and Personality. Special Issue: Handbook of Self-Actualization*, 6(5): 61–74.

Larsen, R.J. (1992) Neuroticism and selective encoding and recall of symptoms: evidence from a combined concurrent–retrospective study. *Journal of Personality and Social Psychology*, 62(3): 480–8.

Lazarus, R.S. (1966) *Psychological Stress and the Coping Process*. New York: McGraw-Hill.

Lazarus, R.S. (1967) Cognitive and personality factors underlying threat and coping. In R. Appley and M.H. Trumbull *Psychological Stress: Issues in Research*. New York: Appleton-Century-Crofts.

Lazarus, R.S. (1968) Emotions and adaptation: conceptual and empirical relations. In W.J. Arnold (ed.) *Nebraska Symposium on Motivation*. Lincoln, NA: University of Nebraska Press.

Lazarus, R.S. (1974) Psychological stress and coping in adaptation and illness. *International Journal of Psychiatry in Medicine*, 5(4): 321–33.

Lazarus, R.S. (1980a) Psychological stress and adaptation: some unresolved issues. In H. Selye (ed.) *Selye's Guide to Stress Research, Volume 1*. New York City: Van Nostrand Reinhold.

Lazarus, R.S. (1980b) The stress and coping paradigm. In C. Eisdorfer, D. Cohen and A. Kleinman (eds) *Conceptual Models for Psychopathology*. New York: Spectrum.

Lazarus, R.S. (1981) The stress and coping paradigm. In C. Eisdorfer, D. Cohen, A. Kleinman and P. Maxim *Models for Clinical Psychopathology*. Lancaster: MTP Press.

Lazarus, R.S. (1982) Thoughts on the relations between emotion and cognition. *American Psychologist*, 37(9): 1019–24.

Lazarus, R.S. (1983) Puzzles in the study of daily hassles. *Journal of Behavioral Medicine*, 7(4): 375–89.

Lazarus, R.S. (1984a) On the primacy of cognition. *American Psychologist*, 39(2): 124–9.

Lazarus, R.S. (1984b) The trivialization of distress. In B.L. Hammonds and C.J. Scheirer (eds) *Psychology and Health*, The Master lecture series, vol. 3. Washington, DC: American Psychological Association.

Lazarus, R.S. (1989) Constructs of the mind in mental health and psychotherapy. In A. Freeman *Comprehensive Handbook of Cognitive Therapy*. New York: Plenum.

Lazarus, R.S. (1990a) Theory-based stress measurement. *Psychological Inquiry*, 1(1): 3–13.

Lazarus, R.S. (1990b) Stress, coping and illness. In H.S. Friedman (ed.) *Personality and Disease*. New York: John Wiley.

Lazarus, R.S. and Launier, R. (1978) Stress-related transactions between the person and environment. In L.A. Pervin and M. Lewis (eds) *Perspectives in Interactional Psychology*. New York: Plenum.

Lazarus, R.S. and Folkman, S. (1984a) *Stress, Appraisal and Coping*. New York: Springer.

Lazarus, R.S. and Folkman, S. (1984b) Coping and adaptation. In W.D. Gentry (ed.) *Handbook of Behavioral Medicine*. New York: Guilford.

Lazarus, R.S. and Folkman, S. (1986) Reply to Deutsch and Green. *American Psychologist*, 41: 715–16.

Lazarus, R.S., Averill, J.R. and Opton, E.M. (1970) Towards a cognitive theory of emotion. In M. Arnold (ed.) *Feelings and Emotions*. New York: Academic Press.

Lazarus, R.S., Cohen, J.B., Folkman, S., Kanner, A. and Schaefer, C. (1980) Psychological stress and adaptation: some unresolved issues. In H. Selye (ed.) *Selye's Guide to Stress Research, Volume 1*. New York City: Van Nostrand Reinhold.

Lazarus, R.S., Coyne, J.C. and Folkman, S. (1982) Cognition, emotion and motivation: the doctoring of Humpty–Dumpty. In R.W.J. Neufeld (ed.) *Psychological Stress and Psychopathology*. New York: McGraw-Hill.

Lazarus, R.S., DeLongis, A., Folkman, S. and Gruen, R. (1985) Stress and adaptational outcomes: the problem of confounded measures. *American Psychologist*, 40: 770–9.

Lecci, L., Karoly, P., Briggs, C. and Kuhn, K. (1994) Specificity and generality of motivational components in depression: a personal projects analysis. *Journal of Abnormal Psychology*, 103(2): 404–8.

Lee, T.W., Locke, E.A. and Latham, G.P. (1989) Goal setting theory and job performance. In L.A. Pervin (ed.) *Goal Concepts in Personality and Social Psychology*. Hove: Lawrence Erlbaum Associates.

Lepore, S.J., Palsane, M.N. and Evans, G.W. (1991) Daily hassles and chronic strains: a hierarchy of stressors? *Social Science and Medicine*, 33(9): 1029–36.

Lepore, S.J., Evans, G.W. and Schneider, M.L. (1992) Role of control and social support in explaining the stress of hassles and crowding. *Environment and Behavior*, 24(6): 795–811.

Lerner, M.J. (1971) Observer's evaluation of a victim: justice, guilt and veridical perception. *Journal of Personality and Social Psychology*, 20(2): 127–35.

Leventhal, H. and Nerenz, D. (1985) The assessment of illness cognition. In P. Karoly (ed.) *Measurement Strategies in Health Psychology*. New York: John Wiley.

Levo, L.M. and Biggs, D. (1989) Cognitive factors in effectively coping with home/career stress. *Journal of Cognitive Psychotherapy: An International Quarterly*, 3(1): 53–68.

Linville, P.W. (1987) Self-complexity as a cognitive buffer against stress-related illness and depression. *Journal of Personality and Social Psychology*, 52(4): 663–76.

Little, B.R. (1983) Personal projects: a rationale and method for investigation. *Environment and Behavior*, 15: 273–309.

Lohr, J.D. and Hamberger, L.K. (1990) Cognitive–behavioural modification of the coronary-prone behaviour pattern. *Journal of Rational–Emotive and Cognitive–Behaviour Therapy*, 8(2): 103–26.

Lu, L. (1991) Daily hassles and mental health: a longitudinal study. *British Journal of Psychology*, 82: 441–7.

MacKay, D.G. (1988) Under what conditions can theoretical psychology survive and prosper? Integrating the rational and empirical epistemologies. *Psychological Review*, 95(4): 559–65.

Maddox, J. (1984) Psychoimmunology: before its time. *Nature*, 309: 400.

Maier, S.F. and Laudenslanger, M. (1985) Stress and health: exploring the links. *Psychology Today*, August: 44–9.

Mann, L. and Janis, I. (1982) Conflict theory of decision making and the expectancy–value approach. In T. Feather (ed.) *Expectations and Actions: Expectancy–Value Models in Psychology*. Hillsdale, NJ: Lawrence Erlbaum Associates.

Marks, D.F. (1994) Psychology's role in The Health of the Nation. *The Psychologist*, 7(3): 119–21.

Markus, H. and Ruvolvo, A. (1989) Possible selves: personalised representations of goals. In L.A. Pervin (ed.) *Goal Concepts in Personality and Social Psychology*. Hove: Lawrence Erlbaum Associates.

Marshall, C., Mitchell, D.E. and Wirt, F. (1985) Assumptive worlds of education policy makers. *Peabody Journal of Education*, 6(4): 90–115.

Marteau, T.M. and Johnston, M. (1987) Health psychology: the danger of neglecting psychological models. *Bulletin of the British Psychological Society*, 40: 82–5.

Martin, R.A. (1984) A critical review of the concept of stress in psychosomatic medicine. *Perspectives in Biology and Medicine*, 27(3): 443–64.

Martin, R.A. (1989) Techniques for data acquisition and analysis in field investigations of stress. In R.W.J. Neufeld (ed.) *Advances in the Investigation of Psychological Stress*. Chichester: Wiley InterScience.

Martin, R.A. and Dobbin, J.P. (1988) Sense of humor, hassles and immunoglobulin A: evidence for a stress-moderating effect of humor. *International Journal of Psychiatry in Medicine*, 18(2): 93–105.

Maslow, A.H. (1970) *Motivation and Personality, 2nd edn*. New York: Harper.

Mason, J.W. (1971) A re-evaluation of the concept of non-specifity in stress theory. *Journal of Psychiatric Research*, 8: 323–33.

Mason, J.W. (1974) Specificity in the organisation of neuroendocrine response profiles. In P. Seeman and G.M. Brown (eds) *Frontiers in Neurology and Neuroscience Research*. Toronto: University of Toronto Neuroscience Institute.

Mason, J.W. (1975a) A historical view of the stress field. Part 1. *Journal of Human Stress*, 1(1): 6–12.

Mason, J.W. (1975b) A historical view of the stress field. Part 2. *Journal of Human Stress*, 1(2): 22–37.

McAdams, D.P., de St. Aubin, E. and Logan, R.L. (1993) Generativity among young, midlife and older adults. *Psychology and Aging*, 8(2): 221–30.

McCann, B.S. and Matthews, K.A. (1988) Antecedents of the coronary-prone behaviour pattern. In T. Field, P.M. McCabe and N. Schneiderman (eds) *Stress and Coping Across Development*. Hove: Lawrence Erlbaum Associates.

McCleod, W.T. (Managing Editor) (1985) *The New Collins Concise Dictionary of the English Language*. London: Guild.

McGuire, W.J. and McGuire, C.V. (1991) The content, structure and operation of thought systems. In R.S. Wyer and T.K. Srull (eds) *Advances in Social Cognition. Volume 4: The Content, Structure and Operation of Thought Systems*. Hove: Lawrence Erlbaum Associates.

McLean, A. (1972) Occupational stress: a misnomer. *Occupational Mental Health*, 2: 12–15.

Meeks, S., Arnkhoff, D.B., Glass, C.R. and Notarius, C.I. (1986) Wives' employment status, hassles, communication and relational efficacy: intra- versus extra-relationship factors and marital adjustment. *Family Relations*, 35(2): 249–55.

Meichenbaum, D. (1977) *Cognitive–behavior modification: an integrated approach*. New York: Plenum.

Miller, C. (1991) Self actualization and the consciousness revolution. In A. Jones and R. Crandall Handbook of Self-Actualization. Special edition of the *Journal of Social Behaviour and Personality*, 6(5): 109–26.

Miller, T.W. (1996) *Theory and Assessment of Stressful Life Events*. Madison, CN: International Universities Press.

Monroe, S.M. (1983) Major and minor life events as predictors of psychological distress: further issues and findings. *Journal of Behavioral Medicine*, 6(2): 189–205.

Montefiore, A. (1989) Philosophical background. In A. Montefiore and D. Noble (eds) *Goals, No-Goals and Own Goals: A Debate on Goal-Directed and Intentional Behaviour*. London: Unwin Hyman.

Montefiore, A. and Noble, D. (1989) *Goals, No-Goals and Own Goals: A Debate on Goal-Directed and Intentional Behaviour*. London: Unwin Hyman.

Moos, R.H. (1992) Stress and coping theory and evaluation research. *Evaluation Review*, 16(5): 534–53.

Morokoff, P.J. and Gillilland, R. (1993) Stress, sexual functioning and marital satisfaction. *Journal of Sex Research*, 30(1): 43–53.

Moser, K., Gadenne, V. and Schroder, J. (1988) Under what conditions does confirmation seeking obstruct scientific progress? *Psychological Review*, 95(4): 572–4.

Mundal, R., Erikssen, M.D., Bjorklund, R. and Rodahl, K. (1990) Elevated blood pressure in air traffic controllers during a period of occupational conflict. *Stress Medicine*, 6: 141–4.

Nakano, K. (1989) Intervening variables of stress, hassles and health. *Japanese Psychological Research*, 31(3): 143–8.

Nakano, K. (1991) The role of coping strategies on psychological and physical well-being. *Japanese Psychological Research*, 33(4): 160–7.

Nickels, J.B., Cramer, K.M. and Gural, D.M. (1992) Toward unconfounding prediction and control: predictionless control made possible. *Canadian Journal of Behavioural Science*, 24(2): 143–6.

Niedenthal, P.M., Setterlund, M.B. and Wherry, M.B. (1992) Possible self-complexity and affective reactions to goal-relevant evaluation. *Journal of Personality and Social Psychology*, 63(1): 5–16.

Novaco, R.W. (1977) Stress inoculation: a cognitive therapy for anger and its application to a case of depression. *Journal of Consulting and Clinical Psychology*, 45: 600–8.

Nowack, K.M. (1989) Coping style, cognitive hardiness and health status. *Journal of Behavioral Medicine*, 12(2): 145–58.

O'Leary, A. (1992) Self-efficacy and health: behavioral and stress–physiological mediation. *Cognitive Therapy and Research*, 16(20): 229–45.

Osman, A., Barrios, F.X., Longnecker, J. and Osman, J.R. (1994) Validation of the inventory of college students' recent life experiences in an American college sample. *Journal of Clinical Psychology*, 50: 856–63.

Paterson, R.J. and Neufeld, R.W.J. (1995) What are my options?: influences of choice availability on stress and perception of control. *Journal of Research in Personality*, 29: 145–67.

Payne, R. (1988) Individual differences in the study of occupational stress. In C.L. Cooper and R. Payne *Causes, Coping and Consequences of Stress at Work*. Chichester: John Wiley.

Pbert, L., Doerfler, L.A. and DeCosimo, D. (1992) An evaluation of the Perceived Stress scale in two clinical populations. *Journal of Psychopathology and Behavioral Assessment*, 14(4): 363–75.

Peacock, E.J., Wong, P.T.P. and Reker, G.T. (1993) Relations between appraisals and coping schemas: support for the congruence model. *Canadian Journal of Behavioural Science*, 25(1): 64–80.

Pearlstone, A., Russell, R.J.H. and Wells, P.A. (1994) A re-examination of the stress/illness relationship: how useful is the concept of stress? *Personality and Individual Differences*, 17(4): 577–80.

Pervin, L.A. (1989) Goal concepts in personality and social psychology: a historical perspective. In L.A. Pervin (ed.) *Goal Concepts in Personality and Social Psychology*. Hove: Lawrence Erlbaum Associates.

Pervin, L.A. and Lewis, M. (eds) (1978) *Perspectives in Interactional Psychology*. New York: Plenum.

Petrie, K., Moss-Morris, R. and Weinman, J. (1995) The impact of catastrophic beliefs on functioning in chronic fatigue syndrome. *Journal of Psychosomatic Research*, 39(1): 31–7.

Pollock, K. (1988) On the nature of social stress: production of a modern mythology. *Social Science and Medicine*, 26(3): 381–92.

Pollock, K. (1993) Attitude of mind as a means of resisting illness. In A. Radley *Worlds of Illness: Biographical and Cultural Perspectives on Health and Disease*. London: Routledge.

Powell, S.S. and Drotar, D. (1992) Postpartum depressed mood: the impact of daily hassles. *Journal of Psychosomatic Obstetrics and Gynaecology*, 13(4): 255–66.

Radley, A. (1993) *Worlds of Illness: Biographical and Cultural Perspectives on Health and Disease*. London: Routledge.

Radloff, R. and Helmreich, R. (1968) *Groups Under Stress*. New York: Appleton-Century-Crofts.

Rahe, R.H. (1974) The pathway between subjects' recent life changes and their near-future illness reports: representative results and methodological issues. In B.S. Dohrenwend and B.P. Dohrenwend *Stressful Life Events: Their Nature and Effects*. London: John Wiley.

Ratcliff-Crain, J., Temoshok, L., Kiecolt-Glaser, J.K. and Tamarkin, L. (1989) Issues in psychoneuroimmunology research. *Health Psychology*, 8(6): 747–52.

Read, S.J. and Miller, L.C. (1989) Inter-personalism: toward a goal-based theory of persons in relationships. In L.A. Pervin (ed.) *Goal Concepts in Personality and Social Psychology*. Hove: Lawrence Erlbaum Associates.

Reich, W.P., Parrella, D.P. and Filstead, W.J. (1988) Unconfounding the hassles scale: external sources versus internal responses to stress. *Journal of Behavioral Medicine*, 11(3): 239–49.

Reynolds, S., Taylor, E. and Shapiro, D. (1993) Session impact and outcome in stress management training. *Journal of Community and Applied Social Psychology*, 3: 325–37.

Rogers, C. (1951) *Client-Centered Therapy*. Boston: Houghton Mifflin.

Rogers, C. (1963) Actualizing tendency in relation to motives and to consciousness. In R. Jones (ed.) *Nebraska Symposium on Motivation.* Lincoln, NA: University of Nebraska Press.

Rose, R.M. (1984) Overview of endocrinology of stress. In G.M. Brown, S.H. Koslow and S.R. Reichlin (eds) *Neuroendocrinology and Psychiatric Disorder.* New York: Raven Press.

Rosenman, R.H., Brand, R.J. and Jenkins, C.D. (1975) Coronary heart disease in the Western Collaborative Group Study. Final follow-up experience of eight and a half years. *Journal of the American Medical Association,* 233: 872–7.

Rotter, J. (1966) Generalised expectancies for internal versus external control of reinforcement. *Psychological Monographs: General and Applied,* 80: whole issue.

Rotter, J.B. (1975) Some problems and misconceptions related to the concept of internal versus external control of reinforcement. *Journal of Consulting and Clinical Psychology,* 43: 56–67.

Rowlison, R.T. and Felner, R.D. (1988) Major life events, hassles and adaptation in adolescence: confounding in the conceptualisation and measurement of life stress and adjustment revisited. *Journal of Personality and Social Psychology,* 55(3): 432–44.

Russell, M. and Davey, G.C.L. (1993) The relationship between life event measures and anxiety and its cognitive correlates. *Personality and Individual Differences,* 14(2): 317–22.

Salovey, P. and Birnbaum, D. (1989) Influence of mood on health-relevant cognitions. *Journal of Personality and Social Psychology,* 57(3): 539–51.

Santiago-Rivera, A.L., Bernstein, B.L. and Gard, T.L. (1995) The importance of achievement and the appraisal of stressful events as predictors of coping. *Journal of College Student Development,* 36(4): 374–83.

Schacter, S. and Singer, J.E. (1962) Cognitive, social and physiological determinants of emotional state. *Psychological Review,* 69: 379–99.

Schafer, J. and Fals-Stewart, W. (1991) Issues of methodology, design and analytic procedure in psychological research on stress. *British Journal of Medical Psychology,* 64: 375–83.

Schank, R.C. and Abelson, R.P. (1979) *Scripts, Plans and Understanding: An Inquiry into Human Knowledge Structures.* Hillsdale, NJ: Lawrence Erlbaum Associates.

Schaubroeck, J. and Ganster, D.C. (1991a) Associations among stress-related individual differences. In C.L. Cooper and R. Payne (eds) *Personality and Stress: Individual Differences in the Stress Process* (Wiley Series on Occupational Stress). Chichester: John Wiley.

Schaubroeck, J. and Ganster, D.C. (1991b) The role of negative affectivity in work-related stress. *Journal of Social Behaviour and Personality,* 6(7): 319–30.

Scheidt, R.J. (1986) Daily hassles and profiles of well-being among older residents of small rural towns. *Psychological Reports,* 58: 587–90.

Scheier, M.F. and Carver, C.S. (1987) Dispositional optimism and physical well-being: the influence of generalised outcome expectancies on health. *Journal of Personality,* 55(2): 169–210.

Scheier, M.F. and Carver, C.S. (1992) Effects of optimism on psychological and physical well-being: theoretical overview and empirical update. *Cognitive Therapy and Research,* 16(2): 201–28.

Scherer, K.R. (1995) In defense of a nomothetic approach to studying emotion-antecedent appraisal. *Psychological Inquiry,* 6(3): 241–8.

Schlenker B.R. and Weigold, M.F. (1989) Goals and the self-identification process: constructing desired identities. In L.A. Pervin (ed.) *Goal Concepts in Personality and Social Psychology.* Hove: Lawrence Erlbaum Associates.

Schmidt, D.D., Zyzanski, S. and Ellner, J. (1985) Stress as a precipitating factor in subjects with recurrent herpes labialis. *Journal of Family Practice*, 20(4): 359–66.

Schroeder, D.H. and Costa, P.T. (1984) Influence of life event stress on physical illness: substantive effects or methodological flaws? *Journal of Personality and Social Psychology*, 46(4): 853–63.

Schulz, K.H. and Schulz, H. (1992) Overview of psychoneuroimmunological stress and intervention studies in humans with an emphasis on the uses of immunological parameters. *Psycho-Oncology*, 1: 51–70.

Schwarz, N. and Clore, G.L. (1983) Mood, misattribution and judgements of well-being: informative and directive functions of affective states. *Journal of Personality and Social Psychology*, 45(3): 513–23.

Schwarzer, R. and Leppin, A. (1989) Social support and health: a meta-analysis. *Psychology and Health*, 3: 1–15.

Selye, H. (1956) *The Stress of Life.* New York: McGraw-Hill.

Selye, H. (1974) *Stress Without Distress.* New York: J.B. Lippincott.

Selye, H. (1980) The stress concept today. In I.L. Kutash, L.B. Schlesinger and associates. *Handbook on Stress and Anxiety.* London: Jossey-Bass.

Selye, H. (1983a) Epilogue to H. Selye (ed.) *Selye's Guide to Stress Research, Volume 2.* New York City: Van Nostrand Reinhold.

Selye, H. (1983b) The stress concept: past, present and future. In C. Cooper *Stress Research: Issues for the Eighties.* Chichester: John Wiley.

Shepperd, J.A. and Kashani, J.H. (1991) The relationship of hardiness, gender, and stress to health outcomes in adolescents. *Journal of Personality*, 59(4): 747–68.

Sherer, M., Maddux, J.E., Mercandante, B., Prentice-Dunn, S., Jacobs, B. and Rogers, R.W. (1982) The self-efficacy scale: construction and validation, *Psychological Reports*, 51: 633–71.

Shibutani, T. (1991) On the empirical investigation of self-concepts. In D.R. Maines (ed.) *Social Organisation and Social Process: Essays in Honor of Anselm Strauss.* New York: Aldine de Gruyter.

Siddle, D.A. (1983) The orienting reflex. In A. Gale and S.A. Edwards *Physiological Correlates of Human Behaviour.* London: Academic Press.

Solomon, G.F., Amkraut, A.A. and Rubin, R.T. (1985) Stress, hormones, neuro-regulation and immunity. In S. Burchfield *Stress: Psychological and Physiological Interactions.* London: Hemisphere.

Staats, A.W. (1991) Unified positivism and unification in psychology: fad or new field? *American Psychologist*, 46: 899–912.

Stadler, M. and Wehner, T. (1985) Anticipation as a basic principle in goal-directed action. In M. Frese and J. Sabini (eds) *Goal Directed Behaviour: The Concept of Action in Psychology.* London: Lawrence Erlbaum Associates.

Stedman's Medical Dictionary (1982) London: Williams and Wilkins.

Steptoe, A. (1991) The links between stress and illness. *Journal of Psychosomatic Research*, 35(6): 633–44.

Steptoe, A. and Appels, A. (eds) (1989) *Stress, Personal Control and Health.* Chichester: John Wiley.

Stone, A.A., Reed, B.R. and Neale, J.M. (1987) Changes in daily event frequency precede episodes of physical symptoms. *Journal of Human Stress*, 13: 70–4.

Strauman, T.J. and Higgins, E.T. (1987) Automatic activation of self-discrepancies and emotional syndromes: when cognitive structures influence affect. *Journal of Personality and Social Psychology*, 53(6): 1004–14.

Sutherland, V.J. and Cooper, C.L. (1988) Sources of work stress. In J.J. Hurrell, L.R. Murphy, S.L. Sauter and C.L. Cooper (eds) *Occupational Stress: Issues and Developments in Research*. London: Taylor and Francis.

Syme, S.L. (1989) Control and health: a personal perspective. In A. Steptoe and A. Appels (eds) *Stress, Personal Control and Health*. Chichester: John Wiley.

Symonds, C.P. (1947) Use and abuse of the term flying stress. In *Air Ministry, Psychological Disorders in Flying Personnel of the Royal Air Force, 1939–1945*. London: HMSO.

Taylor, H. and Cooper, C.L. (1989) The stress-prone personality: a review of the research in the context of occupational stress. *Stress Medicine*, 5: 17–27.

Temkin, N.R. and Davis, G.R. (1984) Stress as a risk factor for seizures among adults with epilepsy. *Epilepsia*, 25(4): 450–6.

Temoshok, L. (1990) On attempting to articulate the biopsychosocial model. In J. Ratcliff-Crain and A. Baum *Individual Differences and Health: Gender, Coping and Stress*. New York: John Wiley.

Theorell, T. (1992) Critical life changes: a review of research. *Psychotherapy and Psychosomatics*, 57: 108–17.

Trzebinski, J. (1989) The role of goal categories in the representation of social knowledge. In L.A. Pervin *Goal Concepts in Personality and Social Psychology*. Hove: Lawrence Erlbaum Associates.

Ursin, H. and Murison, R.C.C. (1984) Classification and description of stress. In G.M. Brown, S.H. Koslow and S.R. Reichlin (eds) *Neuroendocrinology and Psychiatric Disorder*. New York: Raven Press.

Wallston, K.A. (1989) Assessment of control in health-care settings. In A. Steptoe and A. Appels (eds) *Stress, Personal Control and Health*. Chichester: John Wiley.

Wallston, K.A. (1992) Hocus-pocus, the focus isn't strictly on locus: Rotter's social learning theory modified for health. *Cognitive Therapy and Research*, 16(2): 183–99.

Ware, N.C. and Kleinman, A. (1992) Culture and somatic experience: the social course of illness in neurasthenia and chronic fatigue syndrome. *Psychosomatic Medicine*, 54: 546–60.

Warr, P.B. (1987) *Work, Unemployment and Mental Health at Work*. Oxford: Clarendon Press.

Watson, D. and Clark, N.A. (1984) Negative affectivity: the disposition to experience negative emotional states, *Psychological Bulletin*, 96: 465–90.

Weinberger, M., Hiner, S. and Tierney, W.M. (1987) In support of hassles as a measure of stress in predicting health outcomes. *Journal of Behavioral Medicine*, 10(1): 19–31.

Weiner, B. (1982) An attributionally based theory of motivation and emotion: focus, range and issues. In T. Feather (ed.) *Expectations and Actions: Expectancy–Value Models in Psychology*. Hillsdale, NJ: Lawrence Erlbaum Associates.

Weiner, B. (1985) Spontaneous causal thinking. *Psychological Bulletin*, 97: 74–84.

Weinman, J. and Cooper, R.L. (1981) Individual differences in perceptual problem-solving. *Intelligence*, 5: 165–78.

Weinman, J., Elithorn, A. and Cooper, R. (1985) Personality and problem-solving: the nature of individual differences in planning, scanning and verification. *Personality and Individual Differences*, 6(4): 453–60.

Williams, R., Zyzanski, S. and Wright, A.L. (1992) Life events and daily hassles and uplifts as predictors of hospitalization and outpatient visitation. *Social Science and Medicine*, 34(7): 763–8.

Wilson, J.F. (1985) Stress, coping styles and physiological arousal. In S.R. Burchfield *Stress: Psychological and Physiological Interactions*. London: Hemisphere.

Wittkower, E.D. (1977) Historical perspective of contemporary psychosomatic medicine. In Z.J. Lipowski, D.R. Lipsitt and P.C. Whybrow (eds) *Psychosomatic Medicine: Current Trends and Clinical Applications*. New York: Oxford University Press.

Wolf, T.M., Elston, R.C. and Kissling, G.E. (1989) Relationship of hassles, uplifts and life events to psychological well-being of freshman medical students. *Behavioural Medicine*, 15(1): 37–45.

Wolff, H.G. (1953) *Stress and Disease*. Springfield, IL: Thomas.

Wolff, H.G. (1977) Personal communication to Hinkle, L.E. In L.E. Hinkle. The concept of stress in the biological and social sciences. In Z.J. Lipowski, D.R. Lipsitt and P.C. Whybrow (eds) *Psychosomatic Medicine: Current Trends and Clinical Applications*. New York: Oxford University Press.

Wong, P.T.P. (1992) Control is a double-edged sword. *Canadian Journal of Behavioural Science*, 24(2): 143–6.

Wong, P.T.P. (1993) Effective management of life stress. *Stress Medicine*, 9: 51–60.

Woolfolk, R.L., Novalany, R.L., Gara, M.A., Allen, L.A. and Polino, M. (1995) Self-complexity, self-evaluation and depression: an examinaiton of form and content within the self-schema. *Journal of Personality and Social Psychology*, 68(6): 1108–20.

Wortman, C.B., Sheedy, C., Gluhoski, V. and Kessler, R. (1992) Stress, coping and health: conceptual issues and directions for future research. In H.S. Friedman (ed.) *Hostility, Coping and Health*. Washington, DC: APA.

Wyer, R.S. and Srull, T.K. (eds) (1994) *Handbook of Social Cognition. Volume 1: Basic Processes*. Hove: Lawrence Erlbaum Associates.

Wu, K.K. and Lam, D.J. (1993) The relationship between daily stress and health: replicating and extending previous findings. *Psychology and Health*, 8(5): 329–44.

Zajonc, R.B. (1980) Feeling and thinking: preferences need no inferences. *American Psychologist*, 35(2): 155–75.

Zarski, J.J. (1984) Hassles and health: a replication. *Health Psychology*, 3(3): 243–51.

Zika, S. and Chamberlain, K. (1987) Relation of hassles and personality to subjective well-being. *Journal of Personality and Social Psychology*, 53(1): 155–62.

Zimmerman, M. (1983) Methodological issues in the assessment of life events. *Clinical Psychology Review*, 3: 339–70.

Index

PSYCHOLOGY AND HEALTH PROMOTION

Paul Bennett and Simon Murphy

- What part do behavioural and psychological factors play in the health of an individual?
- Which theories contribute to health promotion at the individual and community level?
- How effective are such interventions in improving people's health?

Psychology and Health Promotion is the first book to set out in clear and authoritative terms the role of psychological theory in health promotion. It adopts both structuralist and social regulation models of health and health promotion, considering the significance of psychological processes in each case. The authors examine how behaviour and the social environment may contribute to health status and how psychological processes may mediate the effect of environmental conditions. They go on to consider the theory underlying interventions that are aimed at individuals and large populations, and the effectiveness of attempts to change both individual behaviour and the environmental factors that may contribute to ill-health.

This highly approachable volume is structured as a textbook and includes a summary and further reading at the end of each chapter, as well as a substantial bibliography. It is designed to provide an invaluable resource for advanced undergraduate and postgraduate courses in health psychology, clinical psychology and social psychology as well as students and practitioners in health and social welfare, including health promotion.

Contents

Introduction: why psychology – Part I: Mediators of health and health behaviours – Psychosocial mediators of health – Cognitive mediators of health-related behaviours – Part II: Facilitating individual change – Influencing health behaviour: individual change – Individually targeted interventions – Part III: Facilitating population change – Environmental and public policy approaches – Attitude and communication theories – Population based intervention – Part IV: What next? – Some final considerations – References – Index.

192pp   0 335 19765 5 (Paperback)   0 335 19766 3 (Hardback)

THE SOCIAL CONTEXT OF HEALTH

Michael Hardey

- In what way is health related to our sense of self-identity?
- How do we make decisions about our health in an age of uncertainty?
- Which developments in medical knowledge and the delivery of care change our ideas about health?

The central theme running through this book is the essentially 'social' nature of health. This embraces the way medical knowledge emerged out of a specific set of historical and intellectual circumstances, and the shaping of the health professions by the cultural and political milieu of the nineteenth century. Like non-expert knowledge, the development and application of expert knowledge in health is embedded in social processes. In this accessible text the complex relationships between inequality, race, gender and other social divisions are examined and related to changes in health care. Problems central to the delivery of health care are highlighted and linked to challenges to established health-care professions and systems. Michael Hardey shows the way in which health has become part of our identity, and relates this to the increasing range of health advice and the constant choices available in terms of our health and lifestyles.

Contents

Introduction – The social context of health – Understanding health and constructing illness – The health services and the delivery of care – Caring and curing: the health professions – Social divisions and health – Gender and health – Opportunities and constraints in health – References – Index.

192pp   0 335 19863 5 (Paperback)   0 335 19864 3 (Hardback)

PAIN
THEORY, RESEARCH AND INTERVENTION
Sandra Horn and Marcus Munafò

- What explanations have been advanced for pain and what are their shortcomings?
- How do theoretical models account for apparent anomalies in the experience of pain?
- What are the implications for clinical practice and how has practice guided theory?

Psychology has made an enormous contribution to the understanding of pain and its phenomena, mechanisms, and treatments. This book explores and integrates current research in key areas of pain and pain management from a psychological perspective, and places recent developments in an historical context.

The experience of pain cannot be captured in physiological terms, and treatments based on physical models are often inadequate. This book explores the multidimensional nature of pain mechanisms, including the roles of past experience, culture and personality, and considers the implications for research and treatment. The approach is primarily theoretical, but with a significant emphasis on clinical practice and application. This balance is often lacking in comparable texts, and is enhanced by the professional and research background of the authors.

This clear and approachable text includes self-contained chapters that can be regarded as units of study and a unified glossary of terms completes the package. It is designed to provide a key resource for advanced undergraduate and postgraduate courses in health psychology, clinical psychology and social psychology as well as students and practitioners in health and social welfare.

Contents
Preface – Theories of pain – Pain mechanisms – Laboratory studies – Acute and chronic dimensions – Personal, social and cultural factors – Measurement – Interventions – Conclusion – Glossary of neurophysiological and anatomical terms – Bibliography – Index.

152pp   0 335 19688 8 (Paperback)   0 335 19689 6 (Hardback)